URBAN AND
REGIONAL POLICY
AND ITS EFFECTS

VOLUME TWO

URBAN AND REGIONAL POLICY AND ITS EFFECTS

NANCY PINDUS

HOWARD WIAL

HAROLD WOLMAN

editors

BROOKINGS INSTITUTION PRESS
Washington, D.C.

Library of Congress Cataloging-in-Publication data

Urban and regional policy and its effects / Margery Austin Turner, Howard Wial, and
Harold Wolman, editors.
    p.   cm.
  Summary: "Brings policymakers, practitioners, and scholars up to speed on the state of
knowledge on urban and regional policy issues. Conceptualizes fresh thinking of different
aspects (economic development, education, land use), presenting main themes and
implications and identifying gaps to fill for successful formulation and implementation of
urban and regional policy"—Provided by publisher.

  Includes bibliographical references and index.
  ISBN 978-0-8157-0297-9 (pbk. : alk. paper)
  1. Urban policy—Congresses. 2. Urban economics—Congresses. 3. Urban renewal—
Congresses. 4. Regional planning—Congresses. 5. City planning—Congresses. I.
Turner, Margery Austin, 1955– II. Wial, Howard. III. Wolman, Harold. IV. Title.

HT151.U65 2008
338.973009173'2—dc22   2008016030

9 8 7 6 5 4 3 2 1

The paper used in this publication meets minimum requirements of the
American National Standard for Information Sciences—Permanence of Paper for
Printed Library Materials: ANSI Z39.48-1992.

Typeset in Adobe Garamond

Composition by Peter Lindeman
Arlington, Virginia

Printed by Versa Press
East Peoria, Illinois

Contents

URBAN AND REGIONAL POLICY AND ITS EFFECTS, VOLUME TWO is the second in a series of publications that provides scholars, policymakers, and practitioners with accessible summaries of what is known about the effectiveness of selected urban and regional policies. This volume contains edited versions of the papers presented at a conference held at the Urban Institute on June 5–6, 2008, and arranged by the editors. The conference and this volume are products of collaboration between the Brookings Institution's Metropolitan Policy Program, the George Washington University's George Washington Institute of Public Policy and Trachtenberg School of Public Policy and Public Administration, and the Urban Institute. All the papers represent the views of the authors and not necessarily the views of the staff members, officers, or trustees of the Brookings Institution, the George Washington University, or the Urban Institute.

Conference Participants

Nancy Y. Augustine, *George Washington University*
William Barnes, *National League of Cities*
Alan Berube, *Brookings Institution*
Ajay Chaudry, *Urban Institute*
Dylan Conger, *George Washington University*
Joseph Cordes, *George Washington University*
Stephen Crawford, *Brookings Institution*
Brooke DeRenzis, *Brookings Institution*
Alec Friedhoff, *Brookings Institution*
Howard Lempel, *Brookings Institution*
Robert Lerman, *Urban Institute*
Jessica Menter, *George Washington University*
Christoph Pross, *Brookings Institution*
Martha Ross, *Brookings Institution*
Margaret Simms, *Urban Institute*
Margery Austin Turner, *Urban Institute*
Jennifer Vey, *Brookings Institution*
Garry Young, *George Washington University*

Preface

The *Urban and Regional Policy and Its Effects* series is designed to present evidence about the impacts of urban and regional policies in a format that is accessible to policymakers and practitioners as well as scholars. The series and the conferences on which it is based are the products of a collaboration between the Brookings Institution's Metropolitan Policy Program, the George Washington University's George Washington Institute of Public Policy and Trachtenberg School of Public Policy and Public Administration, and the Urban Institute.

This volume and the 2008 conference on Urban and Regional Policy and Its Effects came about with the support of several people at the sponsoring institutions. At Brookings, Bruce Katz, director of the Metropolitan Policy Program, has provided the program's support for this project. Amy Liu provided us with invaluable intellectual and practical assistance in planning the conference. Alan Berube provided essential intellectual advice and also moderated one of the conference sessions.

At George Washington University, Joe Cordes, director of the Trachtenberg School of Public Policy and Public Administration, provided useful advice throughout. Nancy Augustine not only made important intellectual contributions but also played a major role in organizing the conference.

At the Urban Institute, Robert Reischauer, president, provided institutional support for this project. Margery Turner, one of the founding editors of the *Urban and Regional Policy and Its Effects* series, continued to be a source of sage advice and also moderated one of the conference sessions.

A number of other people were instrumental in making the conference and this volume a reality. Mildred Woodhouse and Latasha Holloway of the Urban Institute managed the conference logistics. Jamaine Fletcher and Elena Sheridan of Brookings and Olive Cox and Kim Rycroft of the George Washington Institute of Public Policy provided administrative support for the conference and throughout the publication process. Rachel Blanchard of the Urban Institute and Pam Blumenthal, Rajeev Darolia, Ana Karruz, and Robert McManmon of the George Washington University took notes on the conference sessions. Alec Friedhoff and Sean Hardgrove of Brookings and Ryan Tang, formerly with Brookings, helped prepare the conference papers for publication. Janet Walker of the Brookings Institution Press expertly and gracefully managed the production of the conference volume.

We are grateful to the John D. and Catherine T. MacArthur Foundation, whose generous support of the Brookings Institution's Metropolitan Economy Initiative made Brookings' cosponsorship of the conference and editorial work on this volume possible. We also thank the Fannie Mae Foundation, George Gund Foundation, Heinz Endowments, and Rockefeller Foundation for providing general support to the Brookings Institution's Metropolitan Policy Program. We thank the George Washington University for providing funding for the conference through its Selective Excellence Program.

URBAN AND REGIONAL POLICY AND ITS EFFECTS

1

Introduction

NANCY PINDUS, HOWARD WIAL, AND HAROLD WOLMAN

U rban and regional policy debates are often long on rhetoric but short on evidence about policy impacts. To redress this imbalance, the Brookings Institution, the George Washington University Institute of Public Policy and the Trachtenberg School of Public Policy and Public Administration, and the Urban Institute held the second in a series of annual conferences on Urban and Regional Policy and Its Effects at the Urban Institute in Washington, D.C., on June 5–6, 2008. Chapters were commissioned for the conference from distinguished social scientists and practitioners. The conference sought to engage authors and discussants in a cross-disciplinary dialogue focused on the central theme—evidence of policy effects. The chapters in this volume are revised versions of those commissioned papers.

Our examination of urban and regional policy and its effects is organized around six key policy challenges that most metropolitan areas and local communities face. Each of the chapters in this volume deals with a specific policy topic under one of these challenges:

—*Creating quality neighborhoods for families*, represented in this volume by "Retail Trade as a Route to Neighborhood Revitalization," by Karen Chapple and Rick Jacobus

—*Governing effectively*, represented by "Correlates of Mayoral Takeovers in City School Systems," by Jeffrey R. Henig and Elisabeth Thurston Fraser

—*Building human capital*, represented by "The Education Gospel and the Metropolis: The Multiple Roles of Community Colleges in Workforce and Economic Development," by W. Norton Grubb

—*Growing the middle class*, represented by "Living Wage Laws: How Much Do (Can) They Matter?" by Harry J. Holzer

—*Growing a competitive economy through industry-based strategies*, represented by "The Next Move: Metropolitan Regions and the Transformation of the Freight Transport and Distribution System," by Susan Christopherson and Michael H. Belzer

—*Managing the spatial pattern of metropolitan growth and development*, represented by "How Might Inclusionary Zoning Affect Urban Form?" by Rolf Pendall

The goal of this volume is to inform scholars, policymakers, and practitioners about the state of knowledge on the effectiveness of the selected policy approaches, reforms, or experiments listed above in addressing key social and economic problems facing central cities, suburbs, and metropolitan areas. Authors were not required to conduct original research, although some did. Rather, their task was to take a fresh and unfettered look at the area and conceptualize (or reconceptualize) the issue and the questions that should be asked to influence intelligent public debate. Given that conceptualization, the authors were then asked to summarize extant research on the topic and, on the basis of that research and their own knowledge, to set forth what is known about the effects of the pubic policy approach under discussion and the public policy implications of what is known. They were also asked to identify what is still not known but important to find out.

Summary of Chapters

Retail trade is a highly visible feature in a community and is often a symbol of economic status. Terms like *upscale retail, strip mall,* or *big box store* convey very different images of retail trade that are widely associated with economic prosperity, or the lack thereof. But, does retail trade really revitalize run-down or neglected neighborhoods? And if so, what are the mechanisms at work, the successful strategies, and necessary conditions that lead to success? In "Retail Trade as a Route to Neighborhood Revitalization," Karen Chapple and Rick Jacobus tackle these questions. They begin by defining the issues and expectations associated with retail development and neighborhood revitalization. The authors state that, from the perspective of residents, there are three types of neighborhood revitalization: approaches that provide more access to services and opportunities for existing low-income populations, residential changes from a low-income neighborhood to a mixed-income neighborhood (due to either an influx of newcomers or increases in incomes for local residents), and gentrification that gradually replaces existing low-income residents with more affluent newcomers. Using a conceptual model, Chapple and Jacobus describe the relationship between retail development and neighborhood revitalization.

Their review of the literature finds mixed evidence for the assumption that low-income neighborhoods are underserved by retailers. It also finds that formal evaluation of the effects of retail development, especially with respect to overall neighborhood improvement, has been limited. The authors acknowledge the challenges to evaluating retail development programs, such as their small scale, the variety of actors involved, and limited neighborhood-level capacity. In reviewing the evidence, Chapple and Jacobus examine three broad strategies to retail revitalization: public-led retail development, private-led retail development, and commercial corridor revitalization. Retail strategies variously target job creation, vacancy rates, private investment, public investment, tax revenues and property values, crime and safety, and community identity. To explore further the relationship between these retail development goals and neighborhood revitalization, Chapple and Jacobus provide a case study of the San Francisco Bay Area, analyzing the relationship between retail and neighborhood revitalization from 1990 to 2005 in a region with unusual increases in income inequality accompanied by significant revitalization. They find that the way the retail sector changes is closely related to the way the neighborhood changes, with increases in middle-income residents (rather than gentrification or other forms of change) most closely associated with retail revitalization.

The chapter concludes with the suggestion that any large-scale impacts of retail development on community economic health occur indirectly, such as through changes in internal and external perceptions of the neighborhood and, ultimately, changes in neighborhood residential composition. However, the authors note that existing studies of the effectiveness of neighborhood retail development strategies have not explored these broader impacts. Chapple and Jacobus also recommend further research to address how outcomes for the poor are tied to the specific character of neighborhood change. Such research might suggest specific retail development strategies that are most likely to benefit the poor and lead to stable mixed-income communities without contributing to displacement of the poor.

IMPROVING LARGE CITY school systems is widely recognized as a critical if not intractable problem. Given its importance, it is not surprising that it has been the subject of a wide range of policy reforms ranging from those within the schools themselves (standards-based education, curriculum reform, smaller class size, performance testing, improving teacher training, and so on) to challenges to the traditional public school system as the monopoly provider of elementary and secondary school education (such as vouchers and charter schools). Over the past two decades, structural change in school governance—in particular, providing the mayor, rather than an independent school board, with the ultimate control of the school system—has also emerged as a possible means of improving central city elementary and secondary education. In "Correlates of Mayoral Takeovers in City School Systems," Jeffrey R. Henig and Elisabeth Thurston Fraser examine why this has occurred, what has changed as a result, and the implications of this governance reform in the major urban school districts in which it has occurred.

The authors begin by considering *why* mayoral control has become a popular approach and the logic that underlies its appeal. On the "push" side, they note the frustration with the performance of existing school systems and the "anything must be better than what we are doing now" approach. On the "pull" side, they review the arguments on why mayoral control ought to be more effective than traditional school board control. In particular, they note theoretical reasons that mayoral control should, by centralizing authority in the office of an elected mayor, improve democratic accountability, broaden the constituency for education, reduce the power of existing entrenched interests, reduce micromanagement, and increase coordination between schools and other local agencies serving youth.

The authors argue that mayoral control might accomplish these objectives because school district policies might be expected to differ as a result of the different agendas and constituencies of a mayor compared with those of an elected school board. School systems controlled by mayors might be expected to "do things differently" than school systems controlled by traditional school boards. Do they?

The authors' review of the existing literature indicates that mayorally controlled school systems are more likely to appoint nontraditional school superintendents with experience outside of education, to experiment with privatization of at least some elements of traditional school system functions, and to shift spending somewhat from administrative purposes to instructional purposes. However, the literature also indicates that school systems with mayoral control have less public interaction and transparency in terms of contested public debate.

The authors' own research indicates that, controlling for other factors, school systems with mayoral control have greater revenues per pupil than do traditional school districts and that virtually all of the additional revenues come from higher levels of state and federal aid. They speculate that mayors may be better at the "politics of grantsmanship." However, given their expectations that mayoral control should broaden the constituency for education in the city, the authors are surprised that mayoral control is not associated with a higher level of locally raised revenue. They suggest that this might result from the substitution of intergovernmental funds for local funds, thus freeing up previously allocated local funds for other uses.

Henig and Fraser recognize that the expected big payoff of major reforms such as mayoral control is in better student educational outcomes, usually measured through test scores. They observe that research on the effects of mayoral control on outcomes is difficult to conduct and interpret, partly because there is a lag between imposition of mayoral control and consequent changes of policy and behavior that must be taken into account and partly because the expected lag between changes in school system policy and behavior and effects on student outcome is unknown. They cite a major study by Kenneth Wong and others, who concluded that giving mayors power to appoint the majority of the school board is associated with outcome gains, but giving them even more power has a negative effect. Wong and his colleagues also found that mayoral control is associated with an increase in the performance gap between low-performing and high-performing schools, a finding they believe may be attributable to the attempts of mayors to stem the brain drain from city public schools to suburban schools by addressing the concerns of a potentially middle-class populace before tackling issues involving redistribution.

The authors also report on their own research conducted in New York City after the shift to mayoral control. They found that the percentage of students meeting state proficiency levels was higher two years after the imposition of mayoral control than before mayoral control and that the effects were greater for lower grades than for higher grades. Henig and Fraser caution that the proficiency gains might reflect a tactic of concentrating attention on children just below the proficiency threshold, suggested by the fact that gains in student scale scores were not as strong as gains in the percentage crossing the proficiency bar, and they note that the city does not show the same evidence of relative gains on national exams.

Henig and Fraser conclude their chapter by observing that "the theoretical rationales for why mayoral control might lead to more comprehensive, coordinated, focused, and responsive education policies are more compelling, at this point, than is the evidence to support them."

TECHNOLOGY AND GLOBALIZATION, as well as the decline of heavy industry and manufacturing in this country, have focused economic development on high-skill jobs. Education, particularly occupational preparation, has come to be considered a key to improving economic performance. W. Norton Grubb offers a note of skepticism and a call for evidence over rhetoric in "The Education Gospel and the Metropolis: The Multiple Roles of Community Colleges in Workforce and Economic Development." The *education gospel* refers to the faith that turning to education to provide more occupationally oriented preparation will solve many individual and social problems. As Grubb describes, the emphasis on education and skills development includes the transformation of high schools and adult education, shifts in two- and four-year colleges toward increases in occupational programs, the rise in professional education in many forms, and increases in job training and other short-term training, all accompanied by narrower conceptions of the purposes of education. States and localities have turned to education and training as tools for economic development, offering their efforts to train a skilled workforce as incentives to attract employers. Grubb's chapter addresses the role of education in economic development from three perspectives: the supply side, represented primarily by community and technical colleges; the demand side, represented by employers; and the policy side, which considers program effectiveness and the justification for public subsidies.

Community colleges are major providers of education and training, but they have multiple roles and missions. Grubb divides the occupational offerings of community colleges into initial preparation (for those who have not yet entered the adult labor force), upgrade training, retraining, and remedial training. He also distinguishes between education, which usually connotes longer periods of academic preparation, and training, which is usually short term and more job specific. Community college courses may be credit or noncredit, and most community colleges also offer customized or contract training tailored to the needs of specific employers. Grubb notes that community colleges have several advantages or potential advantages, including a wide variety of offerings and schedules, a connection to pedagogical issues that can result in innovative approaches to instruction, lower cost due to public subsidy, and their spatial distribution across the country. An important question Grubb considers is how responsive community colleges are to local labor market conditions.

With respect to meeting the needs of employers, there has been concern in this country that firms provide too little training for their workers, particularly lower-level workers, but Grubb notes that this assumption is hard to evaluate. Community colleges primarily serve the middle-skilled labor market, occupations that require some post–high school education or training but less than a baccalaureate degree. This labor market, like community colleges, is local in nature. It is characterized by cyclical demand, a predominance of smaller firms and informal hiring practices, and job requirements that are not always clear. Grubb concludes that this labor market is more chaotic than the market for professionals and managers and that both its workers and its employers are underinformed about sources of education and training.

As for policy initiatives, Grubb finds that the field of workforce and economic development has usually been unclear about what justifies public involvement. The largest public subsidies for postsecondary occupational education come through community college systems. Other state and federal programs support customized training, postsecondary occupational education, and job training. In addition, the federal government provides a number of tax credits for education and training. Grubb poses two key questions: Is there justification for public spending on education and training, rather than requiring individuals and employers to bear the costs? Second, under what conditions might education and training lead to economic development? Grubb reviews existing evidence on returns to education for credit courses and programs in community colleges, but he notes the lack of data on noncredit enrollments and the limited studies and methodological problems associated with evaluations of state customized training. Grubb's chapter concludes with recommendations for educational and training providers, states, and the federal government. He acknowledges that a lack of skills is only one factor affecting economic growth and cautions against putting too much faith in the education gospel.

IN RECENT YEARS many municipalities and counties throughout the nation have enacted *living wage laws*, which require businesses that benefit from government contracts or other forms of public financial assistance to pay wages well above the federal minimum wage, and sometimes benefits, to their workers. A diverse set of concerns motivated these laws—including desires to raise the earnings of low-wage workers, prevent the outsourcing of municipal work to lower-wage providers, support union organizing, limit local governments' use of economic development subsidies to attract large firms, mobilize a broad social movement to combat low wages and inequality, and make a symbolic statement about fair wage levels and the appropriateness of government efforts to raise low wages. Campaigns in favor of living wage laws began to grow in a context of dramatically widening income inequality in the United States and at a time when minimum wage laws, labor unions, and other policies and institutions that had traditionally been used in efforts to limit such inequality were declining in the private sector.

In "Living Wage Laws: How Much Do (Can) They Matter?" Harry J. Holzer focuses on the impacts of living wage laws on labor market outcomes such as wage levels, employment rates, poverty, and inequality. Advocates of these laws often view them as ways to raise the earnings of low-wage workers and reduce wage inequality. Opponents often believe that the laws reduce the number of jobs available to low-wage workers and drive businesses away from the jurisdictions that enact them.

Holzer begins by describing the living wage laws that exist in the 140 municipalities and counties that had such laws as of May 2006. These laws affect very few workers directly, because few work for firms that are subject to living wage laws. Most studies suggest that the laws cover only 2–3 percent of the bottom tenth of wage-earners. Even in a city of 1 million people, only about 1,500 workers are likely to be covered. However, it is possible that the impacts of living wage laws spill over to other workers who do not work for covered employers.

Holzer then addresses some of the basic economic issues that the laws raise, including the possibility of trade-offs between improved quality of jobs and reduced quantity of jobs for low-wage workers. He finds that living wage laws have modest benefits and modest costs for low-wage workers. Living wage laws raise the wages of the lowest-wage workers. They may also result in lower turnover, better worker morale, and modest reductions in poverty. However, they lead to modest reductions in employment for the lowest-wage workers and may also result in reductions in training and in the use of part-time or overtime work.

Holzer concludes that living wage laws can be useful but that meaningful increases in the earnings of low-wage workers and reductions in poverty require more powerful public policies. Because of their limited coverage and modest effects on wages, living wage laws cannot have a large impact on low wages or poverty. Other public policies, such as those to expand collective bargaining, education and training, publicly financed health insurance, and parental leave, are likely to have more impact. Living wage laws can be useful if they raise awareness of pay disparity issues and build support for more powerful policies to raise the earnings of low-wage workers, but they are not a substitute for such policies.

IN MANY METROPOLITAN areas, industry-based, economic development strategies emphasize attracting and growing high-technology industries such as information technology and biotechnology, which provide few job opportunities for workers with less than a bachelor's degree. Policymakers in some metropolitan areas, including Louisville, Kentucky, and Riverside, California, have embraced an alternative development strategy centered around freight transportation, including long-distance trucking, logistics and distribution, and air freight. These industries offer many more jobs for less-educated workers, leading some observers to hail them as replacements for the manufacturing jobs that the nation's metropolitan areas are continuing to lose.

In "The Next Move: Metropolitan Regions and the Transformation of the Freight Transport and Distribution System," Susan Christopherson and Michael H. Belzer assess the prospects for different types of metropolitan areas to become freight transportation centers. They begin by describing the economic, technological, and national public policy forces that have shaped those prospects over the course of the last three decades. Trade liberalization, the deregulation of the trucking industry and other transportation industries, the decline of union bargaining power within the trucking industry, and the adoption of new technologies such as bar codes, radio frequency identification, and containerization helped lower the price of long-distance freight transportation substantially. As a result, freight shipment became more time sensitive. Trade liberalization also spurred the growth of imports, leading suppliers of manufactured goods increasingly to cluster geographically around their major customers (assemblers of finished products or major retailers). Seaport activity became more concentrated in a few major ports on the East and West coasts, which became more self-contained and less capable of generating spillover benefits for their metropolitan regional economies. New inland ports centered on large intermodal distribution facilities arose, especially in metropolitan areas in the Midwest and South. These facilities were developed mainly in exurban areas where land was cheap and highway and air freight access was good. Metropolitan areas that are not currently either seaports or inland ports, or whose geographic locations are not conducive to seaport or inland port activities, are not likely to become freight transportation centers unless one or more of the forces that created today's economic geography of the freight industry is reversed.

Christopherson and Belzer describe the extent to which freight transportation is geographically concentrated within metropolitan areas. They distinguish between *metropolitan areas with large concentrations of freight transportation jobs* (those that specialize to a great extent in freight transportation, as indicated by a high location quotient in freight transportation) and *metropolitan areas that have large numbers of freight jobs* (but that may or may not have high location quotients in freight transportation). Metropolitan areas with large numbers of such jobs are generally large metropolitan areas, although there are some exceptions. Metropolitan areas with large concentrations of such jobs are ones in which freight transportation is an important export industry, bringing in large amounts of income from outside the region rather than primarily serving local residents. Metropolitan areas with both large numbers and large concentrations of freight transportation jobs, such as Memphis and Indianapolis, are the nation's major freight centers.

Although freight transportation can be an important export industry for metropolitan areas that are currently either seaports or inland ports, or that have the geographic characteristics necessary to become one or the other, the authors note that freight-led economic development has important drawbacks. These include low wages for most workers in the industry, reduced highway safety, air pollution, traffic congestion, highway deterioration, poor employment opportunities for women and minorities, and the acceleration of job growth at the geographic fringes of a metropolitan area.

The authors conclude by considering what would happen to the prospects for the development of new freight transportation centers if there were a long-term increase in fuel prices. In that case, they argue, rail transportation would become more important relative to trucking and airlines, and freight transportation by truck and air would become even more concentrated in existing freight centers.

AN INCREASING NUMBER of communities over the past two decades have adopted inclusionary zoning laws. While these ordinances are clearly directed toward achieving affordable housing goals, they might also affect the shape, form, and density of urban areas. To what extent and in what ways are inclusionary zoning laws affecting urban form, and can these laws be utilized to promote compact, walkable, and mixed land-use development as well as affordable housing? Rolf Pendall's chapter, "How Might Inclusionary Zoning Affect Urban Form?" examines this question.

Pendall begins by defining inclusionary zoning narrowly as "a mandate in which local governments require residential builders to provide a share of housing that will be affordable over a long term to people earning low to moderate incomes." He notes that a broader definition would include programs, such as incentive density bonuses, which encourage affordable housing but do not require it. Pendall is interested in the effect of both definitions of inclusionary zoning on *urban form*, by which he means the density of urban development and the mix of land use and housing types at the neighborhood level.

There are a variety of design features and choices in structuring an inclusionary zoning program, each of which may lead to different effects, not only on developer decisionmaking but on urban form. These design features include, among other things, the share of units in the development that must be affordable and the number of years for which they must be kept as affordable; whether permitted densities will be increased to offset the inclusionary mandate; what the target level of affordability for the units will be; whether the mandate will be aimed at renters, homeowners, or both; whether there is a minimum development size below which the mandate will not be in effect; and whether the developer can avoid the mandate by contributing to a development fund or constructing affordable housing elsewhere.

In answer to the question of how might inclusionary zoning affect urban form, the author responds, "it depends." "Even for a single jurisdiction, inclusionary zoning might increase, have no effect on, or decrease a jurisdiction's total new residential supply, density, and unit mix," depending on the characteristics of the jurisdiction's housing market, the inclusionary zoning program design, and the availability for development of alternative locations that lack inclusionary zoning laws.

The condition of the local housing market is particularly important. To be effective, inclusionary zoning laws must not put such a substantial burden on developers that they will decide not to engage in residential development in the area. When demand in the local housing market is modest, Pendall argues that developers will likely avoid the market if inclusionary zoning requirements are imposed. Indeed, he observes that on the one hand, except in very hot housing markets, an inclusionary zoning law whose program design did not include off-sets would probably result in developers' seeking alternative locations. The effect of inclusionary zoning on urban form would in these cases depend on what landowners and developers do with the land instead of developing housing, relative to what they would have done with the land had an inclusionary zoning law not been in effect. He speculates that landowners might try to develop the land for nonresidential uses, which might, depending on other uses in the area, contribute to a more mixed-use urban form.

On the other hand, a program with a substantial high-density bonus in a relatively hot housing market might result in large numbers of high-density units and multifamily units and thus contribute to more compact urban form. However, there may be areas that adopt inclusionary zoning laws to pursue slow growth objectives, that is, adopting such laws with the expectation of driving development to other areas. In these cases, the effect on urban form would be to prevent more compact development that otherwise would have occurred.

Pendall cites Gerrit-Jan Knaap's study that indicates inclusionary zoning laws shifted production from single-family to multifamily housing by 6 percent in those California cities that had inclusionary zoning laws, thus increasing compact development. The research does not suggest that inclusionary zoning, on average, displaces development to other areas, though this may well indicate that jurisdictions adopt inclusionary zoning only if there is substantial demand for housing and displacement is thus unlikely to occur. However, the author notes that when inclusionary zoning does succeed in bringing about more dense development, it may also produce substantial political opposition on the part of established residents of lower-density single-family units, as has occurred in Berkeley, California.

Pendall concludes by observing that inclusionary zoning "starts and ends as a zoning tool . . . like zoning in general, it can foster compact development; it can kill development entirely." Because its major, intended objective is to accomplish something else—housing affordability—it is not likely to have as direct an impact on urban form as other land use regulatory tools. However, given its increasing usage and its potential, Pendall ends by urging that inclusionary zoning "should absolutely continue to be one of the elements in local and regional programs to promote compact, mixed-use, pedestrian-friendly development."

Cross-Cutting Themes

In selecting the topics for this volume and for the conference, we sought to acknowledge the broad scope of urban and regional policy issues, foster interdisciplinary discussion, and focus attention on policy effects and challenges. The topics and backgrounds of the authors and conference participants were diverse. Yet several issues cut across many of the chapters and pose shared challenges for both researchers and policymakers.

The Goals of Public Policies

Some policies may have an explicit (or apparently explicit) single goal. Others may have multiple goals, and these may or may not all be explicit. However, there is usually a single goal that researchers and evaluators take to be *the goal* of the policy and on which they focus exclusively. Several of the chapters in this volume deal with policies that are conventionally evaluated with respect to an explicit goal. Inclusionary zoning laws are usually evaluated for their impact on housing affordability for low- and moderate-income households, living wage laws for their impact on earnings and poverty, mayoral control of public schools for its impact on student achievement. Yet policies may also have unstated implicit goals as well as unintended consequences that may or may not be desirable. Thus, regardless of the effect of inclusionary zoning on housing affordability or living wage laws' effects on poverty, the efforts to put in place such policies may have contributed to the social mobilization of a constituency around the goal and, in the case of inclusionary zoning, made affordable housing an acceptable policy goal for a community. Regardless of whether mayoral takeovers of big-city schools raise students' test scores, they may mobilize business support for education as well as for the mayor's broader policy agenda.

Evaluating a policy's effectiveness with respect to only one apparently explicit goal is important, but it may not be sufficient to fully assess the policy's desirability or effectiveness. The chapters that consider alternative policy goals take different approaches to this issue. The chapter on living wage laws notes that a variety of objectives exist but devotes most of its attention to the labor market impacts of living wage laws. The chapter on mayoral takeovers considers a variety of potential policy objectives. The primary focus of the chapter on inclusionary zoning is the policy's impact on metropolitan spatial structure, although the chapter also considers the more conventional goal of housing affordability.

The Influence of Policy Design and Context on Policy Effectiveness

Nearly all the chapters conclude that the answer to the question of whether a policy is effective is "we don't know" or "it depends." To a large extent this is because the policies included in this volume are general strategies that are difficult to assess without considering specific elements of program design or the context in which policy is used. For example, the specific design characteristics of mayoral control, inclusionary zoning, or a living wage law can be important determinants of the impacts of these policies. Whether a mayor has the authority to privatize parts of public school operations or convert public schools to charter schools may affect the outcome of mayoral control of a school system. The strictness of an inclusionary zoning law's affordable housing requirement and the size of its density bonus may be important determinants of whether the law promotes the construction of affordable housing for low- and moderate-income households or whether it simply halts almost all new development. Whether a living wage law covers firms that receive government subsidies may influence its impact on employment and wages, as may the size of the geographic area to which the law applies. The challenge in such cases is to identify the design features that work to achieve the policies' objectives.

In addition, the effects of a public policy may depend on external circumstances on which the policy itself may have little or no effect. For example, whether policies to promote retail trade in a neighborhood encourage gentrification and displacement of low-income residents or make the neighborhood's existing low-income residents better-off without displacing them depends in part on what is happening to income inequality within the broader metropolitan area. Whether an economic development policy that depends heavily on attracting and retaining freight transportation facilities is feasible for a metropolitan area depends on whether the metropolitan area has the geographic characteristics necessary for it to become either a seaport or an inland port. The challenge here is to identify the circumstances under which a particular policy may be appropriate.

Policy Mechanisms

To understand a policy fully and to assess its effectiveness, it is important to understand the causal mechanism through which the desired change is expected to occur. For example, even proponents of mayoral control of large-city public school systems do not believe that simply changing control in and of itself will bring about desired change. Instead the mechanism by which proponents believe the policy will produce change is that mayoral control will lead to a series of other changes in school systems that are expected to result in better outcomes. Similarly, proponents may think inclusionary zoning will produce more affordable housing and more dense development because its density bonus will motivate developers to build affordable units at higher densities than what they would otherwise have built without such an incentive. A living wage law may raise the earnings of low-wage workers by spurring unionization or mobilizing a broader social movement that leads to the enactment of other antipoverty policies. Publicly supported workforce development programs at community colleges may improve the skills and earnings of workers who do not have bachelor's degrees if they provide general training for which individual employers would not otherwise pay.

Income Inequality as a Motivator and Target of Public Policy

Municipal and metropolitan policymakers are frequently faced with problems that are not of their own making but to which they try to respond. For all the policies considered in this volume, rising income inequality at the national level, the metropolitan level, or both levels played a role either as a motivator of the policy or as a problem that the policy was intended to address. Inclusionary zoning is generally thought of as a response to a reduced supply of affordable housing for low- and moderate-income households, which is in part a consequence of growing income inequality within metropolitan areas. Similarly, neighborhood retail development policies are in part a response to neighborhood decline in low-income areas, which is due in part to the decline or stagnation of the incomes that residents of those neighborhoods earn. One objective of living wage laws is to reduce economic inequality by raising the earnings of low-wage workers. Economic development strategies led by freight transportation are sometimes motivated by a desire to replace lost high-wage manufacturing jobs and provide good jobs for less-educated workers, although they may actually provide low-wage jobs for those workers. Community college workforce development programs are sometimes motivated by a concern with the earnings prospects of workers without bachelor's degrees and may affect those prospects. Mayoral takeovers of big-city school systems are in part a response to low student achievement, which is partly a consequence of the concentration of low-income students in those districts.

History Matters

In several of the chapters, the historical development of the policy was important and helped to explain, at least partly, why the policy was put in place and what it was expected to do. For example, the fact that inclusionary zoning arose in large part because of exclusionary zoning practices increases the understanding of inclusionary zoning as a policy and provides a yardstick for the evaluation of inclusionary zoning. Similarly the fact that living wage laws grew in part out of an effort to combat outsourcing by municipal governments provides another goal by which they could be assessed. An understanding of the national-level policies that affected transportation costs and wages in long-distance trucking contributes to an understanding of why an economic development policy based on freight transportation is or is not feasible for a particular metropolitan area. The impacts of mayoral control of schools may depend on whether mayoral control was a long-standing feature of school district governance or whether it was adopted as part of the recent wave of mayoral takeovers as well as on whether it came about as a result of a mayoral initiative or a state mandate to which the mayor was opposed or indifferent.

Policy Evaluation under Less than Ideal Conditions

Many of the chapters in this volume conclude that the policy under discussion had not fully accomplished its goals or had made only a small dent in the problem(s) it was ostensibly intended to address. Alternative policies may be more effective than the policies the authors analyze. For example, a combination of relaxed zoning regulations, widespread housing subsidies for low-income residents, and more vigorous national policies to raise the incomes of low-income households would probably be more effective than inclusionary zoning as a means of improving housing affordability. The adoption of better instructional methods by elected school boards working in cooperation with teachers and school administrators may have a greater impact on student achievement than mayoral school takeovers. A combination of higher federal or state minimum wages, greater unionization of low-wage workers, a more generous Earned Income Tax Credit, more public support for education and training, publicly financed health insurance, and parental leave would likely do more to raise the living standards of low-wage workers than would living wage ordinances. National and regional policies to retain and expand high-wage manufacturing employment (for example, expanded efforts to assist manufacturers in improving productivity and creating new products, complementary workforce policies to upgrade the skills of incumbent workers, and trade and exchange rate policies), combined with effective policies to raise the wages of less-educated workers in all industries, may do more to provide less-educated workers with good jobs than policies to attract or expand the freight transportation industry.

However, these alternative policies may be politically infeasible or at least not subject to the control of urban and regional policymakers. In such circumstances, when the ideal policy or mix of policies cannot be implemented at the urban or regional level, the nonideal policies analyzed in this volume should be compared not with the ideal policies but with other nonideal policies that are feasible for urban and regional policymakers. This does not mean that it is worthless to note that superior policies exist. Nor does it mean that it is useless to advocate for more effective federal policies or to find ways to loosen the political constraints that inhibit the adoption of superior policies. However, it does mean that urban and regional policies should be evaluated in a way that takes account of the options that are feasible for urban and regional policymakers.

Geographic Spillovers

Urban and regional policies are usually intended to produce effects within a particular geographic area, such as a neighborhood, municipality, or metropolitan area. However, many such policies have effects, positive or negative, that extend beyond the geographic areas to which they are targeted. These effects are usually unintended and policy analysts often fail to consider them. Thus, inclusionary zoning in one or a few municipalities in a metropolitan area may induce people of various income levels to move into or out of other municipalities in the same region. A living wage ordinance in one or a few municipalities similarly may induce some businesses to move elsewhere. A new retail development in one neighborhood may draw business away from other neighborhoods in the same metropolitan area. A freight-based economic development strategy in one metropolitan area may affect air pollution, traffic congestion, and road safety in other regions. It is important to evaluate the impacts of such policies not only on the geographic areas at which they are targeted but also at broader metropolitan or national scales.

Public-Private Bargaining and Collaboration

It is conventional in public policy analysis to assume that the public and private sectors have an arm's-length relationship in which the government sets a policy and private actors make decisions in reaction to that policy. The policies discussed in this volume either explicitly or implicitly involve public-private interactions that depart from this assumption.

In some cases the design of policy involves bargaining between public and private sectors. The public sector strives to structure incentives or regulations in ways that promote private sector activity consistent with public purposes, and the private organizations seek to shape those incentives or regulations in accordance with their own interests. The design features of living wage laws, such as the level of the living wage and the kinds of firms and workers covered, often result from bargaining among living wage advocates outside government, business interests, and government policymakers (who variously may be sympathetic to living wage advocates or opponents). The specifics of inclusionary zoning laws may depend on bargaining among housing affordability advocates, developers, existing property owners, and government policymakers. Similarly, bargaining among neighborhood residents of various income levels, developers, retailers, and government policymakers may shape the nature of efforts to revitalize neighborhoods through retail trade. This type of bargaining contrasts with the conventional model of government regulation in which the government, without any direct interaction with private actors, estimates how those actors will react to a proposed policy and then adopts the policy that induces those actors to behave in a way that the government deems desirable. Information asymmetry factors into these negotiations because the government lacks the information used by the private sector for strategic decisionmaking but needs to strike a balance between incentives and oversubsidy.

Some of the policies described in this book involved direct collaboration between the public and private sectors. Workforce development programs at community colleges are often developed through collaboration between the colleges and one or more employers. Retail trade strategies to revitalize neighborhoods may involve collaboration among local governments, retailers, and developers. In some cases mayoral control of public schools may include contracting out school operations to private firms or establishing charter schools that are run by private organizations.

The crosscutting themes that we have identified suggest two broad ways in which future research on urban and regional policy should be reoriented so that it is of greater use to policymakers. First, research analyzing the impacts of urban and regional policy should move away from an exclusive preoccupation with identifying "the" exclusive impacts of "a" particular policy and embrace a more multifaceted approach to policy analysis. Such an approach would include attention to multiple goals that may exist for a particular policy, the ways in which specific elements of policy design influence policy outcomes, the causal mechanisms by which policies produce their effects, the roles of history and context in shaping policies and their effects, and the feasibility of policy alternatives at the urban and regional levels. Although researchers sometimes mention these issues within the context for their analyses of policy impacts, they do not typically integrate them into their analyses.

Second, our crosscutting themes suggest that empirical research on urban and regional policy should adopt more realistic conceptions of the behavior of private sector actors. It should pay explicit attention to the geographic spillover effects of public policies, which often come about because the initial impacts of policies on households and firms in particular places give rise to out-migration from those places by some of those households and firms or immigration to those places by others. Empirical research should also incorporate strategy, bargaining, and uncertainty, as well as collaboration, into its treatment of public-private relationships. Theoretical research in urban and regional economics pays a great deal of attention to geographic spillovers (though in highly stylized ways), but empirical policy-oriented research typically does so only on some issues, often because of data limitations. Strategy, bargaining, uncertainty, and collaboration are important issues in nonspatial economic theory, political economy, and some applied fields of economics and political science. However, they do not figure prominently in either theoretical or applied research on urban and regional problems.

We hope that the emergence of these themes across the topics of the following chapters will move research and policy forward in ways that promote collaborative solutions to the many challenges of urban and regional policy.

2

Retail Trade as a Route to Neighborhood Revitalization

KAREN CHAPPLE AND RICK JACOBUS

At the end of World War II, most American neighborhoods were serviced by neighborhood commercial districts populated with stores selling food, clothing, household goods, jewelry, and other items. The strongest of these districts successfully competed with downtowns as locations for major department stores. But rapid suburbanization and the development of automobile-oriented shopping centers led to the decline of most of these historic commercial districts.[1] In low-income and minority neighborhoods, the decline of neighborhood retail coincided with dramatic shifts in residential housing patterns as middle-income minorities and white families of all income levels moved out of urban neighborhoods, leaving behind increasingly concentrated poverty and racially segregated neighborhoods. By the 1980s, growing income inequality was contributing to a "spiral of decay" in which declining incomes and population losses led to declining retail and other neighborhood conditions, which, in turn, caused further out-migration.[2] This was especially true in communities of color. While the 1990s saw the return of some more affluent and white residents to the inner city, neighborhood commercial strips have been slower to revitalize.[3] By 2000, half as many central city neighborhoods had a middle-income profile as in 1970, suggesting that these areas epitomize national patterns of growing income inequality.[4] Disinvestment has remained so pervasive

We gratefully acknowledge suggestions from Karl Seidman and the excellent research assistance from Lauren Lambie-Hanson. Any errors are, of course, our own.
1. Fogelson (2001).
2. Wilson (1987).
3. Wilson (1987).
4. Booza and others (2006).

that policymakers (urged on by Michael Porter) paradoxically consider these older neighborhoods to be "new" or "emerging" markets.

Neighborhood commercial disinvestment stems not only from population shifts but also from shifting consumption patterns. Most obvious, the rise of big box retail, now commonly called the Wal-Martization of retail, has vastly increased the type and quantity of goods available to consumers, for the most part at lower prices. "Big box" means larger market areas and stores, but rarely in the traditional commercial corridor locations. The need for larger sites and freeway access means that this type of retail generally must locate in industrial or commercial areas distant from residential neighborhoods, most often requiring the use of an automobile. Moreover, as consumers increasingly purchase goods in bulk from discounters, the car has become essential to the shopping trip. Though the debate is ongoing about whether big box outlets cannibalize or complement small local stores, this overall shift in retailing has undoubtedly discouraged retailers from locating in neighborhood retail strips.[5]

Across the country, local governments and community-based organizations are operating a wide variety of programs that seek to reverse this decline. These programs intervene in neighborhood retail markets by attracting new retail businesses or supporting existing businesses, building new commercial real estate, or improving quality-of-life conditions that stand in the way of retail development. Although these programs are part of a broader attempt to revitalize disinvested urban neighborhoods, their proponents have generally not articulated the specific mechanisms through which they are expected to contribute to revitalization. This chapter will fill that gap by describing how retail reinvestment might, at least in theory, lead to neighborhood revitalization.

Are retail strategies successful? As this chapter will show, few formal evaluations have been completed, and even those tend to measure discrete outcomes such as job creation rather than the contribution of programs to overall neighborhood well-being. Evaluating retail development programs is difficult, first, because of their small scale, and second, because of the variety of actors involved. Generally, retail development programs are very local efforts—targeting a single neighborhood or, in some cases, areas as small as one or two city blocks. The relative shortage of neighborhood-level capacity (including community-based organizations, or CBOs, and private market actors such as realtors and real estate developers focused on inner-city neighborhoods) makes it difficult to develop and sustain programs. Moreover, many revitalization efforts are relatively small-scale pilots implemented for limited periods of time, with minimal funding. Finally, different stakeholders move in and out of retail revitalization, depending on foundation fashions and political conditions. Alter-

5. Artz and Stone (2006); Basker (2005); Stone (1997); Civic Economics (2002).

natively, the federal government, the mayor's office, the redevelopment agency, intermediaries such as the Local Initiatives Support Corporation (LISC) or Main Street programs, merchants' associations, local chambers of commerce, and local business development centers may get involved in commercial corridors in joint or separate efforts.

The evaluations to date use anecdotal and program outcome data to show that these efforts do result in some increased market activity, increased sales tax revenue, and even an improved sense of community pride. But since very few studies have looked at these outcomes in the context of comparison neighborhoods, it is hard to know if the intervention, rather than other factors, caused the improvement. Only studies of empowerment zones tend to employ quasi-experimental designs with control neighborhoods.[6]

Though it is possible that programs are creating overall economic growth, there are several plausible alternative explanations as well. First, retail development strategies may be causing retail activity to shift between neighborhoods: rather than creating net new activity, resurgence in one place means decline in another. Second, retail consumption may be shifting back to more traditional neighborhood-based patterns. Third, the return of higher-income residents to urban neighborhoods may be stimulating improvements in retail activity. In other words, just as the flight of the urban middle class caused the decline of retail, its return is generating a resurgence.

If some part of this third explanation is accurate—that is, improvements in neighborhood retail conditions are associated with changes in the housing preferences of U.S. households and in the widespread strength of the housing market in the early part of this decade—an interesting chicken-and-egg question arises. In addition to population shifts fueling the retail sector, might improvements in neighborhood retail be stimulating residential revitalization? If so, the case for retail revitalization becomes much more compelling, and one key question becomes what kind of revitalization is occurring: an influx of upper-income households replacing lower-income residents, a diversification of household incomes, or income improvements for existing residents?

This chapter begins by outlining the relationship between retail and neighborhood revitalization, presenting a conceptual model of how changes in one shape the other. We then examine the issue of the retail gap: although interest in retail revitalization is based upon a presumption that low-income neighborhoods are underserved, the evidence on this point is conflicting, and measurement is generally poor. Next, we examine three broad strategies for retail revitalization: public-led retail development, private-led retail development, and commercial corridor revitalization. As the following section shows, each has had

6. See, for example, Oakley and Tsao (2006).

varying effects on revitalization outcomes, from job creation to improving neighborhood identity. We then provide a case study of revitalization in the San Francisco Bay Area, analyzing the relationship between retail and neighborhood revitalization from 1990 to 2005 in a region with unusual increases in income inequality accompanied by significant revitalization. A conclusion offers thoughts for further research.

How Does Neighborhood Revitalization through Retail Work?

Proponents of retail development programs cite a wide range of sometimes conflicting reasons for pursuing these strategies. These programs can raise local and state tax revenues, often with just minimal expenditures, since they typically use underutilized infrastructure. New retail projects or revitalized corridors act as catalysts for further public and private development. They also provide entrepreneurship opportunities and create jobs for neighborhood residents.

Successful commercial development can make low-income neighborhoods more attractive places to live for working families and individuals, while also stemming the outflow of the low-income population—thus diversifying income levels in communities. But making neighborhoods more desirable might also spur gentrification—the attraction of new middle- and upper-income residents into previously decaying neighborhoods, typically associated with an increase in property values and sometimes the displacement of lower-income households as well. In the following section, we first examine the debate over neighborhood revitalization and gentrification and then turn to the question of how retail revitalization might be connected to neighborhood revitalization.

What Is Neighborhood Revitalization?

At the outset, it is important to distinguish among different forms of revitalization. By definition, revitalization can only take place in areas that are initially declining or low income. In these neighborhoods, the process of revitalization might lead to three different types of outcomes for residents. Some low-income areas might remain essentially low income but with improved access to services and opportunities. One example of this is the Dudley Street Neighborhood Initiative in Boston, which seems to have stabilized and revitalized the neighborhood without a substantial influx of more affluent residents.[7] Another form of revitalization occurs as a low-income neighborhood becomes mixed income, either through an influx of more affluent residents or through improvements in the incomes of existing residents (or both). Of particular interest are neighborhoods that gain middle-income, rather than upper-income, residents; although

7. Medoff and Sklar (1994).

the majority of U.S. neighborhoods are diverse, most are losing their middle-income households (which is due, in part, to increasing income inequality nationwide).[8] Research has documented how revitalization strategies from small-scale community interventions to physical redevelopment can benefit existing residents and stabilize diverse communities; however, it should be noted that these studies focus more on racial rather than on income diversity.[9]

If the community does not remain mixed income, but continues to attract more affluent residents who gradually replace the existing low-income residents, then a third form of revitalization, *gentrification*, has occurred, often without benefit to existing residents. Though definitions of gentrification vary, these neighborhoods generally experience disinvestment followed by an influx of reinvestment and households of higher socioeconomic status and educational attainment.[10] Such neighborhood change transforms the "essential character and flavor of the neighborhood."[11]

Gentrification has been widely documented, with most commonly cited examples in New York, Chicago, Boston, and San Francisco.[12] However, a debate still flourishes about the extent to which this process is accompanied by displacement. Particularly in the hottest real estate markets, with rising rents and property taxes, redevelopment of existing housing, condo conversions, or even outright evictions can result in displacement of existing residents. Yet, there is some evidence that household mobility rates are relatively lower in gentrifying neighborhoods (perhaps as more households choose to stay), and even those who dispute that finding admit that only a small share of renters move because of displacement.[13]

If middle-income residents depart as well, then the neighborhood may well become *bipolar*, with growth in the share of both very low- and very high-income households.[14] Public policies promoting revitalization may help set in motion these processes of gentrification and bipolarity. Yet, ironically, the stated intent of many of these policies is to facilitate the creation of *mixed-income* communities.

William Julius Wilson suggested that the income mix in a community was key to the life outcomes of poor residents.[15] The concentration of poverty left poor communities without the stabilizing influence of middle-income house-

8. Galster and others (2005).
9. Goodman and Monti (1999); Nyden and others (1997).
10. Freeman (2005); Wyly and Hammel (2004).
11. Kennedy and Leonard (2001).
12. See Wyly and Hammel (1999).
13. Freeman and Braconi (2004); McKinnish, Walsh, and White (2008); Newman and Wyly (2006). Newman and Wyly find that from 1989 to 2002, 6.6 percent to 9.9 percent of all local moves among renter households were due to displacement.
14. Galster and Booza (2007).
15. Wilson (1987).

holds. A growing consensus of policymakers and academics suggests that policies that promote the formation of more mixed-income communities will benefit poor families. There are essentially three ways in which the low-income benefit from the presence of more affluent neighbors; the first two generally are accepted, and the third is still hotly debated. First, residents may gain from the better resources and services available in neighborhoods with more middle- and upper-income residents; second, such neighborhoods have better mechanisms for informal social control; and third, social interaction with more affluent neighbors may (but probably will not) improve access to opportunity.[16] While debate continues about the most effective policies, federal, state, and local programs have begun to focus on deconcentrating poverty by, for example, offering housing vouchers in place of public housing complexes, incorporating into market-rate developments low-income housing in scattered sites, and redeveloping public housing projects to include moderate-income units.

Although the term *gentrification* has been used positively to refer to any community where overall income composition changes to include more higher-income households, increasingly the term is used as a pejorative to refer to only the negative consequences of such change.[17] This leaves advocates for mixed-income communities in a difficult bind. If any influx of higher-income households is considered gentrification and therefore harmful to the existing community, any improvements to the neighborhood (including reductions in crime or blight or new retail development) will inevitably make the neighborhood more attractive to higher-income residents and result in the displacement of existing residents. Community leaders are left to debate whether it is possible to achieve any measure of development without displacement.

Whereas concerns about gentrification are focused more often on residential change than on the influx of new businesses displacing existing stores, this kind of commercial gentrification seems to happen as well and has consequences for the broader character of a neighborhood. Businesses serving higher-income cus-

16. None of the HUD mixed-income policies (Gautreaux and the other consent decrees to desegregate housing, Moving to Opportunity [or MTO], and HOPE VI) have had a demonstrable positive effect on economic opportunity, as measured by employment, earnings, or income of individuals. In the Gautreaux program in Chicago, the outcome for families who moved to the suburbs was that there was no change in employment or wages (Rosenbaum and Popkin 1991). This failure is repeated for individuals in the MTO program, every HOPE VI study thus far completed, and even in HUD's Welfare-to-Work Voucher Program. Clampet-Lundquist (2004); Goering and Feins (2003); Goetz (2002); Levy and Woolley, 2007; Rubinowitz and Rosenbaum (2000); Turney and others (2006); Curley (2006). See also Emily Holt, "The Impact of Urban Neighborhood Revitalization on the Self-Sufficiency of Public Housing Residents" (http://hdl.handle.net/1961/4255 [2007]); Joseph (2006).

17. Freeman (2006).

tomers (either new residents or outsiders attracted into the neighborhood by businesses like art galleries or restaurants) may be able to pay higher rents than established neighborhood businesses can, which may then be pushed out to make way for the new businesses. This commercial transformation can itself play a role in the process of residential change. Lance Freeman interviewed lower-income residents in gentrifying neighborhoods in New York City who pointed to changed or increased retail activity as a key sign of neighborhood change.[18] Some residents clearly resented the new businesses. One reported, "We don't eat there. I went in there for a piece of cake and it was like four bucks! I can get a whole cake for four bucks. Obviously they don't want too many of us in there."[19] Others welcomed the same changes, even the arrival of stores that were clearly catering to the neighborhood's new demographic.

> I just like the change. . . . You know, you get to see, different people, differ-
> ent stores being opened . . . me and my kids, go up on DeKalb Avenue to
> the different restaurants. Then we went to the sushi restaurant. My son was
> like, what is this? I was like, let's just try it, 'cause I've never had it before.[20]

But Freeman found that when asked about neighborhood changes, most residents, rather than commenting on the arrival of expensive stores or restaurants, mentioned instead the return of supermarkets and drugstores. One said:

> [I] like the new stores and shops. . . . I appreciate that. Like I know there's
> a Pathmark [grocery store] that's opening up on 145th and 8th Avenue.
> That's like unheard of. I was really surprised at that, and then up the block
> it's Duane Reade [drugstore] opening up. 'Cause we used to have to travel
> so far just to get prescriptions filled.[21]

While Freeman cites these reactions to suggest that gentrification may offer very significant underappreciated benefits to lower-income residents, they also suggest that the impact on lower-income residents may not be the same for all types of commercial improvement. Some businesses are more likely to provide key services for existing residents and improved economic stability, while others may further marginalize the poor and undermine economic stability by fueling speculation and displacement. A new, upscale restaurant sends a different kind of signal than does a new drugstore, and both are quite different from the message that a new art school would send.

---

18. Freeman (2006).
19. Freeman (2006, p. 64).
20. Freeman (2006, p. 63).
21. Freeman (2006, p. 66).

How Does Retail Revitalization Lead to Neighborhood Revitalization?

One of the key debates in community development concerns the relative effectiveness of place-based versus people-based strategies.[22] The basic argument for targeting place is that since most disadvantaged groups are spatially concentrated, programs (such as redevelopment or enterprise zones) to intervene in these neighborhoods will have the most direct impact. But since not all locals will benefit, and some may in fact prefer to leave the neighborhood, others argue that community economic development programs should target the disadvantaged directly. Another critique of place-based economic revitalization argues that revitalization is based on a false assumption that neighborhood-level economic growth could have a significant impact on the well-being of low-income, inner-city residents; because labor markets are regional, this view sees the neighborhood's increased participation in regional economic growth as key to any positive future for these households.[23] Others reject the need to choose between people and place, seeing social norms and networks as the major obstacles to opportunity for low-income households, making a combination of people-based and place-based strategies necessary to repair inner-city norms and networks.[24]

Policymakers typically conceptualize commercial development programs in terms of their impact on place, rather than on its residents. But there is also an argument that these programs can build connections to new social networks and the regional economy. Neighborhood-based development efforts may be necessary to overcome employment and investment obstacles so that neighborhood residents can benefit from regional economic growth.[25] Likewise, commercial district strategies can help address inner-city poverty "by creating a stronger and more positive environment for residents, promoting more social interaction and helping to change resident self-perceptions and norms."[26]

Beyond its impact on existing residents, neighborhood retail development can have an impact on the residential composition of a neighborhood (positively or negatively) The relationship between neighborhood-level commercial markets and residential markets in the same neighborhoods is unclear; in particular, no research has addressed the chicken-and-egg question of whether neighborhood residential revitalization leads to retail revitalization or vice versa. It is clear that demographic changes among neighborhood residents should eventually lead to altered retail conditions, given perfect information in the market. How-

22. For an effective reframing of the debate, see Crane and Manville (2008).
23. See, for example, Teitz (1989).
24. Dickens (1999) provides a useful review of this position.
25. Dickens (1999).
26. Seidman (2002, p. 24).

ever it is also clear that the presence of retail centers or strips and the absence of blighted commercial properties can influence the location decisions of households. Hedonic housing price models have shown that amenities play an important role in residential location, and the literature on the back-to-the-city movement also suggests that easy access to time-saving household services and retail has led residents to value inner-city locations.[27] In this way, new commercial development can have an impact on the residential market.

In addition to the direct impact that the presence or absence of stores has on potential neighborhood residents, retail has an indirect impact on the overall perception of a neighborhood. Retail strips, commercial corridors, and neighborhood shopping centers serve as a kind of "front door" to any community. On the one hand, if the strip is run down and partially abandoned, it sends a negative signal about the quality of the whole neighborhood. If, on the other hand, the neighborhood commercial district is improving, people are likely to see this as a strong sign that the whole neighborhood is improving. In this sense, neighborhood retail serves to signal the market about the direction and specific type of change in a community. This signal then affects the location choices of potential neighborhood residents and ultimately the overall composition of the neighborhood.

Figure 2-1 summarizes the various indicators used to measure retail revitalization, the outcomes associated with neighborhood revitalization, and the relationship between the two. With the exception of improvements to individual well-being such as gaining employment and better health, most of these revitalization measures are mutually reinforcing: for instance, declining retail vacancy rates can transform neighborhood identity, but also, transformed neighborhood identity (due to new residents) can result in declining vacancy rates.

The Retail Gap: Myths and Realities

Porter's article "Competitive Advantage of Inner Cities" brought wider attention to the economic potential of inner cities. Among the competitive advantages he identified was the relatively untapped local market demand of inner-city residents. Yet, as this section describes, there is still considerable debate over whether this gap exists and whether it is being measured accurately, as well as whether inner cities present significant barriers to retail development.[28]

---

27. Artz and Stone (2006); Basker (2005); Stone (1997); Civic Economics (2002); Birch (2005); Smith (1996).

28. Porter (1995).

Figure 2-1. *Synergistic Relationship between Retail and Neighborhood Revitalization*

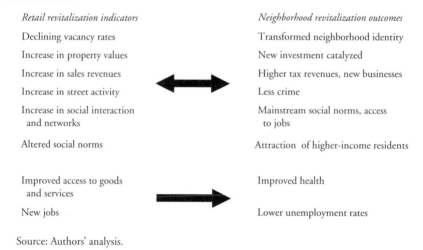

Source: Authors' analysis.

Are Low-Income Urban Neighborhoods Underserved?

Porter noted that in inner-city Boston "spending power per acre is comparable with the rest of the city despite a 21 percent lower average household income," which is due to higher average housing densities in the inner city.[29] And yet, as Porter and others noted, retail sales in inner-city areas fall far below the level of local demand. Porter called for a new era of market-led, inner-city economic development in which self-interested businesses would step in to take advantage of this real market opportunity. Porter's Initiative for a Competitive Inner City estimates that inner cities represent a $122 billion retail market, and it finds that inner-city residents are making one-third of their retail purchases (totaling $40 billion) outside of inner-city areas.[30] A Chicago study confirmed this, finding that its neighborhoods experienced an average leakage of 37 percent of retail spending, with individual low-income areas leaking between 60 and 70 percent.[31]

How has the retail industry missed this dramatic economic opportunity? In a 2004 survey, 88 percent of retail industry professionals indicated that "insufficient concentration of your target population" was a significant barrier to development of new retail in inner-city areas.[32] While low-income households do,

29. Porter (1995).
30. Coyle (2007).
31. Weissbourd and Berry (1999).
32. International Council of Shopping Centers (2004).

obviously, have less spending power, the retail industry may be overlooking much of the real economic potential of lower-income neighborhoods. Problems with data collection and common methods of analysis may ultimately prove to be a bigger barrier to inner-city development than an actual lack of spending power on the part of low-income residents. The market power of low-income neighborhoods is notoriously hard to evaluate for three reasons: First, the census fails to count many households, especially low-income and immigrant households. As much as 6 percent of the population was not counted in some neighborhoods in Los Angeles.[33] Second, many lower-income households receive significant income that is not reported in government data. While some of this income comes from illegal activity, most is probably from legal but informal activity like childcare. One study showed that families with reported incomes of less than $10,000 per year reported *spending* over $25,000 on goods and services.[34] Third, because most market data are based on the decennial census, economic forecasts often fail to reflect more recent changes in a neighborhood's character. A comparison of projections by market research firms for Milwaukee neighborhoods for 1999 (projected forward from the 1990 census) with the actual 2000 census numbers found significant discrepancies, particularly in low-income neighborhoods.[35] Several neighborhoods were shown as having rapidly declining populations, but they turned out to be experiencing steady growth.

Even if the underlying data were fully accurate, many urban neighborhoods might be disadvantaged by the traditional reliance by market researchers on indicators of economic potential that fail to account for the real economic power of urban neighborhoods. Much of the retail industry, accustomed to suburban locations, has focused on neighborhood *median income* rather than aggregate income as a simple metric for comparing potential locations.[36] Retailers hoping to serve middle-income consumers may overlook real concentrations of these households by focusing on the percentage of an area that is middle class rather than on the total number of middle-class households (which may be higher in a dense area with a low middle-class percentage than in a lower density but predominantly middle-class area).[37] Similarly, widely used "lifestyle segmentation" systems such as Tapestry and PRIZM offer a shortcut for retailers hoping to quickly understand the demographics of a given area, but often these systems present lower-income consumers in inaccurate, biased, and dismissive terms.[38]

33. Ong and Houston (2002).
34. Weissbourd and Berry (1999).
35. Pawasarat and Quinn (2001).
36. Porter (1995); Weissbourd and Berry (1999); HUD (1999).
37. International Council of Shopping Centers (2004).
38. These systems, and others like them, group an area's diverse population into relatively homogeneous segments on the basis of demographic traits, such as race, gender, and income,

Although much of the discussion of Porter's inner-city work has accepted the premise that inner-city neighborhoods are underserved, others question that assertion.[39] One study of retail location patterns in Chicago found that poor areas are in fact home to fewer retail establishments (especially drugstores, supermarkets, and banks), but when the authors controlled for lower aggregate spending power, poor areas have just as many stores per million dollars of spending power as other parts of town. Thus, in spite of a growing concern that low-income neighborhoods are underserved by supermarkets, these areas generally have the number and size of supermarkets that their spending power alone would indicate that they could support. However, beyond supermarkets and banks, there are significant differences, including shortages (relative to spending power) of large-format drugstores, clothing stores, and restaurants, as well as fewer large stores in general. The authors conclude that this difference in retail structure is evidence that "retailers and service providers are underserving poor areas and are not responding to profit opportunities" but also that the situation is "not as bleak as many would paint it."[40]

In spite of the recent emphasis on better documentation of the untapped spending power of inner-city neighborhoods, there is some evidence that the importance of consumer demand in predicting retail locations may be overstated. Theodore Koebel studied the change in the number of neighborhood-serving retail and service firms reported by the Census Bureau's Zip Code Business Patterns file for six cities between 1981 and 1995.[41] Selecting a subset of retail and service firms (using Standard Industrial Classification, SIC, codes) that were thought to primarily serve neighborhood markets rather than regional consumer markets, he compared the growth (or decline) in the number of firms by zip code with a very wide range of neighborhood characteristic variables and found little correlation. Koebel's findings are consistent with other results in suggesting that noneconomic factors including racial discrimination contribute more to changes in neighborhood commerce than do economic factors like population and income growth.[42] Some of Koebel's neighborhoods saw rising numbers of retail firms in spite of falling populations or falling incomes, while others experienced drops in the number of retail firms in spite of rising incomes.

There is also some debate about whether the fact that at least one-third of the retail spending of lower-income communities is leaking out of these neighbor-

---

and attribute similar consumer preferences, hobbies, and other lifestyle traits to members of these segments. See Pawasarat and Quinn (2001).

39. Alwitt and Donley (1997).
40. Alwitt and Donley (1997).
41. Koebel (2002).
42. Immergluck (1999).

hoods should be seen as cause for concern at all. Every residential neighborhood must experience significant leakage, and there has been little analysis of how much leakage is normal. Because of the shift in preferences to large discount stores, low-income consumers may not be underserved at all; instead, shoppers of all income levels are simply driving to large-format stores outside of residential neighborhoods. However, as Kelly Clifton notes, these alternatives may not serve the poor well because they are not only price-sensitive but also time-sensitive; with a combination of income, time, and mobility constraints, low-income groups may not be able to patronize stores as regularly as more affluent clientele.[43]

Moreover, the retail structure of low-income communities may have public health consequences. Although it is debatable whether these neighborhoods have more or less retail than they can economically support, many community advocates and researchers point to health problems associated with poor access to fresh food as a sign that more grocery stores are needed. Many studies document the lack of large supermarkets in low-income neighborhoods and the associated health challenges.[44] However, recent research on "food deserts" in disadvantaged neighborhoods has found that smaller grocery stores, many with decent produce and prices, may substitute for supermarkets.[45] A recent study found that Latino consumers in particular were effectively meeting their fresh food needs through small (under 3,000 square feet) full-service stores, but that even in mixed-race neighborhoods with an adequate supply of these small stores, African American households were not being served adequately.[46] Cultural differences in the patterns of consumer demand and store-type preferences are an overlooked aspect of the "food deserts" problem.

Ultimately, consumers themselves may be the best judges of whether their neighborhoods are underserved. The Boston Consulting Group's study of retail opportunities in the inner city, for example, documents the dissatisfaction of many residents of low-income neighborhoods with the local retail offerings in terms of price, quality, and selection.[47] In such a context, it is not surprising that Freeman found that some residents perceived gentrification positively.[48]

43. Clifton (2003, 2004).

44. Chung and Myers (1999); Mari Gallagher Research and Consulting (2006); Moore and Diez Roux (2006).

45. Short, Guthman, and Raskin (2007); Raja, Ma, and Yadav (2008).

46. Short, Guthman, and Raskin (2007).

47. Boston Consulting Group (1988).

48. Freeman (2006).

Barriers to Retail Development

If inner-city neighborhoods are underserved, and real market opportunities exist, why are retailers slow to return to these areas? Unmet social needs or even untapped spending power alone are unlikely to motivate firms to open stores. The location preferences of any given retailer will be influenced by a large list of factors, some quite technical, beyond spending power, including

—traffic patterns;

—the availability of suitable sites in terms of size, freeway access, and other factors;

—the presence of compatible cotenants in a shopping center or commercial district;

—the perception of crime;

—the cost of development or occupancy of retail space;

—likely preferences of the local consumers for the given retailer's brand or products.

Many retailers have designed their store formats, their product selection and pricing, and their overall brand identity specifically to appeal to suburban middle-class customers. Capturing the untapped inner-city market will often require changes to the retailer's format or operating practices to meet the needs of consumers with different preferences and needs. In addition, low-income urban neighborhoods suffer from a number of unique challenges that make retail development more difficult even for those businesses that understand the market, in particular, the challenges and costs associated with developing large retail projects in the inner city; quality-of-life issues, particularly crime; and poor management.

Development Challenges

One commonly cited challenge for urban retail development is the relative lack of large development sites. Most urban residential neighborhoods are made up of many smaller lots, but current retail development patterns demand the large sites that are much more common in suburban areas. The need expressed by many retailers for large parking lots greatly exacerbates the challenge of finding suitable sites. Even when assembling multiple lots into a single site is possible, the process can add significantly to the overall cost of urban projects. Whereas there has been some progress in convincing retailers to experiment with new store formats that better fit into the existing urban fabric, retailers and many consumers continue to express strong preferences for larger-format retail.[49]

49. International Council of Shopping Centers (2004).

A study of the challenges faced by nineteen shopping center development projects found that the most common challenges faced by the sponsoring community development corporation (CDC) were issues related to identifying appropriate sites for new shopping centers and assembling multiple smaller parcels for larger-scale development.[50] The New Community Corporation in Newark had to take absentee property owners to court to force the sale of parcels that were key to the development of its center, while the Community Development Corporation of Kansas City had to defeat plans to build a minimum security prison before it could proceed with development of a shopping center on a key parcel in its neighborhood.

Further, developers report that retail projects in urban neighborhoods are significantly more expensive to develop because of higher land costs, greater likelihood of environmental contamination, more frequent community opposition, more complex planning and zoning regulations, and higher wages.[51]

Crime and Cleanliness

A 2004 survey of retail professionals found widespread agreement within the industry regarding the most significant barriers to new retail development in underserved markets.[52] The most commonly identified barrier, cited by 93 percent of respondents, was crime and the perception of crime. High crime rates affect business operating costs through the direct cost of theft and the higher associated security costs; but perhaps more important, high crime makes it harder to attract customers. And even areas with relatively modest *actual* crime rates often suffer from a misperception that they are high crime areas. Retailers recognize that even when they are wrong, these perceptions affect shopping behavior.

The "broken windows" theory suggested that people's sense of safety is not so directly connected to the crime rate as it is to the overall level of public order.[53] Factors such as the cleanliness of streets and sidewalks, the condition of public infrastructure, the presence or absence of graffiti, and dozens of other small factors may have a large influence over which retail locations consumers choose. Whether or not they suffer from high crime rates, urban neighborhods often suffer from lack of investment in the streetscape, buildings, and other physical infrastructure and insufficient maintenance and cleanliness efforts. Overcoming these conditions may, in some cases, be more difficult than reducing the crime

---

50. Abell (2002).
51. International Council of Shopping Centers (2004).
52. International Council of Shopping Centers (2004).
53. Wilson and Kelling (1982).

rate because they require changing the behavior of many public and private actors and changing social norms on the street.[54]

Management Factors

Management issues, from poor skills to other complications, also create barriers to retail development. Many of the retail businesses serving low-income communities suffer from a lack of management capacity and difficulties accessing financing and supplier networks.[55] Immigrant and low-income entrepreneurs are less likely to succeed in part because they have lower levels of education and prior business experience, as well as less capital to invest in the business.[56]

Retailers also point to higher than average operating costs for inner-city stores due to factors such as higher tax rates, higher insurance costs, greater security costs, and losses due to theft.[57] Higher average operating costs mean that many types of inner-city stores must rely on a greater than average sales volume to be profitable. As a result, inner-city commercial strips generally offer a limited variety of stores frequently offering lower-quality goods, less customer service, and higher prices—and they are less likely to survive.[58]

Strategies to Promote Neighborhood Retail Development

Local governments and community-based organizations that want to strengthen neighborhood retail markets undertake a wide range of strategies. These include commercial real estate development projects supported by the public sector through direct financing or various tax incentives, market-led development strategies that rely on market research and promotion to attract new retailers to underserved areas, and coordinated commercial revitalization programs that combine business attraction with softer activities such as safety and cleanliness efforts, consumer marketing, business assistance, and smaller-scale improvements to the physical infrastructure.

Public-Led Commercial Development

The most direct intervention in neighborhood retail markets is simply to develop new commercial real estate projects. Retail development projects range from supermarket-anchored neighborhood shopping centers to smaller-scale "infill" retail development including ground-floor retail space developed in

---

54. Hoyt (2005).
55. Rauch (1996).
56. Bates (1997).
57. Initiative for a Competitive Inner City (2002).
58. Loukaitou-Sideris (2000).

mixed-use projects with housing above. A recent trend has been transit-oriented development projects that combine higher-density housing and retail around transit stations. These projects are frequently referred to as "catalysts" of further neighborhood development, with the expectation being that public investment in one or more key initial projects will lead to greatly increased private (unsubsidized) development activity. There is often an unstated expectation that these projects will generate jobs for neighborhood residents, offer key services to residents, and improve neighborhood safety and contribute to other quality-of-life factors.

Local governments frequently provide grants, subsidized loans, or tax or regulatory incentives to encourage development of new commercial real estate projects by private or nonprofit developers. A recent survey of planners working for thirty-two local government agencies in major U.S. cities asked about efforts to attract retail (especially supermarkets) to inner-city neighborhoods.[59] Thirteen of these cities offered some kind of financial incentives to supermarket developers; ten offered fast-track permitting, fee waivers, or parking or public safety assistance; and seven conducted or paid for market studies to help attract retailers to target sites. Another key form of local government assistance for commercial development is site assembly. A number of public agencies have undertaken the complex task of assembling several smaller parcels into a large enough site to attract outside retail developers into urban neighborhoods. This approach reduces the risk and the cost that the shopping center developer would otherwise face alone.[60]

Often local governments turn to CDCs to manage the development of neighborhood shopping centers or other retail projects designed to respond to unmet retail demand and catalyze neighborhood revitalization.[61] Several studies of CDC development have attempted to gauge the extent of this type of commercial development, with the most recent finding that 62 percent of CDCs were engaged in commercial real estate activity.[62]

Historically local governments relied on Urban Development Action Grants to fund commercial development, but since that program was terminated, they have used a variety of local and federal sources to fund these projects.[63] In 2002 an Urban Institute study found that local governments used Department of Housing and Urban Development (HUD) block grant funds to make or guar-

59. Pothukuchi (2005).
60. Abell (2002).
61. Abell (1998).
62. Gross (2005). Servon and Melendez (2006) found that 46 percent of CDCs were involved in commercial real estate development, while 72 percent conducted commercial rehab activity.
63. Abell (2002).

antee $2.2 billion in loans to private businesses during the second half of the 1990s. The majority of this loan volume was made through the Section 108 loan guarantee program, which allows local governments to provide 100 percent loan guarantees for economic development projects with any future loan losses repaid from the community's annual Community Development Block Grant (CDBG) funds. Local governments frequently use Section 108 loans to facilitate larger business development or commercial real estate development projects. Of the Section 108 loans, 18 percent went to retail businesses and 32 percent to service businesses.[64] Many projects also benefit from tax incentives of some kind.

Redevelopment and tax increment financing. Redevelopment typically occurs through tax increment financing (TIF), which spread across the country in the wake of the urban fiscal crises of the 1970s, and is now utilized in forty-nine states and the District of Columbia. TIF allows redevelopment agencies to use the projected additional property taxes to be generated by redevelopment to finance certain development costs within a designated district. Cost-benefit analyses generally find positive results for TIF, with its primary benefit being its ability to finance infrastructure development.[65]

EZ-EC programs. Federal and state enterprise zones (EZ) and empowerment communities (EC) generally provide a set of tax incentives to encourage businesses to locate in targeted disinvested areas and hire local residents. While these programs generally do not focus primarily on retail businesses, many include retail development as one of several goals. Overall the impact of these programs has been mixed at best, with several studies demonstrating that the designated EZ-EC zones did not experience greater reduction in unemployment, more job creation or business growth, or a greater reduction in poverty than that experienced by comparison areas.[66] When enterprise zones are successful, they are typically located in neighborhoods that are still economically viable and have a substantial manufacturing component.[67]

Historic preservation tax credits. Enacted in 1976, the federal Historic Preservation Tax Incentives program offers a 20 percent tax credit for private investors rehabbing historic properties. Many states have enacted their own tax credit program to supplement the federal incentive. The literature suggests that these credits (and historic preservation in general) have a strong positive impact and multiplier effect, but measurement of that is complicated.[68]

---

64. Walker and others (2002).
65. Johnson and Man (2001).
66. Oakley and Tsao (2006); GAO (2006); Rich and Stoker (2007); Eisinger (1988).
67. Wilder and Rubin (1988); Dowall and others (1994).
68. For a review, see Mason (2005).

New Markets Tax Credits. More recently the New Markets Tax Credit (NMTC) program has used tax policy to provide federal subsidies to induce private investment in targeted low-income areas. However, unlike the EZ-EC incentives that generally benefit employers, the NMTC credits are given to investors in qualified businesses. The result may be a closer correspondence between federal subsidy and private market activity—in other words, more of a market-led approach. By the beginning of 2007, the NMTC program had led to the investment of about $5.3 billion.[69] Although the tax credits can be used to fund business loans, industrial facilities, and many other eligible uses, the majority of this investment to date seems to have been directed toward commercial real estate projects, especially those in retail.[70] While it is too soon to gauge the economic impact of this investment in urban communities, the Government Accountability Office's (GAO) initial report on the program suggests that, at a minimum, the program is spurring new investment and shifting resources away from less needy areas.[71] Yet, there may be a mismatch between lengthy development processes and the relatively quick turnaround required for NMTC projects. As a result, this funding may go to projects already in the pipeline rather than to projects that would not have happened but for the funding. The Department of the Treasury is tracking direct impacts such as the volume and type of investment, but Treasury is also interested in indirect neighborhood impacts such as increases in employment, increases in property values, and access to needed services.

Market-Led Business Attraction

Porter lamented the slow progress of publicly led retail development and called on local government to "shift its focus from direct involvement and intervention to creating a favorable environment for business."[72] Porter's work contributed to a growing sense that government subsidies might be part of the problem and that more commercial development might result if the neighborhoods were promoted on the basis of their assets rather than their liabilities. Expanding on Porter's work, researchers began documenting the dramatic market opportunities that were being overlooked by retailers.[73] The potential of this new approach was seen as so significant that two separate organizations were launched to focus primarily on developing new tools to help retailers identify market opportuni-

69. GAO (2007).

70. New Markets Tax Credit, "New Markets Tax Credits Progress Report 2007" (www. newmarketstaxcreditcoalition.org/reportsETC/newfiles/2007%20NMTC%20Progres%20 Report%20-%20Final.pdf [2007]).

71. GAO (2007).

72. Porter (1995).

73. Weissbourd and Berry (1999); HUD (1999).

ties in underserved inner cities. MetroEdge, founded as a subsidiary of Shore-bank and later sold to the Local Initiatives Support Corporation, focused on developing new metrics that would represent the real spending power in urban neighborhoods more accurately. For example, when traditional market analysis focused on the median income, MetroEdge encouraged retailers to look instead at total spending per square mile. The other firm, Social Compact, developed new tools for identifying undocumented spending resulting from inaccurate government statistics or informal economic activity. The unstated assumption behind these two programs seems to be that better information about the real market opportunities in underserved neighborhoods will encourage developers to build new projects and retailers to open new stores for reasons of their own self-interest. These new projects and stores would then be expected to have the same kinds of community impacts as the government-led commercial real estate projects. But where government-subsidized projects might reinforce the idea that a neighborhood is not ready for private investment, market-led development projects might be more likely to catalyze further private investment because they would signal to other developers and retailers that these markets could be profitable on their own.

Over the past decade, MetroEdge and Social Compact, together with Porter's own Initiative for a Competitive Inner City (ICIC), have produced a steady stream of reports that have called attention to the spending power of inner-city neighborhoods in one city after another. The reports regularly receive media attention and renewed calls for retailers to take a closer look at the business opportunities in these areas. While this market-led approach has successfully realigned the philanthropic, and to a lesser extent municipal, strategy toward these neighborhoods, it has yet to affect retailer behavior dramatically. A 2006 study by ICIC found that the gap between retail supply and retail demand in inner-city neighborhoods in 100 of the largest U.S. cities has "remained approximately the same for the past decade."[74] However, ICIC found dramatic differences between cities, with some experiencing 30 to 50 percent growth in retail jobs in inner-city neighborhoods during the decade while others experienced comparable declines. ICIC attributes this difference in part to the fact that "several cities with aggressive entrepreneurial mayors developed strategies for attracting retail establishments" and concludes that "national retailers, impressed with market data and the absence of competition, moved more confidently to open branches in select cities."[75]

74. Coyle (2007, p. 1).
75. Coyle (2007, p. 9). However, a brief review of the websites of Social Compact, MetroEdge, and ICIC indicates that, of the cities that have been the focus of inner-city market research, just as many fall into the group that Coyle identified as experiencing retail declines.

The city of Indianapolis developed a "minimalist" program that followed Porter's approach by identifying sites for retail development, researching untapped spending power, and organizing local public and private sector actors to promote these opportunities. A study suggests that the effort would have been more likely to succeed if the city had identified public sector resources to help offset some of the increased cost of inner-city locations.[76] Several communities have developed more intensive programs to coordinate outreach to retailers in an effort to bring new stores into existing or planned private developments in target neighborhoods.[77] These programs are frequently developed alongside programs to support commercial real estate development. Retail Chicago is perhaps the premier example of this type of program. Staff of Retail Chicago serve as a one-stop resource for retailers interested in locating in Chicago's disinvested neighborhoods. The agency contracts with LISC MetroEdge to compile market data about the target neighborhoods, maintains a list of opportunity sites, organizes annual retailer tours, and markets inner-city retail opportunities through national and regional retail trade conventions. The program also coordinates a suite of city incentives and support programs designed to reduce the cost of opening new stores in the targeted neighborhoods. Other cities that have used retail attraction successfully are Rochester, New York, and Dallas.[78]

One assumption underlying this approach is that inner-city markets are growing. And in fact, a growing literature demonstrates how an influx of immigrants can revitalize retail, by providing both new entrepreneurs and markets.[79] However, while ICIC found that most of the inner-city areas that experienced retail growth also experienced population growth and increased household density, it identified a few cities with declining inner-city populations that nonetheless managed net growth in inner-city retail jobs. Deirdre Coyle points to Columbus, Ohio, and its "aggressive initiative to build a retail destination and attract retailers" as accounting for that city's retail growth in the face of declining inner-city population.[80] However, she notes that rather than simply promoting the untapped market potential to retailers and developers, as many cities do, Columbus also committed to locating a government building at the site, assembled parcels, offered financing for the developers, and streamlined permitting. The result was that between 1995 and 2003 Columbus's inner-city areas experienced an 8 percent increase in retail sales and a 14 percent increase in retail sec-

76. Nunn (2001).
77. Including Indianapolis under a subsequent administration (see www.focusindy.com).
78. Pothukuchi (2005).
79. Ball (2002); Min and Bozorgmehr (2000).
80. Coyle (2007).

tor employment in spite of a 3 percent drop in population. This may indicate
that market-led business attraction works best when accompanied by either
strong population growth (often led by immigrants) or very significant public
sector investment.

Commercial District Revitalization Programs

Comprehensive efforts to improve the strength of existing commercial districts
have become increasingly popular. Either together with or instead of building
new shopping centers, these programs attempt to revive the historical pattern of
neighborhood-serving retail—generally small-format retail arranged along
major arterials and accessed on foot with adjacent on-street parking or district-
oriented public parking lots. A large number of these programs are organized
according to the National Trust for Historic Preservation's Main Street model.[81]
The Main Street model involves committees of local merchants, residents, property owners, and other stakeholders undertaking a long-term, coordinated strategy for district revitalization including design, promotion, economic restructuring, and organizing. There are currently more than 1,200 active Main Street
programs across the country. Although the vast majority of these programs focus
on downtowns of smaller cities, a growing minority of Main Street programs are
focused on revitalization of urban neighborhoods. An evaluation of seven Main
Street programs found that the successful programs had adapted the traditional
model to the local context; of interest, it found that a program was most effective when the local government played a proactive role and also provided financial support for large-scale infrastructure or development projects.[82]

Many, but not all, Business Improvement Districts (BIDs) operate similarly
comprehensive programs. BIDs are special tax assessment districts that are
formed to provide special services to targeted districts. The property owners (or
sometimes the businesses themselves) pay the special assessment and have the
right to participate in governance of the BID, which then generally uses the
funds to pay for additional public safety, cleanliness, or promotional services
that benefit the entire district. BIDs are still rare in underserved urban neighborhoods but are becoming more common. In general, although BIDs are considered effective, studies have not focused on BIDs in low-income areas.[83] One
exception is a study of New York's forty-one Business Improvement Districts, of
which ten serve predominantly low-income neighborhoods.[84] These BIDs, however, tended to be less well funded and offered significantly less comprehensive

81. Seidman (2004).
82. Seidman (2003).
83. Houstoun (2004); Mitchell (2003).
84. Gross (2005).

services, with most focusing exclusively on district upkeep and maintenance rather than on the promotion and capital improvement activities common in higher-income BIDs.

A number of CDCs have undertaken comprehensive commercial district revitalization programs as well. Some of these CDC programs follow the Main Street model, while others are organized as BIDs, but many are less formally structured. LISC has supported several dozen CDC commercial revitalization programs throughout the country.[85] Whether or not they are formally recognized as Main Street programs, CDC revitalization programs tend to be more focused on crime and safety and to use commercial real estate development as a key strategy than non-CDC programs.[86]

The specific activities undertaken by any individual BID, Main Street Program, or CDC-led revitalization program will depend largely on local circumstances and priorities. Commercial revitalization programs frequently make improvements like new street lighting, benches, trash receptacles, bicycle racks, sidewalks, curbing, street trees, bus shelters, entryways, signage, banners, murals, and pedestrian signage. These programs also undertake efforts to improve code enforcement against property owners with blighted properties, to remove graffiti in a timely manner, and to increase neighborhood greenspace. Some programs offer façade improvement loans or grants to merchants or property owners to make physical improvements to the exterior of their street-front retail spaces. These programs frequently require some level of matching financial commitment from the merchant or property owner. Less common, some communities operate tenant improvement loan or grant programs that help finance the cost of custom build-outs of retail space in targeted revitalization areas.

Crime is a major barrier to retail success in inner-city locations, and commercial revitalization programs frequently invest significant resources to reduce the level of crime and, just as important, to change the perception of safety on the part of customers and merchants by taking actions such as hiring private security firms or safety ambassadors to patrol the sidewalks, removing pay phones used in the drug trade, installing security cameras, organizing merchants, and implementing principles of "defensible space."[87] Lorlene Hoyt argues that in addition to direct safety activities like these, investments such as streetscape improvements, façade improvements, and increased street cleaning also have a direct impact on crime rates.[88]

85. Carlson (2003).
86. Carlson (2003).
87. International Council of Shopping Centers (2004); Houstoun (2004); Stokes (2007); Carlson (2003); Seidman (2004).
88. Hoyt (2005).

Many revitalization programs also organize promotional activities intended to change consumer perceptions of the commercial district. Three-fourths of BIDs in one study reported conducting direct consumer marketing programs on behalf of district businesses—their most common activity.[89] However, a study of BIDs in lower-income areas found that they tended to focus their more limited marketing budgets on promoting special events, while BIDs in higher-income areas invested in broader marketing efforts to alter the identity of the district.[90] Another study found that urban main street districts have difficulty identifying a unique image that differentiates them from other areas.[91] Nonetheless many urban main street programs have succeeded in significantly changing perceptions and increasing sales through conscious branding programs.[92]

Many commercial corridor programs offer resources for improving and expanding existing retail businesses. These programs include training for business operators, assistance in accessing financing, and real estate search assistance. A recent large-scale survey of CDCs found that 65 percent had worked in the business enterprise development area.[93] Karl Seidman evaluated ten CDC-led business assistance programs participating in Boston's Community Business Network and found that, though most did not focus on specific commercial districts, several programs targeted Boston Main Street districts, and many businesses receiving assistance reported participating in district revitalization programs.[94]

Measuring the Impact of Retail Development Programs

Although the retail development approaches described above are quite different in scope and scale, they generally share a common underlying set of goals. Each of these strategies seeks to increase the level of retail activity in targeted underserved neighborhoods. Public-led commercial development and market-led business attraction both focus on bringing in new catalyst real estate projects with new stores; in contrast, the revitalization programs generally seek more incremental change, improving the quality and competitiveness of existing businesses and attracting new stores to fill existing vacancies. But in either case, expanded retail activity is likely to be seen as a means to a broader set of changes in the neighborhood as a whole. There is, however, very little agreement about how to measure the impact of these projects and programs on neighborhood revitalization and probably even about what kind of neighborhood change

89. Mitchell (2003).
90. Gross (2005).
91. Dane (1988).
92. Jacobus and Hickey (2007).
93. Servon and Melendez (2006).
94. Seidman (1999).

would be considered desirable. For the most part, evaluations have focused instead on documenting the impact of the projects on a set of intermediate indicators including job creation, tax revenue, new investment, higher property values, additional services for neighborhood residents, access to healthy food and other essential goods, reduced crime, improved perception of the neighborhood, and increased neighborhood pride. Studies have not attempted to draw direct connections between any of these indicators and overall neighborhood change, although the implication generally seems to be that changes in these factors should lead to other (presumably positive) changes in the neighborhood.

However, if retail growth in one neighborhood is indeed associated with a decline in nearby areas, then this focus on intermediate indicators may be problematic. Studies have generally neglected to look at the impact of these projects within a citywide or regional context or to evaluate whether job growth, crime reduction, and other outcomes in the target neighborhoods are associated with corresponding changes in neighboring districts.[95] This kind of interneighborhood transfer or geographic spillover would not necessarily undermine the claim that retail development is contributing to neighborhood revitalization, but it would suggest the need for better measures of neighborhood-level impact. Currently, while it is possible to evaluate whether these strategies create jobs or reduce crime, it is hard to know whether those limited changes add up to meaningful change in the overall health, attractiveness, or competitiveness of a neighborhood—or whether these strategies actually benefit existing neighborhood residents.

Job Creation

The Urban Institute study of HUD-funded local economic development loans found that only 56 percent of CDBG-funded borrowers and 52 percent of Section 108–supported borrowers met or exceeded their job creation goals. However, since a small number of borrowers exceeded their job creation goals by large margins, overall, the total number of jobs created by all HUD-funded loans amounted to 93 percent of the combined job creation goals. The same report found that the Section 108 program generated one new job for every $38,000 lent. By comparing Section 108 loan terms with prevailing private market loans, the researchers estimated that these below-market loans represented an average public subsidy of approximately $7,865 per job. Although considerably lower than the cost per job of tax incentives provided to corporations, this is considerably higher than the average grant per job created by other

95. Even studies of enterprise zones, which compare the zones with comparable nonzones, generally do not discuss whether the different outcomes are due to shifts in activity between these areas.

federal programs identified in similar studies.[96] Furthermore, the study showed that jobs created by Section 108 loans in high-poverty neighborhoods required 25 percent more subsidy per job than those created by loans outside high-poverty areas.[97]

Many financing programs, such as TIF, do not evaluate job creation outcomes. A number of case studies have shown, though, that new supermarket development projects have led to the creation of significant numbers of new jobs and that neighborhood residents are frequently able to fill the majority of these new jobs.[98] In addition to the direct employment created in the new stores, retail development is likely to have some multiplier effect, stimulating local economic activity that results in additional neighborhood jobs beyond the new retail development.[99] Yet, there has been little research on the extent of this multiplier effect for neighborhood retail development.

Studies of empowerment zones have found few positive employment effects. In a study of six cities with federal empowerment zones, the only city whose zone neighborhoods had a significantly different outcome than the corresponding control group was New York City; the New York census tracts fared worse in reducing unemployment than the control group counterparts.[100] These and other studies have long found that the hiring tax credits are ineffective, because of unwillingness of employers to alter their hiring habits, and a more recent study of California empowerment zones detailed the abuse of the hiring tax credit, which rarely goes to disadvantaged workers.[101]

Many commercial district revitalization programs also attempt to track job creation outcomes. This is difficult because of the large number of businesses that must be contacted. Seidman found that the average urban Main Street program generated 38 net new jobs per year, a total that was comparable with the national average for Main Street programs outside of urban areas considered successful.[102] LISC documented 1,490 net new jobs created by its six pilot neighborhood Main Street programs over a four-year period—an average of 62 jobs per district per year.[103] Studying the results of new Main Street programs in Boston between 1996 and 2000, Seidman found wide variation in the total

96. Markusen (2007).
97. Walker and others (2002).
98. Abell (1998); Food Marketing Institute (1993).
99. Dixon (2005).
100. Rich and Stoker (2007).
101. California Budget Project, "California's Enterprise Zones Miss the Mark" (www.cbp.org/pdfs/2006/0604_ezreport.pdf [2006]).
102. Seidman (2004).
103. Carlson (2003).

number of jobs created, with the Hyde Park program generating 166 net new jobs while the Hyde/Jackson Square program created only six.[104]

Whether they are created by new real estate development or revitalization programs, it is likely that some of these jobs are being filled by neighborhood residents.[105] A 2000 study of the economic impact of the Fruitvale Main Street program in Oakland, California, found that 58 percent of district retail employees lived in the immediate neighborhood.[106] Neighborhood retail jobs are less than ideal, however: not only do they pay low wages and rely on part-time or temporary workers, but retailers offer the least on-the-job training of any business sector and offer relatively few supervisor positions, thus failing to facilitate upward mobility.[107] Nevertheless, they may serve as an entry point to the workforce for young or discouraged workers, and they provide key work experience, which leads to better jobs later. The Initiative for a Competitive Inner City cites lower employee turnover in inner-city retail stores as an advantage for businesses but low turnover may also occur because employees in these stores are using these opportunities as permanent career jobs instead of moving up.[108] Further research is needed to determine the extent to which neighborhood residents are moving successfully from local retail jobs into other career paths.

Vacancy Rates

A common goal of commercial development programs is to fill vacant commercial space. Despite this, it appears that comprehensive data have not been collected on the impact of new commercial real estate development projects on occupancy rates of surrounding commercial properties.

Commercial district revitalization programs, however, seem to have had more success in evaluating their impact. Jerry Mitchell conducted a survey of BID managers and found that the majority (55 percent) of BIDs are tracking vacancy and occupancy rates, which is the most frequently used benchmark for BID success.[109] Suzanne Dane's report on Main Street programs (mostly in rural areas) documented an average decline in vacancy rates from 21 percent to only 5 percent over a nine-year period.[110] Seidman studied the reported results of fourteen urban Main Street programs and found an average of eight net new businesses were created each year in the Main Street districts.[111] Seidman's earlier study of

104. Seidman (2001).
105. Abell (2002); Dunford (2006).
106. Marketek (2000).
107. Bernhardt (1999).
108. Initiative for a Competitive Inner City (2002).
109. Mitchell (2003).
110. Dane (1988).
111. Seidman (2004).

Boston Main Street programs found that between 55 and 88 percent of businesses reported that the Main Street program had improved their performance.[112] During the first four years of the Main Street pilot in Oakland's Fruitvale neighborhood, ground-floor, street-front commercial vacancy rates declined from 12 percent to less than 1 percent.[113]

Private Investment

Investment of public or charitable resources into retail development projects or programs is thought to lead to greater private investment in the same areas. Commercial real estate projects are frequently referred to as catalysts, with the implication being that one or two key projects with public subsidy can lead to a self-sustaining process of private reinvestment in distressed neighborhoods. Commercial corridor programs similarly describe increased private investment as a likely outcome of activities such as street cleaning, façade improvement, and safety improvements.

Of commercial district programs, one study showed that formation of a BID in Maplewood, New Jersey, led to a significant increase in private building permit activity.[114] Seidman found that successful urban Main Street programs had similar effects and generated an average of $1 million in public and private investment each year.[115] Much of this investment was associated with building projects ranging from major renovations to minor storefront improvements. Seidman found that urban Main Street districts experienced an average of eleven such projects per year. Between 1996 and 2000, LISC and the National Main Street Center undertook a pilot Neighborhood Main Street Initiative that involved an investment of just over $3 million to create and sustain six new urban Main Street programs. During a four-year period, these demonstration sites closely tracked outcomes and documented more than $35 million in new public and private investment in the target areas. One site, Frankford Avenue in Philadelphia, generated nearly $10 million in private investment as a result of thirty new businesses that opened on the avenue during this time.[116]

For commercial real estate development projects, tracking the impact on investment in surrounding properties is uncommon. Yet, there have been several studies that have shown that direct public investment in these projects leverages significant private investment in the same projects.[117] But the type of investment matters. For instance, in the survey of local government supermarket attraction

---

112. Seidman (2001).
113. Marketek (2000).
114. Seidman (2004).
115. Seidman (2004).
116. Carlson (2003).
117. Walker and others (2002); GAO (2007).

programs, twelve of the nineteen cities with EZ or EC designations reported efforts to attract new supermarkets, but only three targeted those efforts within the EZ-EC boundaries. These three (Buffalo, Atlanta, and Bridgeport, Connecticut) all reported no success in leveraging EZ-EC resources to attract new supermarket development.[118]

Historic preservation is generally thought to leverage private investment. Yet, while historic district designation has been associated with large increases in residential property values, there is apparently no correlation between historic district designation and increased commercial property values.[119] That may be due to any number of factors and seems to suggest that even the relatively more generous historic preservation tax credits are not sufficient to generate significant increases in economic activity or dramatically alter the location decision of most private businesses. But preservation tax credits, when combined with a Main Street program, do seem to have a significant impact.[120]

Public Investment

Urban neighborhoods compete for attention and support from local government. Commercial revitalization advocates argue that increased attention and organization at the community level combined with increased private investment should result in increased investment on the part of local governments. A key function of BIDs is their ability to "negotiate with politicians and municipalities on behalf of business owners" and "work to garner additional services."[121] Among Main Street programs nationwide (mostly in rural towns), only 37 percent report that the program led to increased investment in the district by local government; but LISC's evaluation of its Neighborhood Main Street Initiative and Seidman's evaluation of Boston's Main Streets Program both suggest that urban Main Street programs are far more likely to succeed in increasing service levels and public capital investment.[122] This may be due to the fact that urban commercial revitalization programs are unlikely to be launched at all in the absence of political support from local government.

Tax Revenue

Successful commercial development should result in immediate increases in local sales tax revenue and longer-term increases in property tax revenue, from the development project and from the surrounding properties. Apart from an

118. Pothukuchi (2005).
119. Asabere and Huffman (1991).
120. Listokin, Listokin, and Lahr (1998).
121. Hoyt (2005).
122. Carlson (2003); Seidman (2001).

evaluation of the Faneuil Hall project in Boston, which found significant but very small positive changes in land prices and rents in the vicinity of the project, there is only very anecdotal evidence for this positive impact of commercial real estate development projects on property values and sales in the surrounding district.[123] One study found, for example, that a new Stop & Shop supermarket in the Hyde/Jackson Square neighborhood attracted new shoppers, raised rents, and led to increased sales by nearby businesses—including increased sales for half of the existing independent grocery and convenience stores.[124]

Studies of redevelopment typically measure impact in terms of property values (and tax revenues), finding that TIFs generally cause growth beyond what would be expected in the absence of redevelopment finance.[125] However, critics charge that TIF districts generally fail to generate enough revenue to pay back for the lost property tax revenue and that the programs fail to reimburse local governments adequately for lost revenue.[126]

By contrast, commercial district revitalization programs have repeatedly documented positive impacts on districtwide sales and sales tax receipts. A study of California Main Street programs (mostly in rural areas) found that during a period when statewide sales taxes increased by 77 percent, the sixteen Main Street districts increased tax revenues by an average of 105 percent.[127] Surprisingly, only 19 percent of BIDs reported tracking taxable retail sales as a benchmark of BID success.[128] Nonetheless, many BIDs report increased sales tax revenue as a result of BID activity. In Boston's Hyde Park Main Street district, for example, 40 percent of businesses reported that their sales increased by 25 percent or more during the first five years of that program.[129] It is unknown whether these increases were accompanied by decreases in neighboring districts.

Crime and Safety

By increasing capital investment, removing blight, and improving cleanliness, commercial corridor programs are thought to reduce the liklihood of crime. And in fact, a study of BIDs in Philadelphia found that, relative to comparison neighborhoods, the BID areas experienced fewer crimes and, in particular, fewer thefts and other property crimes or crimes that typically would be directed at retail district visitors.[130] Commercial development projects may also have a posi-

---

123. Sagalyn (1989).
124. Hernandez (2001), cited in Seidman (2002).
125. Dardia (1998); Johnson and Man (2001).
126. Dardia (1998); Weber (2003).
127. Kelley (1996).
128. Mitchell (2003).
129. Seidman (2001).
130. Hoyt (2005).

tive impact on crime rates in the surrounding areas because of the presence of paid security and as a result of additional "eyes on the street," but there appears to be no research into this aspect of these projects.

Some BID critics have suggested that crime reductions in BID districts are not due to actual reductions in overall crime but are merely the result when crime moves to other areas, another reason why establishing a regional unit of analysis is needed.[131] This is an important point but one that has been scarcely studied. If crime reduction is itself a goal, then such a finding would undermine some of the value of commercial district programs. However, if crime prevention is seen as a means to the end of improving the relative competitiveness of a given commercial district or neighborhood, then even relocating crimes might be considered evidence of neighborhood revitalization.

Community Identity

Commercial revitalization may reshape community identity in two ways: individual or neighborhood. Recent work on the sociology of social exclusion may shed some light on how neighborhood retail development might affect resident self-perception. *Retail exclusion* also has important implications for self-identity.[132] Shopping is increasingly seen as a means of self-expression and as a tool for constructing a personal identity. Consumers who are unable to participate in this aspect of our culture may define themselves as "excluded shoppers." Even consumers with enough income to purchase essential goods may come to see themselves as being excluded because of the mode through which they purchase. In a situation when goods were acquired informally, the consumer would have preferred to purchase from a traditional retailer but was unable to do so because of cost and the inaccessibility of retail stores.[133]

Many urban consumers are either discouraged from accessing stores outside their neighborhood or feel uncomfortable in these environments.[134] Social exclusion works in both directions to disadvantage lower-income communities: low-income residents, minorities, the youth, and seniors may all feel unwelcome in mainstream stores outside their neighborhood, and similarly, outsiders are less likely to patronize stores in inner-city communities because of the presence

131. Briffault (1999).
132. Williams and Windebank (2002).
133. This section is based on research by Williams and Windebank (2002), who conducted in-depth interviews with 400 consumers in low-income neighborhoods about their methods of acquiring various essential household goods and found that a large number of these consumers are purchasing products such as TVs, cars, clothing, and furniture through informal channels or secondhand stores rather than through traditional retail outlets.
134. Turner (2004).

of these groups.[135] In this sense the retail patterns in lower-income communities may have social implications beyond the purely economic factors that are typically considered.

However, many commercial development programs point to changes in the neighborhood's identity as a key outcome. Many Main Street programs and BIDs regularly measure consumer perceptions of the commercial district and document improvements over time.[136] To the extent that successful retail development requires overcoming this kind of self-segregating behavior on the part of consumers, these programs can be seen as affecting not only neighborhood identity but individual self-identity.

Overall, this review of retail strategies and their impact suggests that commercial district revitalization strategies have a demonstrably positive effect on retail revitalization. Less is known about the effectiveness of public-led commercial development and market-led retail attraction strategies (see table 2-1). In terms of the impact of these strategies on neighborhood revitalization, we can really only speculate, since there is very little evidence. In general, it seems that leveraging public investment is key no matter which strategy is followed. Commercial district revitalization programs are the most promising in terms of improving neighborhoods, perhaps because they focus more directly on quality-of-life issues such as crime. This example suggests the importance of incorporating desired outcomes into program design. If crime is a major obstacle to business attraction, then attraction programs should include security as a design feature. Although the business cycle will affect the ability of programs to achieve some outcomes, such as reductions in vacancy rates and increases in property tax revenue, policymakers can clearly design programs to be more effective. They can easily build incentives into programs to leverage more private or public investment, by requiring matching funding. They can also help spur more job creation for local residents, for example, by requiring local hires or partnering with job training or apprenticeship programs.

A Quantitative Analysis of Retail Development and Neighborhood Change

What is the relationship between retail development and neighborhood revitalization? As discussed previously, research suggests that retail growth may not respond to changes in household income—in other words, as upper-income residents move into an area, retail revitalization does not necessarily follow.[137]

---

135. Turner (2004).
136. Seidman (2001); Mitchell (2003).
137. Koebel (2002); Immergluck (1999).

Table 2-1. *Retail Strategies, Goals, Impacts, and Unknowns*

Goal	Impact on retail revitalization	Impact on neighborhood revitalization	Remaining questions
Job creation	Commercial developments create many jobs but often at a high public investment per job created. Revitalization programs are more cost-effective but generate only modest job growth.	Residents are likely to fill many of the new jobs, particularly in corridor projects. However, job quality is likely to be poor.	What are the multiplier effects for local retail jobs? What is the overall economic impact of new retail jobs? To what extent do neighborhood retail jobs provide an avenue to better jobs?
Vacancy rate	Corridor programs have a documented impact on occupancy and appear to be an effective strategy for filling vacant space.	Declining vacancies can alter perceptions of an entire neighborhood.	What is the impact of new shopping center development on surrounding occupancy?
Private investment	Real estate projects all involve direct private investment, and there is some evidence that commercial corridor programs can lead to increased private commercial investment as well.	Retail revitalization programs are associated with an increase in residential building activity.	Do commercial real estate projects lead to increased private investment in neighboring properties?
Public investment	Commercial development projects frequently involve increases in public investment in the target area.	Infrastructure development related to commercial projects can help revitalize neighborhoods as well.	How does leveraging from all sources work?
Tax revenue (and property values)	Increased retail activity clearly increases sales tax revenue and likely adds to property tax revenue.	Retail revitalization may increase residential property values as well as commercial values.	Is the increase enough to offset investment in these programs? Are tax increases in one district offset by decreases in nearby retail districts?
Crime and safety	Revitalization programs can clearly cause reductions in crime within targeted commercial areas, though some of this crime may simply be moved to other areas.		Is the documented crime reduction due to safety programs or to the impact of economic development (that is, more stores, eyes on the street, and so on)? What impact do commercial real estate projects have on crime?
Community identity	The extent to which retail development affects the overall image of the community and the self-image of neighborhood residents is still largely unexplored.	From a sociological perspective on exclusion and a planning perspective on activity patterns, local retail should help improve individual and community image.	How much does the presence or absence of retail influence who chooses to live in the neighborhood?

Source: Authors' analysis.

Research has yet to examine the converse: the type of neighborhood revitalization that follows retail revitalization. Models suggest that job creation, private and public investment, rising property values, better access to services, and improved community identity will benefit residents, either directly or indirectly. Yet, to what extent do these benefits accrue to existing residents instead of newcomers? Will neighborhood revitalization take the form of transformation from a low-income to a moderately low-income, mixed-income, or upper-income neighborhood? Is retail best seen as a tool for attracting upper-income residents or retaining and developing the middle class?

In the following discussion, we look in more detail at the association between retail and neighborhood revitalization in the San Francisco Bay Area (the Bay Area) by linking zip code–level data on retail change (measured in terms of establishments, employees, sales, business mix, start-ups and deaths, and chains or stand-alone stores) to census tract–level data on neighborhood change. One of the most affluent regions in the country, with some of the highest income inequality, the San Francisco Bay Area has unique concentrations of neighborhoods either gentrifying or becoming more bipolar, and thus it offers the opportunity to look at a variety of patterns of retail revitalization. This pilot study reveals a surprisingly strong relationship between retail revitalization and an increase in middle-income households.

Methodology

For this analysis, we start with recent definitions of neighborhood change from George Galster and Jason Booza as well as Freeman to create a typology of neighborhood change from 1990 to 2000 that includes the following categories: "bipolar," "gentrified," "more middle income," "more lower income," "more upper income," and "other."[138] We use the Neighborhood Change Database (NCDB) developed by Geolytics, Inc. The NCDB provides 1990 census data for normalized 2000 census tract definitions, allowing us to compare 1990 neighborhood characteristics with those of 2000.

To construct the typology, we first had to convert the census data on household income from ten to sixteen irregular categorical variables (in 1990 and 2000) into consistent and meaningful groups. Following Galster, we create six income categories that are relative to the area median income (AMI) for the nine-county San Francisco Bay Area.[139] These categories are the following:

—very low income (less than 50 percent of AMI)
—low income (50 percent to 79.9 percent of AMI)
—moderate income (80 percent to 99.9 percent of AMI)

138. Freeman (2005); Galster and Booza (2007).
139. Booza, Cutsinger, and Galster (2006).

—high to moderate income (100 percent to 119.9 percent of AMI)

—high income (120 percent to 149.9 percent of AMI)

—very high income (150 percent of AMI and above)

Following Berube and Tiffany and Galster and others, we use two different methods to aggregate the finer (census) distribution into our six categories.[140] First, we calculate the area median income using the linear interpolation method.[141] Then, for each census tract in the Bay Area, we calculate the share of households in each of the census categories and their cumulative density.[142] Galster and Booza identified neighborhoods that are bipolar using a formulation based on the entropy index.[143] The entropy index is based upon the thermodynamic principle that any system will naturally trend toward evenness. The amount of entropy in a system refers to how far along a system is in reaching complete evenness. In the social sciences, researchers have developed an index that ranges from 0 (lowest entropy, meaning that the entire population is in the same category) to 1 (highest entropy, meaning that the population is evenly spread among all categories) to measure entropy of a population across social categories.[144]

In addition to this nominal entropy index, Galster and Booza constructed a new ordinal entropy index and used the ratio of the two to measure *bipolarity* in a tract, that is, the extent to which the population is disproportionately concentrated in the lowest and highest of the six income groups. There are 220 bipolar tracts in the San Francisco Bay Area, about 16 percent of the total (see figure 2-2).

To determine the extent of gentrified neighborhoods, we use the compound measure from Freeman, including tracts that have

140. Berube and Tiffany (2004); Galster and others (2005).

141. We chose to calculate this figure from the Geolytics tract-level data instead of using the raw overall figure from the census summary files for consistency reasons. Specifically, there is a small possibility of measurement error introduced by Geolytics' spatial interpolation of data from pre-2000 tract geography to a consistent geography. Comparing such interpolated tract-level data to an externally obtained median could introduce additional error.

142. In aggregating to our six categories, we used linear interpolation to find breakpoints within a census category for those at or below the median income. However, we assumed that the distribution of households within the higher-income categories follows a Pareto distribution. This assumes that there is more density toward the lower cutoff.

143. Galster and Booza (2007).

144. This index, also called the Shannon-Weaver Index, is defined as

$$H = \frac{-\sum_{i}^{k} \pi_i \ln \pi_i}{n},$$

where H is the index, π is the proportion of the population in each category, and k is the number of categories.

Figure 2-2. *A Typology of Neighborhood Change in the San Francisco Bay Area, 1990–2000*

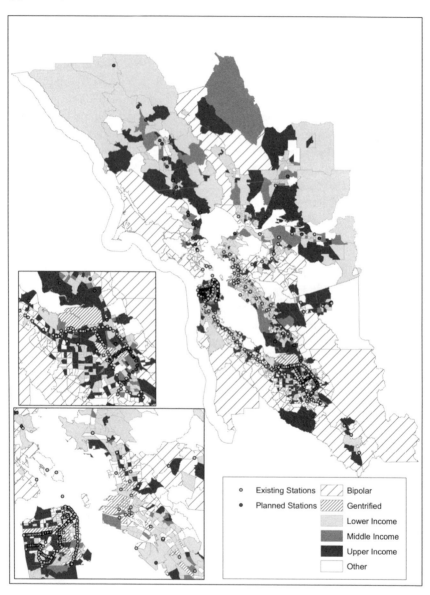

Source: Authors' analysis.

—a median income less than the 40th percentile for the Bay Area as a whole in 1990 ($33,670),

—a proportion of housing built from 1980 to 2000 that is lower than the proportion found at the 40th percentile for the Bay Area (10.7 percent),

—a percentage increase in educational attainment (that is, some college) that is greater than the median increase in educational attainment for the Bay Area between 1990 and 2000 (7.4 percent),

—an increase in real housing prices from 1995 to 2002 that is greater than the median for the Bay Area (70.2 percent).

Freeman also includes a central city designation in his definition, but since the Bay Area includes some neighborhoods that may be gentrifying outside of its few central cities (such as Berkeley and Richmond), we excluded this criterion. There are 102 gentrified tracts in the Bay Area, more than 7 percent of the total. It is interesting that there is little overlap between the bipolar and gentrified tracts, just as Galster and Booza have suggested: only three tracts are in both categories (which we classified as gentrified).

We use a relatively simple calculation to identify neighborhoods that are becoming more middle income, lower income, or upper income. Change in middle-income neighborhoods occurs when the share of population in the two middle-income categories is greater in 2000 than in 1990 and is more than 25 percent by 2000. Ten percent (141) of Bay Area tracts are becoming more middle income; just eight overlap with the gentrifying category, and we classified them as gentrified. Likewise, lower-income change (448 tracts, 32 percent of the total) occurs when the share in the two lower-income categories is greater in 2000, and the ending point is at least 25 percent, and upper-income change (300 tracts, 21 percent) occurs when the share in the top two income categories is greater in 2000, with an ending share of 25 percent or more. "Other" (185 tracts) is a residual category and seems to consist of a mix of tracts where there is no systematic pattern of change.

Of these six forms of neighborhood change, three relate directly to neighborhood revitalization. Neighborhoods that gentrify are shifting from low-income to upper-income status, which is a common definition of revitalization. Neighborhoods that become bipolar are gaining at both ends of the distribution, simultaneously revitalizing and declining. Neighborhoods that become middle income are revitalizing by gaining in the middle, often becoming more mixed income in the process. Also of interest, but less pertinent to our discussion, are two of the other neighborhood change types. Neighborhoods that become upper income are in a sense revitalizing, but from a higher-income base than that of the gentrifying neighborhoods. Neighborhoods becoming lower income are actually declining.

For the retail database, we use a private sector–generated time series database of individual establishments, the National Establishment Time-Series database (NETS), which combines annual Dun and Bradstreet entries into a time series from 1990 through 2005. This database provides us with detailed data on individual establishments over time, from establishment births (if post 1989) through current operations or deaths. Whereas government sources can provide some similar research opportunities, barriers to access to the disaggregated forms of these data are high. Further, the NETS database offers access to detailed data relevant for creating a clean database of retail establishments; for instance, we can eliminate headquarters and identify chains.

In this analysis, we include a variety of retail and service establishments, most locally oriented, based on a list of industry codes used by the Local Initiatives Support Corporation's commercial corridor program. To exclude outliers from home-based businesses to national headquarters, we include only non-headquarters establishments having more than one employee and less than $50 million in sales. We look at retail revitalization by zip code. Although the zip code is not an ideal proxy for a retail market area, it can give a sense of retail opportunities in and adjacent to neighborhoods. Since zip codes may include multiple census tracts, we weight each zip code by the share of housing units in each category of neighborhood change. For instance, 79 percent of San Francisco's Mission District (94110) is becoming more gentrified, and 21 percent is becoming purely upper income.

Findings

We first examine some simple indicators of retail revitalization—an increase in retail and service establishments, in sales, and in employees—in relation to neighborhood change. We focus in particular on the relationship of retail to the neighborhoods that become more middle income, since this type of change seems to be what most are referring to when they speak of neighborhood revitalization.

Retail and service establishments grew generally throughout the region (by about 16 percent), with much less growth in bipolarizing and gentrifying neighborhoods and an overconcentration of growth in the neighborhoods becoming middle income (table 2-2). This shows an association that might go either way: the growth of middle-income groups might have attracted new establishments to the area, or retail and service growth might have attracted new middle-income residents.

Of note, the difference in growth in total sales was quite dramatic across neighborhoods, with just 19 percent and 23 percent growth in bipolarizing and gentrifying neighborhoods, respectively, compared with 34 percent in neighbor-

Table 2-2. *Change in Establishments, Sales, and Employment, by Neighborhood-Change Type*

Neighborhood-change type	Number of establishments			Percent change 1990–2005	
	1990	*2005*	*Percent change*	*Sales*	*Employment*
Bipolar	21,466	23,629	10	19	3
Gentrified	9,564	10,544	10	23	9
Middle income	9,761	11,626	19	34	13
Lower income	32,193	38,068	18	35	12
Upper income	23,254	27,532	18	38	14
Other	12,783	14,934	17	32	10
Overall	111,012	128,339	16	34	12

Source: Authors' analysis.

Table 2-3. *Change in Retail Establishments, Employment, and Sales for Middle-Income Neighborhoods in 1990*

Neighborhood-change type	Percent change 1990–2005		
	Establishments	*Employment*	*Sales*
Middle income in 1990	23	20	48
Not middle income in 1990	16	11	31

Source: Authors' analysis.

hoods becoming middle income, 35 percent in neighborhoods becoming lower income, and 38 percent in neighborhoods becoming upper income. Likewise, growth in employment occurred disproportionately in these three types of neighborhood change. Again, although it is not clear whether neighborhood revitalization led retail revitalization or the reverse, it is interesting to note that middle-income neighborhoods started with much higher average sales per establishment ($605,000 compared with $567,000 across all types). This provides some evidence that a concentration of retail was attracting new middle-income residents.

To analyze the chicken-and-egg question more directly, we next looked at how neighborhoods that were middle income at the start, in 1990, fared in terms of retail revitalization. Table 2-3 suggests that retailers are strongly attracted to middle-income neighborhoods; areas that were middle income in 1990 saw more than 50 percent higher growth in both establishments and sales, and almost twice as much growth in employment, relative to the corresponding growth in non-middle-income neighborhoods. Thus, it seems likely that the existing middle-income composition of the neighborhood in 1990 sent a signal to retailers as much as did the influx of more middle-income residents in subsequent years

Overall, these indicators suggest that retail revitalization is more likely to occur in neighborhoods that are becoming middle income or upper income than in those that become bipolar or gentrified (or vice versa: middle-income neighborhood revitalization is occurring where retail revitalization is significant). One explanation for this that warrants further exploration is whether retailers respond more positively when a group, such as middle-income residents, concentrates, since retailers then know what market niche to fill. Another theory is that neighborhoods that are becoming bipolar or gentrified are sending some sort of negative or mixed signal to the market. That the "other" type, a residual category with no clear change pattern, also experiences disproportionately low revitalization suggests that this confused signal may be the problem. A third possibility is that the types of areas that are becoming more middle income or upper income are simply more likely to house the types of retail that are growing, such as the big box store (because of urban design factors).

Though the NETS data do not allow us to explore these theories systematically, they do offer potential when one considers four other hypotheses:

—Neighborhood revitalization is related to the share of independent establishments (as opposed to chains).

—Neighborhood revitalization is more likely to occur when there is a supermarket in the beginning period.

—Neighborhood revitalization occurs because of start-up businesses.

—Neighborhood revitalization is related to the mix of businesses in the neighborhood.

As it turns out, middle-income change areas not only housed a disproportionate share of chains at the beginning of the period, but also they were substantially more likely to see new chain stores come in (table 2-4). This suggests that the availability of chain stores may positively affect neighborhood revitalization.

However, areas in which the middle-income groups are growing do not need a supermarket to do well. Overall, areas that had a supermarket in 1990 experienced far greater sales growth; the one exception was neighborhoods with a growing middle class, which experienced roughly the same sales growth even without a local supermarket (table 2-5).

One reason that areas that are becoming middle income may fare better than bipolarizing and gentrifying neighborhoods is their ability to attract start-up businesses. Table 2-6 shows that start-ups are more attracted to middle-income—and, interestingly, lower-income—neighborhoods than to bipolarizing or gentrifying areas.

Table 2-4. *Share of Chain Stores, by Neighborhood-Change Type, 1990–2005*

Percent

Neighborhood-change type	1990	2005
Bipolar	8.7	11.0
Gentrified	8.9	11.6
Middle income	11.8	14.9
Lower income	10.4	13.2
Upper income	9.1	12.0
Other	9.7	12.7
Overall	9.4	12.3

Source: Authors' analysis.

Table 2-5. *Change in Average Sales, by Neighborhood-Change Type, with and without a Supermarket, 1990–2005*

Percent

	Change in average sales, 1990–2005	
Neighborhood-change type	With supermarket in 1990	Without supermarket in 1990
Bipolarizing	42	9
Gentrifying	41	11
Becoming middle income	17	17
Becoming lower income	34	20
Becoming upper income	44	19
Other	42	17
Overall	35	16

Source: Authors' analysis.

Table 2-6. *Share of Start-ups, by Neighborhood-Change Type*

Percent

	When establishment started			
Neighborhood-change type	Before 1950	1951–90	1991–2000	2001–05
Bipolar	4	54	33	9
Gentrified	6	52	34	8
Middle income	3	50	35	12
Lower income	4	51	34	11
Upper income	4	51	35	10
Other	4	51	34	11
Overall	4	51	34	10

Source: Authors' analysis.

Finally, areas that are becoming middle income tend to have a similar retail and service mix compared with that of other neighborhoods, with similar shifts to services and nonprofits from 1990 to 2005. However, they tend to be more diverse across the sectors: based on an entropy index ranging from 0 (perfectly homogeneous) to 1 (perfectly diverse), the neighborhood-change types score from a high of 0.90 for middle-income areas to a low of 0.87 for bipolarizing and gentrifying neighborhoods.

In sum, this exploration suggests that the way the retail sector changes is closely related to how the neighborhood changes, with middle-income revitalization most closely associated with retail revitalization. Further research should explore the dynamic in more detail.

Conclusion and Thoughts for Further Research

If neighborhood retail development contributes to broader community revitalization, it seems unlikely that it does so by dramatically increasing the employment or wage levels, the labor force participation rates, or the overall level of financial assets, although these changes can help. It seems that certain kinds of public investment in retail development (particularly corridor programs) can catalyze further private commercial development and, in at least some situations, this public investment can be recaptured through increased tax revenues. However, none of this activity indicates that there is a much broader impact on the well-being of the surrounding community. It may not even have a positive impact on the local economy as a whole, since the retail activity generated by new commercial development, business attraction programs, or corridor revitalization programs may simply be shifting economic activity between places. Despite this, the persistent call for these programs is itself a strong indication that there are real needs to which these programs are effectively responding— even if those needs are not always that well articulated by program advocates.

If retail development has large-scale impacts on community economic health, it may be through more indirect outcomes including changes in internal and external perceptions of the neighborhood and ultimately changes in neighborhood residential composition. Because neighborhood-level retail growth is closely associated with middle-income growth, retail development may be a key component to building the kind of stable mixed-income communities that are most likely to positively affect existing low-income residents. However, existing studies of the effectiveness of neighborhood retail development strategies have not explored these broader impacts.

Rather than assuming that any neighborhood improvement leads ultimately to displacement of the poor, this research suggests that more than one kind of neighborhood change is possible. Further research is necessary to establish whether low-income residents face better outcomes living in middle-income or bipolar neighborhoods, but it seems likely that middle-income neighborhoods would offer more amenities because of their ability to attract more retail growth. It is unclear to what extent this association is due to retailers' following middle-income households as opposed to middle-income consumers' strongly preferring locations with nearby retail. It seems likely that both factors play a role, though certainly a community that starts out as middle income sends a clear signal of a sound investment opportunity to retailers. The limited time frame of the NETS data (1990 to 2005) limits our ability to explore whether the retail or the residential growth comes first.

If outcomes for the poor are tied to the specific character of neighborhood change, then further research might suggest specific retail development strategies that most likely will benefit the poor and lead to stable mixed-income communities without contributing to displacement of the poor. This research suggests that chain stores are associated with neighborhoods that are becoming more middle income—and thus, attracting chain stores may be one way to stabilize the neighborhood. Further research is needed to better understand, for example, whether certain types of establishments (restaurants, bars, and so forth) are more likely to contribute to gentrification while others (drugstores, groceries, and the like) lead more often to middle-income neighborhoods.

We have explored the relationship between neighborhood demographic change and the subsequent change in retail activity, but further research might allow us to better understand the relationship between the beginning level of retail and subsequent demographic changes. Does the presence or absence of retail (or, again, certain types of retail) lead to subsequent changes in income composition?

In spite of the recent academic literature and public effort focused on better documenting retail demand in low-income neighborhoods, it may be the case that demand is not the key factor that determines retail locations. This research suggests, in fact, that the existing composition of the neighborhood matters, and shifts in demand, such as increases in the high and low end of the markets, may be confusing retailers. If much of the neighborhood-level retail growth is due to the competitive dynamics between neighborhoods, with activity shifting between nearby locations, what accounts for these shifts? Future research should focus more on the contribution of supply-side factors, particularly business mix, to retail location decisions. To generate more meaningful policy implications, it will be necessary to drill down to the corridor level, rather than analyzing business patterns at the zip code level as is most commonly done in this type of research.

To understand these questions and craft more effective policy interventions, better data are necessary. The NETS data are a convenient source of the address-based longitudinal data that are required to understand retail markets, but they fall short in several regards. First, because this database is developed by a private vendor, its cost is prohibitive for many researchers. Second, researchers report that its employment numbers may be inaccurate.[145] Finally, research on retail revitalization needs to take into account many different outcomes, including changes in crime, tax revenue, vacancy rates, indirect investment, and other indicators. To advance this field, it would be helpful to have government agencies, such as the Small Business Administration and the Department of Housing and Urban Development, work together to collect data on these revitalization outcomes at the level of the address and neighborhood. Until the collection of data becomes more systematic, our studies of revitalization will remain mostly speculative.

145. Panel discussion on "Employment Dynamics, Firm Movement, and Establishment-Level Time-Series Data," Association of Collegiate Schools of Planning Annual Conference, Chicago, July 9, 2008. For the Dun and Bradstreet data, phone surveyors ask employers to estimate numbers of employees, and if they decline to provide new data, surveyors simply use the total from the previous year. Further, employers may give a total number of employees, rather than the number employed at one specific location.

References

Abell, Barbara. 2002. *Overcoming Obstacles to CDC Supermarket Development: A Guide.* Washington: National Congress for Community Economic Development.

———. 1998. *Supermarket Development: CDC's and Inner City Economic Development.* Washington: National Congress for Community Economic Development.

Alwitt, Linda F., and Thomas D. Donley. 1997. "Retail Stores in Poor Urban Neighborhoods." *Journal of Consumer Affairs* 31, no. 1: 139–64.

Artz, Georgeanne, and Kenneth Stone. 2006. "Analyzing the Impact of Wal-Mart Supercenters on Local Food Store Sales." *American Journal of Agricultural Economics* 88, no. 5: 1296–303.

Asabere, Paul K., and Forrest E. Huffman. 1991. "Historic Districts and Land Values." *Journal of Real Estate Research* 6, no. 1: 1–7.

Ball, Jennifer. 2002. *Street Vending (PAS 509): A Survey of Ideas and Lessons for Planners.* Chicago: American Planning Association Planning Advisory Service.

Basker, Emek. 2005. "Job Creation or Destruction? Labor-Market Effects of Wal-Mart Expansion." *Review of Economics and Statistics* 87: 174–83.

Bates, Timothy. 1997. *Race, Self-Employment, and Upward Mobility: An Illusive American Dream.* Johns Hopkins University Press.

Bernhardt, Annette. 1999. "The Future of Low-Wage Jobs: Case Studies in the Retail Industry." IEE Working Paper 10. New York: Institute on Education and the Economy.

Berube, Alan, and Thacher Tiffany. 2004. *The Shape of the Curve: Household Income Distributions in U.S. Cities, 1979–1999.* Living Cities Census Series. Brookings.

Birch, Eugenie L. 2005. "Who Lives Downtown." Brookings, Metropolitan Policy Program.

Booza, Jason, Jackie Cutsinger, and George Galster. 2006. *Where Did They Go? The Decline of Middle-Income Neighborhoods in Metropolitan America.* Brookings.

Boston Consulting Group Inc. 1998. "The Business Case for Pursuing Retail Opportunities in the Inner City." Boston: Initiative for a Competitive Inner City.

Briffault, Richard. 1999. "A Government for Our Time: Business Improvement Districts and Urban Governance." *Columbia Law Review* 99, no. 2: 265–477.

Carlson, Neil. 2003. "A Road Map to Revitalizing Urban Neighborhood Business Districts." New York: Local Initiatives Support Corporation (October).

Chung, Chanjin, and Samuel L. Myers Jr. 1999. "Do the Poor Pay More for Food? An Analysis of Grocery Store Availability and Food Price Disparities." *Journal of Consumer Affairs* 33, no. 2: 276–96.

Civic Economics. 2002. *Economic Impact Analysis: A Case Study, Local Merchants vs. Chain Retailers, Executive Summary.* Report prepared for LiveableCity Austin and Austin Independent Business Alliance. Austin (December).

Clampet-Lundquist, Susan. 2004. "Moving Over or Moving Up? Short-Term Gains and Losses for Relocated HOPE VI Families." *Cityscape* 7, no. 1: 57–80.

Clifton, Kelly J. 2003. "Examining Travel Choices of Low-Income Populations: Issues, Methods, and New Approaches." Paper presented at the 10th International Conference on Travel Behaviour Research. Lucerne, Switzerland, August.

———. 2004. "Mobility Strategies and Food Shopping for Low-Income Families: A Case Study." *Journal of Planning Education and Research* 23, no. 4: 387–401.

Coyle, Deirdre M. 2007. "Realizing the Inner City Retail Opportunity: Progress and New Directions, An Analysis of Retail Markets in America's Inner Cities." *Economic Development Journal* 6, no. 1: 6–14.

Crane, Randall, and Michael Manville. 2008. "People or Place? Revisiting the Who versus the Where in Community Economic Development." Working Paper. Cambridge, Mass.: Lincoln Institute of Land Policy.

Curley, Alexandra M. 2006. "HOPE and Housing: The Effects of Relocation on Movers' Economic Stability, Social Networks, and Health." Ph.D. dissertation, Boston University.

Dane, Suzanne G., ed. 1988. *New Directions for Urban Main Streets.* Washington: National Trust for Historic Preservation.

Dardia, Michael. 1998. "Subsidizing Redevelopment in California." San Francisco: Public Policy Institute of California.

Dickens, William T. 1999. "Rebuilding Urban Labor Markets: What Community Development Can Accomplish." In *Urban Problems and Community Development*, edited by Ronald F. Ferguson, pp. 381–436. Brookings.

Dixon, Timothy J. 2005. "The Role of Retailing in Urban Regeneration." *Local Economy* 20, no. 2: 168–82.

Dowall, David E., and others. 1994. "Urban Residential Redevelopment in the People's Republic of China." *Urban Studies* 31, no. 9: 1497–516.

Dunford, Jenny. 2006. "Under-served Markets." *Local Economy* 21, no. 1: 73–77.

Eisinger, Peter K. 1988. *The Rise of the Entrepreneurial State: State and Local Economic Development Policy in the United States.* University of Wisconsin Press.

Fogelson, Robert M. 2001. *Downtown: Its Rise and Fall, 1880–1950.* Yale University Press.

Food Marketing Institute. 1993. *Joint Venture in the Inner City—Supermarket General Corporation and New Community Corporation.* Washington.

Freeman, Lance. 2004. "There Goes the Hood: The Meaning of Gentrification to Long-Term Residents." Paper presented at annual meeting of American Sociological Association. San Francisco, August.

———. 2005. "Displacement or Succession? Residential Mobility in Gentrifying Neighborhoods." *Urban Affairs Review* 40, no. 4: 463–91.

———. 2006. *There Goes the Hood: Views of Gentrification from the Ground Up.* Temple University Press.

Freeman, Lance, and Frank Braconi. 2004. "Gentrification and Displacement in New York City." *Journal of the American Planning Association* 70, no. 1: 39–52.

Frieden, Bernard J., and Lynne Sagalyn. 1989. *Downtown, Inc.: How America Builds Cities.* MIT Press.

Galster, George, and Jason Booza. 2007. "The Rise of the Bipolar Neighborhood." *Journal of American Planning Association* 73, no. 4: 421–35.

Galster, George, and others. 2005. *Low-Income Households in Mixed-Income Neighborhoods: Extent, Trends, and Determinants.* Report prepared for the U.S. Department of Housing and Urban Development. Washington: HUD.

Goering, John, and Judith D. Feins. 2003. *Choosing a Better Life: Evaluating the Moving to Opportunity Social Experiment.* Washington: Urban Institute Press.

Goetz, Edward G. 2002. "Forced Relocation vs. Voluntary Mobility: The Effects of Dispersal Programs on Households." *Housing Studies* 17, no. 1: 107–23.

Goodman, Michael D., and Daniel J. Monti. 1999. "Corporately Sponsored Redevelopment Campaigns and the Social Stability of Urban Neighborhoods: St. Louis Revisited." *Journal of Urban Affairs* 21, no. 1: 101–27.

Gross, Jill S. 2005. "Business Improvement Districts in New York City's Low-Income and High-Income Neighborhoods." *Economic Development Quarterly* 19, no. 2: 174–89.

Hernandez, Manuel. 2001. "The Impact of Commercial Development on Inner City Revitalization: An Analysis of Projects in Boston." Master's thesis, Department of Urban Studies and Planning, Massachusetts Institute of Technology.

Houstoun, Lawrence O., Jr. 2004. "Business Improvement Districts." *Economic Development Journal* 3, no. 3: 48–54.

Hoyt, Lorlene M. 2005. "Do Business Improvement District Organizations Make a Difference?" *Journal of Planning Education and Research* 25, no. 2: 185–99.

Immergluck, Daniel. 1999. "Neighborhoods, Race, and Capital: The Effects of Residential Change on Commercial Investment Patterns." *Urban Affairs Review* 34, no. 3: 397–411.

Initiative for a Competitive Inner City. 2002. *The Changing Models of Inner City Grocery Retailing.* Boston.

International Council of Shopping Centers. 2004. *Developing Successfull Retail in Underserved Urban Markets.* Report produced in cooperation with Business for Social Responsibility. New York.

Jacobus, Rick, and Maureen Hickey. 2007. "Commercial Revitalization Planning Guide: A Toolkit for Community Based Organizations." New York: Local Initiatives Support Corporation, Center for Commercial Revitalization.

Johnson, Craig L., and Joyce Y. Man. 2001. *Tax Increment Financing and Economic Development: Uses, Structures, and Impact.* State University of New York Press.

Joseph, Mark. 2006. "Is Mixed-Income Development an Antidote to Urban Poverty?" *Housing Policy Debate* 17, no. 2: 209–34.

Kelley, Steve. 1996. "The Main Street Program in Mississippi." *Economic Development Review* 14, no. 3: 56.

Kennedy, Maureen, and Paul Leonard. 2001. "Dealing with Neighborhood Change: A Primer on Gentrification and Policy Choices." Discussion Paper prepared for the Brookings Institution Center on Urban and Metropolitan Policy and PolicyLink (www.policylink.org/pdfs/BrookingsGentrification.pdf).

Koebel, Theodore C. 2002. "Analyzing Neighborhood Retail and Service Change in Six Cities." Blacksburg, Va.: Virginia Polytechnic Institute and State University, Center for Housing Research.

Levy, Diane K., and Mark Woolley. 2007. "Relocation Is Not Enough: Employment Barriers among HOPE VI Families." *Policy Brief* 6. Washington: Urban Institute.

Listokin, David, Barbara Listokin, and Michael Lahr. 1998. "The Contributions of Historic Preservation to Housing and Economic Development." *Housing Policy Debate* 9, no. 3: 431–78.

Loukaitou-Sideris, Anastasia. 2000. "Revisiting Inner-City Strips: A Framework for Community and Economic Development." *Economic Development Quarterly* 14, no. 2: 165–81.

Mari Gallagher Research and Consulting Group. 2006. "Examining the Impact of Food Deserts on Public Health in Chicago." Chicago: LaSalle Bank.

Marketek, Inc. 2000. *Economic Impact Assessment of Fruitvale Main Street Initiative.* Report prepared for the Local Initiatives Support Corporation. New York: LISC.

Markusen, Ann R., ed. 2007. *Reining in the Competition for Capital.* Kalamazoo, Mich.: Upjohn Institute for Employment Research.

Mason, Randall. 2005. "Economics and Historic Preservation: A Guide and Review of the Literature." Brookings.

McKinnish, Terra, Randall P. Walsh, and Kirk White. 2008. "Who Gentrifies Low-Income Neighborhoods?" NBER Working Paper W14036. Cambridge, Mass.: National Bureau of Economic Research (http://ssrn.com/abstract=1139352).

Medoff, Peter, and Holly Sklar. 1994. *Streets of Hope: The Fall and Rise of an Urban Neighborhood.* Boston: South End Press.

Min, Pyong Gap, and Mehdi Bozorgmehr. 2000. "Immigrant Entrepreneurship and Business Patterns: A Comparison of Koreans and Iranians in Los Angeles." *International Migration Review* 34, no. 3: 707–38.

Mitchell, Jerry. 2003. "Business Improvement Districts and Innovative Service Delivery." In *New Ways of Doing Business,* edited by Mark A. Abramson and Ann M. Kieffaber, pp. 217–48. Lanham, Md.: Rowman & Littlefield.

Moore, Latetia V., and Ana V. Diez Roux. 2006. "Associations of Neighborhood Characteristics with the Location and Type of Food Stores." *American Journal of Public Health* 96, no. 2: 325–31.

Newman, Kathe, and Elvin Wyly. 2006. "The Right to Stay Put, Revisited: Gentrification and Resistance to Displacement in New York City." *Urban Studies* 43, no. 1: 23–57.

Nunn, Samuel. 2001. "Planning for Inner-City Retail Development." *Journal of the American Planning Association* 67, no. 2: 159–72.

Nyden, Phillip, and others. 1997. *Building Community: Social Science in Action.* Thousand Oaks, Calif.: Pine Forge Press.

Oakley, Dierdre, and Hui-Shien Tsao. 2006. "A New Way of Revitalizing Distressed Urban Communities? Assessing the Impact of the Federal Urban Empowerment Zone Program." *Journal of Urban Affairs* 28, no. 5: 443–71.

Ong, Paul M., and Doug Houston. 2002. "The 2000 Census Undercount in Los Angles County." University of California—Los Angeles, School of Public Policy Social Research.

Pawasarat, John, and Lois M. Quinn. 2001. "Exposing Urban Legends: The Real Purchasing Power of Central City Neighborhoods." Brookings, Center on Urban and Metropolitan Policy.

Porter, Michael E. 1995. "The Competitive Advantage of the Inner City." *Harvard Business Review* 73, no. 3: 55–71.

Pothukuchi, Kameshwari. 2005. "Attracting Supermarkets to Inner-City Neighborhoods: Economic Development outside the Box." *Economic Development Quarterly* 19, no. 3: 232–44.

Raja, Samina, Changxing Ma, and Pavan Yadav. 2008. "Beyond Food Deserts: Measuring and Mapping Racial Disparities in Neighborhood Food Environments." *Journal of Planning Education and Research* 27, no. 4: 469–82.

Rauch, James E. 1996. "Trade and Networks: An Application to Minority Retail Entrepreneurship." Working Paper. New York: Russell Sage Foundation.

Rich, Michael J., and Robert P. Stoker. 2007. "Governance and Urban Revitalization: Lessons from the Urban Empowerment Zones Initiative." Paper prepared for Conference on a Global Look at Urban and Regional Governance: The State-Market-Civic Nexus. Emory University, January 18–19.

Rosenbaum, James E., and Susan J. Popkin. 1991. "Employment and Earnings of Low-Income Blacks Who Move to Middle-Class Suburbs." In *The Urban Underclass*, edited by Christopher Jencks and Paul Peterson, pp. 342–56. Brookings.

Rubinowitz, Leonard S., and James E. Rosenbaum. 2000. *Crossing the Class and Color Lines: From Public Housing to White Suburbia*. University of Chicago Press.

Sagalyn, Lynne. 1989. "Measuring Financial Returns When the City Acts as an Investor: Boston and Faneuil Hall Marketplace." *Real Estate Issue* 14, no. 2: 7–15.

Seidman, Karl F. 1999. *Community Business Network: An Evaluation of Program Outcomes and Operations*. Cambridge, Mass.: Massachusetts Association of Community Development Corporations.

———. 2001. *Wanted: Solutions for America*. Final Research Report, Boston Main Streets Program. Prepared for Pew Partnership and Rutgers University Center for Urban and Regional Policy.

———. 2002. "Urban Inner City Commercial Revitalization: A Literature Review." Unpublished paper. MIT, Department of Urban Studies and Planning (June).

———. 2003. "Inner-City Commercial Revitalization: Applying the Main Street Model." Unpublished paper. MIT, Department of Urban Studies and Planning (March).

———. 2004. *Revitalizing Commerce for American Cities: A Practitioner's Guide to Urban Main Street Programs*. Washington: Fannie Mae Foundation.

Servon, Lisa J., and Edwin Melendez. 2006. "The Evolution of Urban Community Development Corporations." Unpublished paper. The New School, Community Development Research Center.

Short, Anne, Julie Guthman, and Samuel Raskin. 2007. "Food Deserts, Oases, or Mirages? Small Markets and Community Food Security in the San Francisco Bay Area." *Journal of Planning Education and Research* 26, no. 3: 352–64.

Smith, Neil. 1996. *The New Urban Frontier: Gentrification and the Revanchist City*. London: Routledge.

Stokes, Robert J. 2007. "Business Improvement Districts and Small Business Advocacy: The Case of San Diego's Citywide BID Program." *Economic Development Quarterly* 21, no. 3: 278–91.

Stone, Kenneth E. 1997. "Impact of the Wal-Mart Phenomenon on Rural Communities." In *Increasing Understanding of Public Problems and Policies*, pp. 189–200. Oak Brook, Ill.: Farm Foundation.

Teitz, Michael. 1989. "Neighborhood Economics: Local Communities and Regional Markets." *Economic Development Quarterly* 3, no. 2: 111–22.

Turner, Robyne S. 2004. "Troost Avenue Revival: Breathing New Life into Neighborhood Commercial Corridors." Paper presented at annual meeting of American Political Science Association. Portland, November.

Turney, Kristen, and others. 2006. "Neighborhood Effects on Barriers to Employment: Results from a Randomized Housing Mobility Experiment in Baltimore." In *Brookings-Wharton Papers on Urban Affairs*, edited by Gary Burtless and Janet Rothenberg Pack, pp. 137–87. Brookings .

U.S. Department of Housing and Urban Development (HUD). 1999. *New Markets: The Untapped Retail Buying Power in America's Inner Cities*. Government Printing Office.

U.S. Government Accountability Office (GAO). 2006. *Empowerment Zone and Enterprise Community Program: Improvements Occurred in Communities, but the Effect of the Program Is Unclear*. Report GAO-06-727.

————. 2007. *New Markets Tax Credit Appears to Increase Investment by Investors in Low-Income Communities, but Opportunities Exist to Better Monitor Compliance.* Report GAO-07-296.

Walker, Christopher, and others. 2002. *Public-Sector Loans to Private-Sector Businesses: An Assessment of HUD-Supported Local Economic Development Lending Activities.* Report to U.S. Department of Housing and Urban Development. Washington: Urban Institute.

Weber, Rachel. 2003. "Equity and Entrepreneurialism: The Impact of Tax Increment Financing on School Finance." *Urban Affairs Review* 38, no. 5: 619–44.

Weissbourd, Robert, and Christopher Berry. 1999. "The Market Potential of Inner-City Neighborhoods: Filling the Information Gap." Brookings.

Wilder, Margaret G., and Barry M. Rubin. 1988. "Targeted Redevelopment through Urban Enterprise Zones." *Journal of Urban Affairs* 10, no. 1: 1–17.

Williams, Colin C., and Jan Windebank. 2002. "The 'Excluded Consumer': A Neglected Aspect of Social Exclusion?" *Policy and Politics* 30, no. 4: 501–13.

Wilson, James, and George Kelling. 1982. "Broken Windows." *Atlantic Monthly* 249, no. 3: 29–38.

Wilson, William J. 1987. *The Truly Disadvantaged: The Inner City, the Underclass, and Public Policy.* University of Chicago Press.

Wyly, Elvin K., and Daniel J. Hammel. 1999. "Islands of Decay in Seas of Renewal: Urban Policy and the Resurgence of Gentrification." *Housing Policy Debate* 10: 711–71.

————. 2004. "Gentrification, Segregation and Discrimination in the American Urban System." *Environment and Planning A* 36: 1215–241.

3

Correlates of Mayoral Takeovers in City School Systems

JEFFREY R. HENIG AND ELISABETH THURSTON FRASER

Mayoral control of schools involves the relative shift of formal authority over public education systems from elected school boards to mayors. Typically, mayoral control consists of giving mayors power to appoint some or all of the school board members, but in its more extreme versions, it involves broadly incorporating previously separate school districts into general purpose municipal government. Mayoral control of schools in itself is nothing new. Indeed, before the Progressive Era reforms in the early twentieth century, public education in large cities most often was housed in an agency reporting to a mayor much as would be the case with law enforcement or public works. What is new is its reemergence as a favored reform after decades in which a rival vision held sway.

During the Progressive era, many communities removed oversight of schools from the mayor's responsibility in the belief that this would lead to a more professional approach and one less responsive to partisan politics and the temptation to use school jobs and school building contracts as forms of patronage. The strategy for depoliticizing education was to place school governance in the hands of an independently elected school board, often elected off-cycle from general elections and often with a dedicated revenue stream. Some urban districts, such as Chicago; New Haven, Connecticut; and Jackson, Mississippi, never took schools out of the mayor's portfolio of control, but of the large districts currently under mayoral control, most gave their mayors stronger formal roles during the past fifteen years after decades of strong school board governance.

The resurgence of interest in mayoral control of schools began in the 1990s, when four major cities—Boston (1992), Chicago (1995), Cleveland (1998), and Detroit (1999)—moved to put schools under the control of the mayor.

Momentum built slowly but accelerated after the turn of the century, with Harrisburg, Pennsylvania; Oakland, California; Providence, Rhode Island; Philadelphia; Washington, D.C.; and, most prominently, New York City among those that have recently moved to mayoral control to at least some degree.[1] Detroit subsequently revoked the mayoral control model, and the New York State legislature must revisit the issue of whether to continue, revoke, or modify the New York City plan before July 2009, when it is scheduled to sunset.

As often happens in the early cycling of hot reform ideas, core elements of the phenomenon are only vaguely defined, data are thin, and debate and diffusion are driven by a combination of vest-pocket theory, symbol, and anecdote. Such loosely framed discussion is especially common when the intervention—as in this case—entails a systemic shift in governance institutions rather than a discrete policy reform. Discrete policy reforms typically are offered with a relatively tightly woven causal narrative that explains why a particular set of design elements can be expected to result in well-specified changes in targeted outcomes. Changes in governance arrangements, however, involve flipping switches far removed from the social conditions that society ultimately wishes to change. Even the most enthusiastic proponents of mayoral control do not believe that simply changing who sits atop the educational delivery system in and of itself will increase the learning that takes place within classrooms or narrow educational achievement gaps. The hope is that such a shift in governance will stimulate a cascade of changes that will make the system either "do things better"—with more focus; more expertise; more commitment, coherence, and consistency; greater innovation; less malfeasance; less waste—or "do different things" that will be more effective than the policy initiatives politically feasible under the conventional governance arrangements. Not only are the causal linkages often long and loosely specified, but governance changes raise a host of political issues related to competing values and interest groups, issues that can give stakeholders incentives to be purposefully vague about the motivations behind the positions they adopt. These factors make even more vexing one of the key issues animating this volume: the question of policy success with respect to what?

As the cases accumulate and time passes, however, it becomes possible to bring matters into sharper focus, something we attempt to do here. This chapter considers the arguments in favor of mayoral control, defines more precisely what mayoral control is and is not, and reviews the evidence about where it emerges and what difference it makes.

We begin by arguing for an understanding of mayoral control as a political movement and not just an administrative adjustment. Paradoxically, although

1. Henig and Rich (2004); Wong and others (2007).

mayoral control is frequently presented as a refutation of the Progressive reformers—particularly as a rejection of their effort to wrest authority from partisan mayors and vest it in institutions of governance and implementation buffered from political winds—the simple theories that contemporary proponents offer in favor of mayoral control echo in most respects the apolitical framing of their predecessors. The generally apolitical administrative theory, in which the arguments today are most frequently cast, focuses on why mayoral control may allow localities to "do it better." While that is an important issue, we suggest that it is also important to attend to the probabilities that mayoral control may lead localities to "do different things." While administrative theory focuses on collective benefits or benefits likely to accrue most directly to those with greatest need, it is also important to consider ways in which mayoral control may provide greater access and benefits to certain advantaged groups.

We review existing evidence—and contribute some original analysis as well—with this distinction between an apolitical and political framing in mind. This leads us to reconceptualize the issue in several respects. First, although most discussion treats mayoral control as a discrete governance reform, it may be more appropriate to consider it as one manifestation of several larger movements that include the erosion of traditional barriers among the levels of federalism, between the public and private sectors, and between general purpose government and schooling as a specialized arena. Second, rather than driven simply by systematic need (worst performance), adoption of mayoral control may be better understood as an ad hoc strategy of business, civic, and state and national leaders to shift authority into a venue in which they have more access and to individuals in whom they have more personal confidence and closer ties. Third, although there are good reasons to believe mayoral control cities will tend to do some things differently, whether this accrues in higher test scores and smaller educational gaps may depend less on the institutional details and initial mayors and more on the political and fiscal context and bureaucratic capacity of the city.

Why Mayoral Control?

Judging the effectiveness of a policy entails knowing what the policy is intended to accomplish. One way to determine this is to look at what proponents offer as their rationale. The task of winning support for new ideas, however, creates different incentives than do the tasks entailed in establishing an evaluative framework. On the one hand, establishing an evaluative framework calls for specifying clear goals, precisely diagnosing the status quo, and detailing causal mechanisms. Building support, on the other hand, often requires creative ambiguity: alluding to broad benefits without identifying pertinent costs or encouraging disparate groups to imagine that their own values and interests will receive greater attention.

In the case of mayoral control, getting a clear understanding of the forces that are actually driving the movement requires drawing some distinctions. One distinction is between pressures for mayoral control based on a presumed advantage to the *unitary interest* of the city as a whole as opposed to those that rest on advantages to *particular stakeholders*. A second distinction is between *push* factors, which generate dissatisfaction with the standard governance arrangements, and *pull* factors, which account for the specific interest in mayoral control. Proponents of mayoral control often emphasize unitary interests and push factors to build on the broadly shared sense that the current arrangements are flawed and to suggest that the reform will provide benefits to all.

City Interest versus Stakeholder Interest

One tradition of analysis starts with a notion of the collective good of the jurisdiction and then applies efficiency and effectiveness as the key evaluative criteria. This approach was explicitly adopted by Progressive reformers of the early twentieth century, who posed it as an alternative to the particularistic style of politics that characterized the urban machine. It is also generally common among public administration experts and among political economists working in the tradition of Charles Tiebout.[2] Paul Peterson's *City Limits* provides what has been an especially influential elaboration of the political economy approach.[3] "Just as we can speak of union interests, judicial interests, and the interests of politicians," he wrote, "so we can speak of the interests of that structured system of social interactions we call a city."[4]

> The interests of cities are neither a summation of individual interests nor the pursuit of optimum size. Instead, policies and programs can be said to be in the interest of cities whenever the policies maintain or enhance the economic position, social prestige, or political power of the city, taken as a whole.[5]

City interests. Applied to the issue of school governance structures, this unitary interest approach asks whether mayoral control is more likely than traditional institutions to generate policies that promote urban well-being. Those relying on this approach typically focus on economic development as the pri-

2. Tiebout (1956).
3. Peterson (1981).
4. Peterson (1981, p. 17).
5. Peterson (1981, p. 20).

mary unifying interest and argue that, compared with elected school boards, mayors are more likely both to be attuned to the importance of economic development and to have the skills and administrative capacity to implement the appropriate strategies. To account for the seeming paradox whereby contemporary reformers are calling for a return to a governance form that reformers of an earlier era had so aggressively rejected, today's reformers argue that the economic context of urban life has changed in ways that ensure modern mayors will do a better job than their historical predecessors. These changes include globalization and its recognized potential to lead to an exodus of capital, combined with internal political evolution that reduces the reliability of electoral appeals based on race and ethnicity. Together, it is argued, these have led to "new and improved" modern-style mayors who are much more inclined than their machine-oriented predecessors to see schools as a mechanism for attracting corporate investment instead of as a patronage pool.[6]

Stakeholder interests. Contrasting with explanations centered on the cities' unitary interests are those that account for the emergence of mayoral control as a tactical movement by particular interest groups. These more explicitly political explanations start with the observation that in almost every instance the key proponents of mayoral control have been segments of the local business community in alliance with state legislators. Although they invariably present a rationale framed in terms of the broad "public interest," these stakeholders may have more particular reasons for advocating for a shift in governance structure.

The business community, historically, has had a narrow and material interest in schools that is tied to its need for literate and disciplined workers and its self-interest in transferring the costs of producing such workers to publicly funded institutions.[7] To the extent that business leaders consider their investment in a community to be dependent on the overall health of the city and regional economy, they also have a shared interest in improving schools, not just as producers of workers, but as institutions that attract and hold residents and jobs. It is worth mentioning here that the breadth and intensity of the business community's commitment to local school reform can vary substantially; some businesses are less dependent on skilled labor; some that are highly dependent on skilled labor can attract it from elsewhere; some businesses depend less than others on a vital localized economy; some care more than others about limiting taxation even if that means that the schools may suffer.

In addition to a generic commitment to better schools, the business community may have a vision of schooling—that is, its goals and its practices—that dif-

6. Kirst and Bulkley (2000).
7. Bowles and Gintis (1976); Katznelson and Weir (1985); O'Connell (1999); Shipps (2006).

fers from that of other important and legitimate stakeholders. Compared with parents' and teachers' organizations, for example, business actors may be more attracted to policy options that are similar to corporate practices: for example, merit pay, contracting out, and bonuses for meeting performance indicators. In terms of curriculum, it may be willing to pay less attention to the arts and humanities in return for greater attention to math and reading skills that align more directly with what they want in their employees.

Some businesses have a more direct material self-interest at stake. A recent phenomenon is the growing sector of the business community that views public school districts as a source of jobs and contracts. The corporate presence in the education delivery sector, composed of educational management organizations (EMOs), tutoring firms, and the testing and publishing industry, was growing robustly even before the enactment of No Child Left Behind (NCLB), but that federal law's provisions for mandatory testing, and for requiring failing schools to provide private supplemental education services or to be reconstituted if they continue to fail, gave that trend added momentum.[8] A political perspective suggests that this sector of the business community might promote mayoral control in the belief that it is likely to have greater access, leverage, and credibility in that institutional venue than when school governance is conducted by school boards more politically sensitive to parents and teachers unions and that this greater influence will help them expand their markets and increase their profit margins.

Business actors, though, are not the only interests that may support mayoral control for their own purposes. State legislators may prefer to deal with mayors than with separately elected school boards; mayors may see that as a way to expand their clout and potential to move on to higher office, and mayoral candidates may see mayoral control as a tactically astute issue on which to campaign.

States, during the past three decades, have been playing an increasingly active role in overseeing local school districts. This is a process that began in the early 1980s, driven, among other factors, by governors' realization that education reform could be key to economic development and by state court rulings that directed states to play a stronger role in resolving fiscal inequities across districts. As legislatures saw more of the state expenditures going to education, they became increasingly interested in making sure the money was well spent. This dynamic was further accelerated by the passage of NCLB, which imposed new responsibilities on states for funding assessment and oversight systems and for intervening when schools and districts failed to make steady progress. Led by New Jersey, some states thought they could tackle central city school reform themselves by directly taking over failing districts. But one lesson from state

8. Toch (2006); Henig and others (2003); Henig (2007).

takeovers has been that wrestling with the problems of inner-city schooling is more difficult than many had assumed. It is not enough to put a state team in control—even an expert and committed one—if the core bureaucracy is resistant or fundamentally lacks capacity and if local political dynamics are such that the reform effort is seen as externally driven and not a reflection of local values and local democracy. Mayoral control is appealing to state legislators, therefore, as a way to enlist an on-site partner: a partner who could pursue their agenda, bring to bear local knowledge, mobilize a local constituency, and take off their shoulders some of the costs and potential risks of failure.

Sitting mayors historically have been reluctant to accept responsibility for education, out of a belief that education is a political hot potato. Education is closely monitored by a range of divergent single-issue groups, including parents, teachers, religious organizations, and antitax advocates. It is difficult to satisfy all of these interests and easy to anger one or more. And because of the proven difficulty of achieving continuing test score gains, it is hard for politicians to demonstrate a record of success convincingly enough to buffer them from political backlash.

Assessments of the political costs and benefits of taking on the education issue appear to be changing, however. The examples of Mayor Menino of Boston and Mayor Daley of Chicago show that formal control over schools is compatible with long tenure in office, and some recent mayoral candidates have found that a stated willingness to take on the responsibility for schools can help propel them into office. During the campaign season preceding the New York City mayoral election in 2001, candidate Michael Bloomberg urged voters to give him a chance to improve city schools and to *judge his performance* as mayor according to his leadership of the school system. Adrian Fenty, similarly, made his desire to take on this responsibility part of his successful effort to become mayor in Washington, D.C. Fear that failure to realize sharp gains might subsequently come back to haunt such hubris may have been overblown. The Bloomberg administration's first term in office did not produce major advances in test scores, but the fact that the mayor appeared serious and sincere was enough to satisfy many. An editorial endorsement for his reelection by the *New York Times* did not list any specific improvements but did assert that "no mayor has devoted more effort to improving the schools."[9] Mayors who express a strong interest in being held accountable for their local schools may be banking on the hope that a formal association with the education system may prove beneficial in future elections, and at the very least, their governance will likely not prove worse than what existed before.

9. *New York Times*, "An Endorsement for Mayor," October 23, 2005.

Most of the public discussion of mayoral control is framed in terms of unitary interests, but that may reflect, at least in part, the greater political appeal of an initiative that promises to raise all ships. If key stakeholders have narrower objectives in mind, it is incumbent upon analysts to be alert to that fact and to include assessments of redistribution of power and gain among the indicators they study in judging the success of mayoral control. The distinction between push and pull factors also illuminates the challenge of assessing an emergent reform strategy for which its proponents have glossed over the underlying causal theories.

Push and Pull

To some extent, the movement toward mayoral control can be explained as simply the latest in a series of reform impulses broadly characterized as "anything's got to be better than what we have now." Frustration with the nation's results in international tests has been a constant at least since 1983 when *A Nation at Risk* issued its sharp warning that "if an unfriendly foreign power had attempted to impose on America the mediocre educational performance that exists today, we might well have viewed it as an act of war."[10] While education has climbed on the national agenda, and despite the fact that the Bush administration has declared that NCLB has been "working," the level of performance (compared with NCLB's 100 percent proficiency goal and as determined in international competitions) and the racial and economic gaps in performance both remain issues of deep concern.[11]

Push. The sense that there is a need for systemic change has prompted a series of reforms "du jour," including school-based decisionmaking, increased high school graduation requirements, smaller class size, smaller schools, increased performance testing, and charter schools, just to name a handful.[12] This process of sequential but short-lived reforms has been labeled a spinning wheel and criticized as being superficial and largely symbolic in nature.[13]

Although much of the reform impulse has been attached to specific programmatic or curricular ideas, some have argued that the basic governance structure characterizing U.S. education at the local district level is the real source of the problem. Elected school boards, particularly those elected by wards, have been criticized for a range of sins, including petty politics, micromanagement, amateurishness, lack of imagination, kowtowing to the teachers unions, corruption, and waste. The tenor of the discussion is captured by the titles of an edited vol-

10. National Commission on Excellence in Education, Department of Education, April 1983 (www.ed.gov/pubs/NatAtRisk/risk.html).
11. McGuinn (2006).
12. Farkas (1992).
13. Hess (1998).

ume of scholarly analyses of school boards and local school governance—
Besieged—and a more journalistic assessment that appeared in the *Atlantic Monthly*, "First Kill All the School Boards."[14]

Pull. To suggest that the existing governance arrangements need to be changed is one thing. That accounts for the push part of the equation, but it does not necessarily account for the pull toward mayoral control. Indeed, before the emergence of mayoral control, several alternative governance models had their day in the sun. One, as alluded to above, involved state takeovers. As of 2001, twenty-four states had legislation on the books that would allow them to take over failing districts.[15] Another governance reform that has cycled in and out of attention is the notion of decentralizing authority to the school level, which had its spike of attention with the community control experiment in New York City in the late 1960s and in Chicago in the 1980s.[16] Rather than shift power up to the state or down to the school and community, a third alternative to school board governance has been to rely more on market choice as an alternative to bureaucratic control. Vouchers, the extreme form of this model, have proven politically unpalatable in most places where they were subject to public referenda, but charter schools, considered by some to be a warmer and more cuddly form of market-based governance, spread rapidly.[17]

While each of these alternatives continues to have proponents, one of the pull factors leading to increased attention to mayoral control is the realization that none of these are panaceas and all are prone to failure absent healthy local politics and district-level governance capacity. Once it is accepted that good public education requires good local governance—that rival governance structures do not allow this difficult step to be bypassed—mayoral control becomes an attractive alternative, backed by theoretical rationales and direct political incentives. Kenneth Meier summarizes what he labels the "formal *a priori* logic" in favor of mayoral control—"that is, how and why it should work"—as being composed of claims that it improves education by centralizing accountability, broadening the constituency for education, and reducing micromanagement.[18] In addition to the promotion of coordination with other agencies, centralizing authority in the mayor's office in theory increases democratic accountability by reducing the opportunity for school boards and superintendents to blame one another or blame the mayor and city council for failing to provide budgetary and other support. Compared with school board members, who often come

14. For the edited volume, *Besieged*, see Howell (2005); for the *Atlantic Monthly* article, see Miller (2008).
15. Wong and Shen (2001).
16. Bryk and others (1998); Gittell and others (1980).
17. Henig (2008).
18. Meier (2004).

into office because of low-turnout, ward-based elections, mayors have to have pulled together broader electoral coalitions, made up of groups that may not have a direct stake in the public schools. A mayor, so inclined, has the opportunity to enlist that constituency in supporting a school reform agenda; and because he or she is less beholden to the teachers unions and parent organizations that dominate school board elections, the mayor may be open to a wider range of policy solutions and less wedded to the status quo. Finally, because they are generalists, and accordingly know less about the details of education, Meier suggests mayors are more likely to recruit a top-notch superintendent and then give that leader the discretion to shape and implement a reform agenda without micromanaging.

Intermediary Steps and the Mechanics of Change

Improving test scores and reducing achievement gaps are the key outcomes emphasized in contemporary debates on education reform. Most analysts take it as given, though, that even successful interventions take at least three to five years before registering measurable gains. For those evaluating a relatively new initiative, therefore, it can be helpful to identify intermediary steps that provide benchmarks for judging whether things are on or off course. The broad framing of the arguments for mayoral control makes this difficult, however.

Proponents of mayoral control have not been explicit or precise in explaining the causal steps between governance change and improved educational performance. That is partly because they have not had to be. Profound dissatisfaction with the status quo allowed the push elements—the notion that the existing arrangements are so bad that fundamental institutional change is required—to carry most of the burden of establishing political support, and the general evocation of the idea of mayors as protectors of the economic viability of cities in an era of mobile capital and populations has sufficed to pull sentiment in the direction of this particular solution.

But there are a couple of additional factors that account for the vagueness regarding the implied causal model. First, many proponents of mayoral control are not particularly knowledgeable about what happens inside classrooms: the nitty-gritty details of the learning process, the details of cognitive development, the strengths and weaknesses of particular pedagogical approaches, and the intricate details of curriculum and testing. Indeed, to some extent, their promotion of mayoral control is linked to a view that professional expertise in teaching and learning has been overemphasized as a requirement for making good policy and that it has been strategically manipulated by educators to embellish their own power and prerogatives. Rather than stipulate a particular educational plan, they rely on the presumption that devising and implementing such a plan will be relatively straightforward once the corrupting and distracting elements of the existing system are defeated. Second, vagueness about specific educational interventions saves proponents of mayoral control from having to take sides on issues that may be contentious and may even reveal latent splits among their own supporters. Implying that mayoral control simply allows districts to do things better is a "mom and apple pie" presentation; one could hardly muster much of an argument against greater efficiency and effectiveness. But if mayoral control is favored because it is associated with a defined set of policy changes—differential pay for teachers based on performance, expansion of charter schools, contracting with private education providers, broadening access to programs for the gifted and talented, relocating the best teachers into the neediest schools, higher emphasis on test scores—being explicit about that fact might alert and unite an otherwise fragmented opposition.

Despite the vagueness about intermediary steps, we can make some general inferences about what mayoral control is expected to engender along the way to educational gains. Because the charge is that elected school boards diffuse attention by engaging in micromanagement and imposing political and partisan demands upon schools, mayoral control presumably works in part by creating greater focus on the classroom and learning, reflected in more funds' going to instruction. Because the charge is that conventional governance arrangements impede the adoption of new ideas and technologies, mayoral control should lead to the adoption of more comprehensive and up-to-date management and data systems and being more open to contracting with private providers who offer expertise and capacity that is lacking in the existing bureaucracy. Because it is argued that elected school boards are too much under the sway of teachers unions that prioritize the interests of long-term teachers and formal certification processes, mayoral control in principle should result in greater emphasis on recruiting and rewarding new teachers and on creating alternative pathways for teachers and principals. Because the existing governance arrangements are seen as overly responsive to the most politically mobilized constituencies, mayoral control might be expected to redistribute resources and attention from more affluent communities to those with greatest need.

There are other possibilities, of course. One is that any gains along these dimensions are attributable not to the governance change itself but to the confluence of political support, resources, and energies that fuel the initial reform effort. If this is the case, any early signs of progress may be followed by sharp drops as cities move from first-generation to second- and third-generation mayoral control. Another possibility is that mayoral control will alter channels of access and influence, replacing one set of beneficiaries with another but without generating any real change in performance.

Drawing Distinctions: Forms of Mayoral Control

A recurring theme in this volume is that effectiveness can be contingent upon specific design details and the specific context in which the policy is applied. If it is true that "the devil is in the details," the contemporary debate over mayoral control has been doing a good job of staying away from the devil's playground. The umbrella label of mayoral control has been applied to a number of cities with little attention given to the ways in which the particular forms and context differ. Sorting through some distinctions can help us make better sense of the evidence available to date and aid in drawing inferences about the policy implications.

Formal versus Informal Power

Giving formal authority to mayors—to appoint school boards, to hire superintendents, to set school budgets—does not ensure that those mayors will take up the cause of school reform with wisdom or even energy. In Baltimore, for example—where the mayors long held power to appoint the school board and, through their power on the city's Board of Estimates, to tightly control spending—even strong and dynamic mayors like William Donald Schaeffer traditionally preferred to play a minimal role.[19] So, too, was this the case in Chicago, where during the years from 1947 to 1980, while the mayor formally controlled both the board and budget, "most mayors avoided public school debates and disavowed any responsibility for their problems."[20]

Nor does lack of formal authority preclude strong mayoral leadership in the education arena. Michael Kirst and Fritz Edelstein highlight Long Beach as a "prime example of how mayoral involvement in education need not rely on formal changes to governance." There, Mayor Beverly O'Neill has worked closely with the superintendent's office in a partnership that appears to have provided much of the multiagency coordination and public support that proponents of mayoral control talk about. Long Beach won the Broad Prize in Urban Education in 2003.[21] Francis Shlay, mayor of St. Louis, made up for a lack of appointment power by backing a slate of reform-oriented school board candidates and helping them all get elected. Kenneth Wong and others cite Douglas Wilder, mayor of Richmond, Virginia, as an example of a politically skillful mayor who has used his informal power and authority to hold the superintendent accountable to him even when there was no formal line of authority to call upon.[22,]

19. Orr (2004).
20. Shipps (2004).
21. Kirst and Edelstein (2006).
22. Wong and others (2007). The Richmond story took an odd turn in September 2007. The mayor had instructed the school board to move its offices out of City Hall to make room for his economic development department. Backed by the council, the school board refused,

We would argue that the term *mayoral control* should be limited to the issue of formal transfer of powers, reserving a term like *activist mayors* for those who push an education agenda within the existing governance rules of the game. Changing the formal institutions of governance is disruptive to local traditions and expectations and can be hard to undo if its advantages do not materialize. If activist mayors without formal power try to do the same things and have as great a likelihood of success, some of the steam should be let out of the mayoral control movement.

Remnant as Opposed to Contemporary Mayoral Control

Of the major examples of mayoral control listed in table 3-1, five (Baltimore, Chicago, Jackson, New Haven, and Philadelphia) had elements that predated the contemporary era. Three of these have had their governance structure realigned more recently, in the cases of Baltimore and Philadelphia to inject a stronger state role and in the case of Chicago to add some new, formal powers to the mayor's armamentarium. No proponents of mayoral control argue that the districts with long-standing mayoral control structures produced sustained periods of superior education. This raises the question of whether it is formal institutions that matter or something about the historical context in which they are launched.

In cases of contemporary adoption, it can be difficult to distinguish the independent impact of the institutional change from the political and reform pressures that led to its adoption. To the extent that mayoral control tends to emerge in an environment marked by substantial attention to education, a mobilized reform constituency, frustration with past efforts, and a supportive or aggressively enthusiastic legislature, it could be those preconditions that account for any subsequent successes we might observe. If urban districts with residual mayoral control fail to demonstrate the same patterns, it would further suggest that the autonomous consequences of structural change are less certain and more contextually determined than some proponents of governance restructuring would lead us to expect.

Externally Initiated as Opposed to Homegrown Mayoral Control

The existing cases of mayoral control differ in the extent to which the initiating force came from the local community—with the state as an enthusiastic or wary

---

and Wilder evicted them in the middle of the night, dismantling their offices and moving the contents into moving vans. A school board member attributed Wilder's act to his resentment of the fact that they had refused his request that they cede to him power to hire and fire the superintendent. See Lisa A. Bacon, "Famous Mayor under Fire in Virginia," *New York Times*, October 21, 2006, p. 25.

Table 3-1. *Specific Features of Mayoral Governance of School Districts*

City	Start date	Important changes	Specific features
Baltimore	Historical (1899)	Augmented in 1997 to include state involvement	Mayor and governor jointly appoint board and superintendent (from a short list generated by the state superintendent).
Boston	1992	In 1996 voters reaffirmed mayoral control	Mayor appoints all of board (from citizens' panel choices), which appoints superintendent.
Chicago	1995 (historical aspects present before this date)		Mayor appoints all of board (and top five administrators), which appoints the superintendent. Each school has a council (six parents; two teachers; two community members; the principal; and, at high schools, a student) that is responsible for hiring and evaluating principals, developing academic goals, and approving school budgets.
Cleveland	1998	Reaffirmed by referendum in 2002	An eleven-member nominating committee, including three appointed by the mayor, reviews board applications and whittles the list to an agreed-upon number. The mayor then appoints board members from the shortened list. The board appoints a superintendent. (The mayor had the appointment power at first, but the initial legislation provided for this power to revert to the appointed board after thirty months.)
Detroit	1999	Reverted in 2004	While mayoral appointment power was in place, the mayor appointed six of seven board members (governor appointed the seventh and had veto power), which appointed the CEO.
Harrisburg	2000		Mayor appoints a seven-member board of control and selects the superintendent.
Hartford	2005		Mayor appoints the majority of the board (five of nine), which then selects the superintendent. Mayor named himself to the board in December 2005.
Jackson	Historical		Mayor appoints board, which is confirmed by the city council.
New Haven	Historical		Mayor appoints board.

Table 3-1. *Specific Features of Mayoral Governance of School Districts (continued)*

City	Start date	Important changes	Specific features
New York City	2002	Requires reauthorization by the governor in 2009	Mayor appoints the majority of the board (and can fire at will), with the others appointed by borough presidents. Mayor appoints the chancellor. Schools have leadership teams, which are mostly advisory.
Oakland	2000	Fiscal problems led to state intervention in 2003	Mayor appoints three of ten members; the others are elected.
Philadelphia	Historical	2001, state converted to partnership arrangement	Mayor appoints two and governor appoints three to the School Reform Committee. State senate confirms all.
Prince George's County[a]	2002	Reverted in 2006	County executive appoints board, which appoints superintendent.
Providence	2003 (historical aspects present before this date)		Mayor appoints all of board, which appoints superintendent.
Trenton	Historical (1978)		Mayor appoints board, which hires superintendent.
Washington, D.C.	2000 (partial)	2007, augmented to full mayoral control	Mayor appoints chancellor, former local board now to function as a state board.
Yonkers	Historical		Mayor appoints board, which hires superintendent.

Source: Chambers (2006); Moore (2007); Wong and others (2007); individual city websites.

a. Prince George's County Public Schools were managed by the County Chief Executive, a position comparable to mayor.

enabler—or had their primary impetus at the state level, with the mayor as a more reluctant partner. Boston appears to anchor the homegrown end of the continuum. Mayor Raymond Flynn became a proponent of governance change in response to pressure from the business community and civic reformers; the city council supported the request to the state by more than a 2 to 1 margin, and when the issue of whether to maintain the change went to a public vote in 1996, it passed citywide by a margin of 53 percent to 24 percent (with 23 percent leaving their ballots blank on the issue.[23] Detroit would seem to anchor the

23. Portz (2004).

other end. Mayor Dennis Archer initially resisted Governor Engler's proposal that the state disband the local school boards in Detroit (as well as other failing systems), and he acceded only when it became obvious that Republicans in the state legislature had the votes to move in that direction with or without his support.[24] Others can be found at various points along the continuum, differing, for example, in the breadth of local support. New York City, for example, is a case in which the mayor was the key proponent, with much of the local community as well as the state legislature hesitant; in Cleveland, Mayor Michael White was an activist mayor who tried to use his informal powers to effect school reform and came, somewhat reluctantly, to accept the mantle of formal power only after serving two terms without it.[25] In Washington, D.C., the first move toward mayoral control, in 2000, came with a strong push from some forces in Congress, which had for a time instituted a financial control board to oversee most of the local government functions (including schools) and which was reluctant to see a return to the traditional elected board when it returned home rule status to the city.[26] But the recent embrace by Congress in 2007 of an even stronger model of mayor control had broader local support, which was mobilized behind a popular incoming mayor, Adrian Fenty, who had made this a key element of his campaign.

Where mayoral control is put in place without a strong local coalition to embrace and support it, its consequences may differ substantially from those in cities where it is the culmination of a political evolution in which disparate groups have learned to work together and have converged on governance change as a basis for solidifying gains and moving to the next level of reform.

Where Is It Happening?

Patterns of adoption can be interesting in and of themselves, but they also provide information relevant to policy evaluation. To the extent that local context affects policy implementation and outcomes, understanding how the places that enact mayoral control differ from others tells us something about those factors for which we may need to control in order to isolate impacts causally attributable to the formal governance change. Patterns of adoption can also provide clues about the real impulses behind the movement. If mayoral control is a pragmatic response to an objective need and an effort to maximize collective good, for example, we should expect it to appear first and most surely in school districts that are highest in need and lowest in performance. If, instead, adoption paral-

---

24. Mirel (2004).
25. Rich and Chambers (2004).
26. Henig (2004).

lels differences in configurations of interest groups, political culture and institutions, or intergovernmental political alignments, this scenario could indicate that the driving forces have more to do with stakeholder pressures and narrower agendas.

School districts that have adopted mayoral control tend to be among the largest in the nation, within some of the largest cities in the nation. Big cities share a common predicament. In addition to citywide social and economic problems, they are home to consistently low-performing schools; the student population in these schools tends to be largely minority and low-income; and the performance of their schools tends to incite more intense media scrutiny than their smaller counterparts. Diminishing public confidence in public schools and their traditional governance structures has plagued all schools, but urban schools have been among the hardest hit. Cities, because of their declining clout in state and national politics, can be less able to defend themselves against externally leveraged pressures for change.[27]

Achievement

As mentioned earlier, achievement levels in urban districts have been a source of concern for decades. More recently, NCLB has placed attention on gaps as well as on levels, particularly gaps based on race, class, language status, and special needs. The focus on levels and gaps draws attention to the low scores in urban districts, but not all districts proceed to adopt (or have imposed upon them) mayoral control. The reasons districts turn to mayoral control vary, but district achievement may not even be the most important one. When Kenneth Wong and Francis Shen looked at the forty mayoral and state takeovers between 1988 and 2000, they found only one takeover to have been based solely on an academic rationale.[28] The majority of takeovers were based at least in part on concerns about financial and management problems. It is likely that a district's academic status in and of itself does not prompt a takeover, but the combination of low achievement and other factors puts a takeover on the agenda.

District and City Characteristics

We conducted a cross-sectional comparison of school districts with and without mayoral control for the year 2002 using data from the National Center for Education Statistics (NCES) and the 2000 census. Included were the 200 largest districts in the school district universe, as defined by NCES (this same sample is used later for an analysis of district revenue and expenditure patterns). Descrip-

27. Weir, Wolman, and Swanstrom (2005).
28. Wong and Shen (2003).

tive table 3-2 presents the results of *t* tests used to demonstrate statistical significance of group mean differences.

Mayoral control is a big district phenomenon. Enrollment in districts under the control of a mayor by 2002 was more than three times higher than enrollment in districts that had not adopted mayoral control, with means of 199,957 and 60,701 students, respectively.

Mayoral control is also associated with enrollment decline. Though enrollment in mayoral control districts is higher, it has been decreasing annually in many of these districts because of overall population declines in their cities and an exodus of students to charter schools, which are largely independent of the local school system. The Cleveland school district, for instance, lost about 8,000 students to charter schools from 1998 to 2005.[29] The school districts in Baltimore, Oakland, and Detroit are all experiencing heavy enrollment losses as well.

Mayoral control is associated with higher proportions of minorities and the poor. Districts with mayoral control average 84 percent minority enrollment compared with nonmayoral control districts where less than half of students are racial and ethnic minorities. Student populations are significantly poorer in mayoral control districts as well: almost twice as many students are eligible for free or reduced price lunches in districts under mayoral governance than in their nonmayoral control counterparts.

Differences in student characteristics between mayoral control and nonmayoral control districts are attributable, at least in part, to differences between the cities they serve. As table 3-2 demonstrates, the cities that have adopted mayoral control over schools tend to be larger than cities that have not, although there is evidence to suggest that this could change over time. Between 1990 and 2000, nonmayoral control cities grew by about 14 percent, while the populations of mayoral control cities actually *decreased* significantly by an average of 2 percent. Mayoral control cities also tend to be worse off economically than nonmayoral control cities. The average household income in a mayoral control city was $35,781, which is about 20 percent less than the average of $47,951 in nonmayoral control cities. Furthermore, the unemployment rate in mayoral control cities is significantly higher on average than in nonmayoral control cities, at 6 percent and 4 percent unemployed, respectively. Household income and unemployment serve as proxies for social need and the fiscal capacity of local government, suggesting greater need and less capacity in mayoral control cities.

Mayoral control cities, then, are not necessarily the worst in terms of achievement, but they are large, highly visible, and often facing a number of social and economic challenges. It is possible that their very prominence and size makes

29. John Gehring, "Dips in Enrollment Posing Challenges for Urban Districts," *Education Week*, March 2, 2005.

Table 3-2. *Differences in School District and City Characteristics between Nonmayoral Control and Mayoral Control Cities, 2002*

District and city characteristic	Nonmayoral control (n = 188)	Mayoral control (n = 12)
District		
Average enrollment	60,701	199,957-
Standard deviation	(66,142)	(290,271)
Minority enrollment (percent)	45	84***
Poverty enrollment (percent)	34	63***
City		
Total city population	316,817	1,370,608-
Standard deviation	(438,567)	(2,230,697)***
Population change, 1990–2000 (percent)	14	–2***
Household income[a] (dollars)	47,951.43	35,781.66**
Standard deviation	(13,293.97)	(5,807.46)*
Unemployment rate (percent)	4	6***

n = 200

Source: 2002 Common Core of Data from National Center for Education Statistics.

***Statistically significant at the 0.001 level; **statistically significant at the 0.01 level; *statistically significant at the 0.05 level; -statistically significant at the 0.10 level.

a. The 2002 Common Core of Data uses estimates of household income from the 2000 census. These numbers have been inflation adjusted to 2002 dollars.

them more likely to attract the attention of state officials, national advocates, and corporate reformers than other smaller districts that may have education systems in as much or more disarray. Politically, too, the fact that central cities have been losing clout in state legislatures and can be portrayed to suburban, rural, and small city residents as somehow exceptional may make it easier to mobilize support for a radical governance change that might be unwelcome if proposed on a more universal basis.

Do Mayoral Control Districts Do Different Things?

After a change in governing authority, one would expect school district policies and politics to differ systematically on the basis of the different agendas and constituencies of an elected school board compared with one appointed by the mayor. Under the traditional system of elected school board governance, the values of the teachers unions, professional bureaucracy, and activist parents dominate. Far from being apolitical, the resulting system can act as a self-perpetuating bureaucracy, privileging rigidity over innovation and the protection of entrenched power over accountability.[30] Although mayors with formal governing authority over their local school system tend to emphasize efficiency and accountability—the politically less contentious "do it better" rationale—there are also indications that mayoral control may alter the agenda, changing priorities and redistributing opportunities and costs.

Management and Administration

The appeal of mayoral control rests as much on who would no longer be managing the schools as on who would be doing so under the new regime. School boards, once held up as bastions of local control and democracy, have become increasingly beleaguered. In an article titled "Who Needs School Boards?" Chester Finn compares the typical elected school board to a "dysfunctional family, comprised of three unlovable sorts: aspiring politicians for whom this is a stepping stone to higher office, former school-system employees with a score to settle, and single-minded advocates of diverse dubious causes who yearn to use the public schools to impose their particular hang-ups on all the kids in town."[31] For those bemoaning the state of education, particularly in urban schools, school boards make an easy scapegoat, while certain mayors appear uniquely suited to bring efficiency and effectiveness to the schools.

The theoretical underpinnings of mayoral control provide some reasons to expect that mayoral governance will produce different strategies of management and administration. Mayors enter office with a governing coalition composed of a broad array of groups and interests, as opposed to school board members who tend to be dependent on teachers unions. If district policies previously have been responsive to the interests of a few entrenched groups, broadening education's constituency may allow different options to emerge. For instance, the business community may be reluctant to become involved in contentious school board politics but eager to partner with a high-profile mayor on educational initiatives. In this way, mayors may be able to mobilize a broad range of resources throughout the city (and beyond) that would not have been available to a local school board. Mayors are also more apt to view running a school district as akin to managing a corporation, a comparison that often rankles professional educators. With this attitude comes a willingness to hire individuals outside of the educational establishment and atypical management approaches.

30. Wirt and Kirst (2001).
31. Finn (2003).

Superintendent

Whether the mayor has the authority to appoint the district's superintendent directly or whether he appoints board members who in turn hire a superintendent, this role is essential to a mayor's educational regime. In some ways the superintendent in a mayoral control district might have more authority than in a district governed by an elected school board. Elected school boards are often accused of micromanaging and cycling through reform efforts and superintendents at the expense of consistency and sustainable districtwide improvement. It is no wonder then that the average tenure of an urban superintendent in 2006 was a mere three years.[32] Unlike typical elected boards, mayors are generalists whose concerns extend far beyond education. Just as a mayor must be willing to delegate to and at times defer to the expertise of top managers in other departments, such as transportation or housing, mayors are more likely than elected boards to give a superintendent autonomy for as long as the results are favorable.

Traditionally, superintendents worked their way up through the ranks to school, and eventually district, administration—essentially they are career educators. Superintendents' jobs, however, require areas of expertise that extend beyond education. In an era of standards and accountability, the superintendency is a high-profile position requiring cooperation with diverse stakeholders, confidence in the face of unrelenting public scrutiny, and the ability to respond quickly to crises ranging from a snowstorm paralyzing children's buses at the end of the day to textbooks stuck in a warehouse days before school is to begin. In recognition of the nature of the position, a small number of cities have discarded the antiquated title of superintendent and christened the position chief executive officer (CEO) of schools. This movement is increasingly becoming associated with mayoral control districts, where almost one-third of the districts give the title of CEO to their top administrator (table 3-3).

Not only are superintendents in mayoral control districts apt to be given a corporate title, they are also more likely than those in nonmayoral control districts to have experience outside of education. According to Michael Casserly, executive director of the Council of the Great City Schools, about 15 to 20 percent of urban superintendents come from a nontraditional background, such as law, research, business, or even the military.[33] Of those districts that adopted mayoral control after 1990, only New York City had a nontraditional superintendent before mayoral control.[34] Currently, about half of the districts under

32. Council of the Great City Schools (2006).

33. Linda Borg, "School Districts Don't Always Hire Educators as Superintendents," *Providence Journal*, March, 27, 2008.

34. In that case, Chancellor Harold O. Levy, an executive from Citigroup, was hired in response to pressure from the business community to hire a "bottom-line corporate man-

mayoral control have superintendents of a nontraditional or mixed (mixture of a nontraditional and an education career) background; in three districts that currently employ traditional superintendents, the prior superintendent was of a nontraditional or mixed background (table 3-3). This transition to a more corporate style of management is a common first effort toward improving city schools for mayors who gain control. When Mayor Richard Daley was granted full control over the Chicago Public Schools, he immediately cleaned house in the central office, putting 100 staffers from his office in management positions and filling more than half of the top management positions with individuals from outside the education establishment. Paul Vallas, the first CEO under Daley's governing regime, was the city's former budget director, who had no educational experience whatsoever. He proceeded to manage Chicago schools for six years—twice the length of an average urban superintendent's tenure—before being hired to replicate his success as CEO of Philadelphia's mayoral controlled school district.

Given the current emphasis on accountability and measurable results for schools, it is possible that many cities engaged in major school reform efforts would be interested in a nontraditional superintendent or CEO. Even so, this type of district leader is clearly more prevalent in mayoral control districts. It may be the case that nontraditional candidates for the superintendency are more eager to work in partnership with the mayor and an appointed board than with an elected school board. Superintendents may feel more insulated from the public criticisms that are inevitable during a reform effort when they are standing behind a powerful mayor as opposed to an unknown school board. Furthermore, mayoral control offers at least the potential for collaboration and coordination with other city agencies. For example, the Chicago Housing Authority implemented an arrangement in which families with children attending public school would be moved during the summer months so as to not disrupt the school year.[35] Another instance of citywide cooperation occurred shortly after Washington, D.C., mayor Adrian Fenty hired nontraditional superintendent Michelle Rhee. In early August 2007, Rhee made headlines when she announced that, because of flaws in the system she inherited, as many as half of all classrooms might not have their textbooks when schools opened for the new academic year. After a concerted effort on the part of Rhee and the mayor, the

---

ager." See Anemona Harticollis, "The New Schools Chancellor: News Analysis; Hoping an Outsider Plus a Bottom-Line Approach Equals Reform," *New York Times*, July 30, 2002. Levy only served a short two-year term until Bloomberg took office and appointed Joel Klein, also from the business sector. In New York City, the term *chancellor* is used in place of *superintendent*.

35. Tamar Lewin, "For Mayoral Control of Schools, Chicago Has a Working Blueprint," *New York Times*, June 15, 2002, p. B1.

Table 3-3. *Characteristics of the Superintendent and the Board of Education in Mayoral Control Districts*

City	Superintendent or CEO before mayoral control	Current (2008) superintendent or CEO
Baltimore	n.a.	CEO, Andres Alonso (2007–present), mixed; Harvard-trained attorney, then doctorate in education, oversaw instruction in New York City for the year prior
		Replaced Bonnie Copeland (2004–07), mixed; was let go; before that, was president of the Fund for Educational Excellence, a deputy state superintendent of schools, and a public school teacher and administrator
Boston	Lois Harrison-Jones (1991–95), traditional; in a last act of power, the elected board of education hired Jones to a four-year contract	Carol R. Johnson (2007–present), traditional
		Thomas Payzant (1995–2005), mixed; assistant secretary of education during Clinton's first term
Chicago	Argie K. Johnson (1993–95), traditional	CEO, Arne Duncan (2001–present), nontraditional; professional basketball player and then director of the Ariel Education Initiative
		Paul Vallas (1995–2001), nontraditional; city's former budget director
Cleveland	Suzanne Burkholder (interim, 1997–98), traditional	CEO, Eugene Sanders (2006–present), traditional
		Replaced Barbara Byrd-Bennett (former superintendent in New York City), traditional; was the most enduring CEO in Cleveland's history
Detroit	John Gardiner (1983–98), traditional	Connie Calloway (2007–08), traditional; fired when the state proposed to oversee the district's finances
		Replaced William Coleman III (2005–07), mixed; former auditor of New York City schools; title reverted to superintendent during his tenure
		CEO, Ken Burnley (2000–05), traditional; fired after voters chose to return power to an elected school board
Harrisburg	Lucien Yates III, traditional	Gerald Kohn (from 2001, under contract until 2011), traditional
Hartford	Anthony Amato (2001–04), traditional	Steven A. Adamowski (2006–present), nontraditional; senior fellow and managing director at American Institutes for Research
Jackson	n.a.	Earl Watkins (2002–08), traditional
New Haven	n.a.	Dr. Reginald Mayo (1992–present), traditional

(continued)

Table 3-3. *Characteristics of the Superintendent and the Board of Education in Mayoral Control Districts (continued)*

City	Superintendent or CEO before mayoral control	Current (2008) superintendent or CEO
New York City	Harold O. Levy, (2000–02), nontraditional; executive at Citigroup, first New York City chancellor from the business world	Joel Klein (2002–present), nontraditional; chairman and chief executive of Bertelsmann Inc., former assistant attorney general to Clinton
Oakland	Carole C. Quan (1997–99), traditional	n.a.; state administrator, Vincent C. Matthews, mixed; formerly superintendent in San Diego, also educator-in-residence for New Schools venture fund, California operations vice president for Edison Schools
Philadelphia	n.a.	CEO, Arlene Ackerman (2008–present), traditional
		Thomas Brady (interim CEO, 2007), nontraditional
		Paul Vallas (2002–07), nontraditional
Prince George's County[a]	Iris T. Metts (1999–2002), traditional	CEO, John E. Deasy (2006–08), mixed
		Interim CEO Howard A. Burnett, was former personnel officer
		Replaced Andre Hornsby (2003–06), previously was superintendent of Yonkers, fired because of a corruption scandal
Providence	Diana Lam (1999–2002), traditional	Thomas M. Brady (2008–present), nontraditional; interim head of Philadelphia school district and former army colonel.
		Replaced Donnie Evans (2004–07), traditional
		Melody Johnson (2002–2004), traditional
		Diana Lam (1992–02), went to New York City to work with Klein
Trenton	n.a.	Rodney Lofton (2006–present), traditional
		Replaced James Lytle (1998–2006), traditional
Washington, D.C.	Arlene Ackerman (1997–2000), traditional	Michelle A. Rhee (2008–present), nontraditional; founder of the New Teacher Project, untested
Yonkers	n.a.	Bernard Pierorazio (2005–present), traditional

Source: Chambers (2006); Wong and others (2007); individual city websites; Martha T. Moore, "More Mayors Move to Take Over Schools," *USA Today*, March 20, 2007.

"Mixed": mixture of a nontraditional background and an education career.

n.a. Not applicable.

a. Prince George's County Public Schools were managed by the County Chief Executive, a position comparable to that of a mayor.

first day of school went more smoothly than expected, if not perfectly. "When I see the fire department pulling up to deliver copy paper, I know we're on to something," one principal reported, in what could be construed as a perfect advertisement for the notion that mayoral control can produce in the form of interagency collaboration.[36]

Privatization of Schools

In another nod to the corporate values that are seemingly prevalent under mayoral governance, a number of districts under mayoral control have experimented with the privatization of schooling, with varying degrees of success. Four cities with experience with mayoral control—Baltimore, Hartford, Philadelphia, and Chicago—also have been among the nation's leaders in restructuring their school systems to include an aspect of privatization. The first such effort occurred, and ceremoniously failed, in Baltimore. After his 1987 campaign where he aspired to be the "education mayor," Kurt Schmoke hired the for-profit Education Alternatives Inc. to manage twelve failing schools under a five-year, $44-million-a-year contract. This move served to inflame teachers unions and erode the mayor's constituency, causing the district to cancel the contract after three years. Shortly thereafter, in 1997, the Maryland legislature forcefully stepped in, establishing an arrangement in which the mayor must share power with the state.[37] It is interesting that the state brought in for-profit Edison Schools in 2000 to run three Baltimore schools under state control.

Unlike Baltimore, which sought outside management only for a subset of its lowest-performing schools, Hartford became the first district in the nation to hire a private company to manage all thirty-two schools in the district. Education Alternative Inc. entered Hartford in 1994 (before the city's adoption of mayoral control in 2005), but similar to its experiences in Baltimore, it was met with rancor from the teachers unions. After a mere eighteen months, the Hartford Board of Education ended the contract amidst budget disputes. The tumultuous management of the district laid the groundwork for the dismantling of the elected board in the form of a state intervention in April 1997 and eventually the adoption of mayoral control in 2005.[38]

In many ways Philadelphia's foray into privatization mimics those of Baltimore and Hartford, except that the state intervention came first. When Governor Schweiker gained majority appointment power for the Philadelphia School Board in 2001, he quickly turned to the for-profit management company Edi-

36. Theola Labb, "Opening with Optimism: Fresh Paint in Some; Schedule Mix-Ups, Other Issues Elsewhere," *Washington Post*, August 28, 2007, p. B2.

37. Orr (2004).

38. Dale Mezzacappa, "Lessons from School Takeovers: Big Change at Districts, Less So in Classrooms," *Philadelphia Inquirer*, November 4, 2001, p. A1.

son Schools. Edison's initial contract was for the management of twenty low-achieving schools, but unlike other arrangements, they were required to work within the terms of the existing teacher contracts.[39] In addition to the twenty Edison schools, the school board enlisted private operators, including local universities and small for-profit and nonprofit enterprises, for twenty-two other schools. Under this plan, one in six Philadelphia schools were to be managed by outside organizations.[40] The district has experienced achievement gains since the implementation of the model, but after an intensive longitudinal study, researchers from the RAND Corporation reported: "*In sum, with four years of data, we find little evidence in terms of academic outcomes that would support the additional resources for the private managers*" [emphasis in the original].[41] It remains unclear whether the investment in private management corporations really can do the job when resources are limited, capacity is low, and commitment to the task of reform ephemeral. Under Arlene Ackerman, who became CEO of the district in the summer of 2008, there are indications that the district may tighten the reins on the private contractors and sharply reduce reliance on private providers to run special disciplinary schools, but—unlike the Baltimore and Hartford experiments with privatization that ended quickly—Philadelphia so far has remained committed to its "diverse provider model," despite these somewhat lackluster results.

Although Chicago's privatization initiative is far-reaching, it evolved over a longer transitional period and built on a foundation of business involvement that has been deeper and more sustained than in any of the cities discussed so far.[42] Mayor Daley successfully blunted the power of local teachers unions with a 1995 amendment limiting the unions' bargaining power over an array of operational and educational issues, but the ability to operate schools outside of the Chicago Teachers Union contract still held appeal.[43] In June 2004 the mayor announced Renaissance 2010, an initiative to close 60 failing schools and open 100 privately managed schools in their place. The initiative received mixed reviews. Unsurprisingly, teachers unions were less than favorable toward the prospect of one in ten Chicago public schools' operating outside of their contracts, but many parents and community groups protested the plan as well.[44]

39. Sam Dillon, "Chicago Has Nonunion Plan for Poor Schools," *New York Times*, July 28, 2004, p. B7.

40. Jacques Steinberg, "Private Groups Get 42 Schools in Philadelphia," *New York Times*, April 18, 2002.

41. Gill and others (2007, p. 41).

42. Shipps (2006).

43. Catalyst Chicago, "Reform History: Chicago Reform Act Highlights" (www.catalyst-chicago.org/guides/?id=77) (1996).

44. One community group, the Chicago Coalition for the Homeless, even sued the district on behalf of homeless children who had attended two schools that had been closed, vio-

Community members were less concerned with opening new schools featuring innovative practices than with the closing of their local schools. Business groups, however, were enthusiastically in favor of the plan, even spearheading a multi-million-dollar fundraising effort. The Civic Committee, led by R. Eden Martin, the attorney who proposed the initial plan, quickly established an organization called New Schools for Chicago, in partnership with the Chicago Education fund, as well as national and local foundations.[45] They aim to support the initiative with $50 million or more from the private sector to support the new schools.

Chicago's Renaissance 2010 plan is thus far the most successful attempt among those of mayoral control districts to integrate private management companies into local school districts. While Baltimore and Hartford's efforts were unequivocal failures and Philadelphia's continues to earn somewhat lackluster results, Chicago's effort is still going strong.[46] By 2007 Chicago Public Schools had opened fifty-five new schools, which report higher attendance, lower transfer-out rates, and higher graduation rates than those reported by regular district schools.[47] Perhaps the lesson to learn from these endeavors lies in their implementation. As appealing as the prospect of handing over the management of local schools (but still taking credit for their success) must be to politicians faced with a struggling district, enlisting private management companies too often may be a case of "if it seems too good to be true, it probably is." Baltimore, Hartford, and, to a lesser extent, Philadelphia all adopted and attempted to implement these reform efforts almost overnight and expected to make the transition without a new, dedicated funding stream. In spite of early rumblings of discontent from teachers unions and community groups, Mayor Daley was able to enlist the support of a powerful business community from the outset, which secured millions of outside dollars for the initiative. It is much easier to convince reluctant interest groups to join a coalition if it is a well-backed one. The integration of private management companies into school districts may be yet another instance where a strong local coalition must be in place for the reform initiative to take root.

---

lating their right to attend a single school regardless of where they were currently residing (Kelleher 2004).

45. Chicago Business Wire, "Chicago Business Leaders Applaud Renaissance 2010; Pledge Financial and Technical Support" (www.cbia.com/ed/NCLB/zpdf/chicago.pdf) (June 24, 2004).

46. Baltimore's and Hartford's efforts were failures at least on political grounds. Whether or not they were proven *educational* failures is an issue still subject to debate.

47. Office of New Schools, "Chicago Public Schools: Renaissance 2010, General Information" (www.ren2010.cps.k12.il.us/general_info.shtml#gi1) (Chicago Public Schools, August 2008).

It is also important to note that while the decision to enlist the services of a private management company followed the adoption of mayoral control in Baltimore, Philadelphia, and Chicago, it actually preceded mayoral control in Hartford. Privatization and mayoral control have both been on the agendas in these cities, but the relation may be a spurious one. For instance, it may be that privatization and mayoral control are both associated with a business-based reform coalition trying to reshape public school governance and policy in a way that reflects its underlying values.

District Finances

Concern about school district finances may be as important to the impetus behind mayoral control as is academic performance per se. The fiscal health of the city's school district has implications for overall city finances, local property values, and the mayor's electoral standing, and what happens in large cities has fiscal and political aftershocks that ripple through state legislatures. Part of the focus is on reducing costs, but there are also expectations that mayors will use public revenues in more targeted and effective ways.

Beyond the expectation that mayors will be more inclined than elected school boards to focus on school districts' overall fiscal health, however, there are conflicting expectations about how revenue and expenditure patterns are likely to change under mayoral control. On the one hand, urban districts' revenue streams can be viewed as relatively fixed. The adoption of mayoral control is unlikely to affect enrollment or the percentage of low-income students—important factors in state and federal aid formulas. On the other hand, the debate about whether to adopt mayoral control over schools is likely to draw attention to the topic of education, potentially softening public opinion toward educational investments. In addition, a big city mayor is well situated to engage in a "politics of grantsmanship," enabling him or her to secure more intergovernmental aid than a local school board can.[48] Big city mayors, particularly those that emphasize fiscal responsibility and business-like efficiency in city services, are better placed to attract and form partnerships with philanthropies, corporations, and national reform organizations, thereby attracting new resources that they can use to finance their reform efforts without the need to subject their spending to school board or city council oversight.[49]

Revenues

Only a limited number of studies have systematically analyzed the effects of mayoral control on school district finances. Wong and others in particular have

48. Wong and Shen (2003).
49. Reckhow (2008).

analyzed a broad array of fiscal outcomes in the largest urban school districts.[50] Their analyses are an important contribution to a body of literature that otherwise has relied heavily on descriptive case studies. Looking at 104 districts over ten years (1993–2003), Wong and colleagues found that mayoral control was negatively related to total revenues (in both no-lag and five-year lag models), but they did not address revenues disaggregated by federal, state, and local sources. However, these results differ from ours (presented below).[51]

Our analyses focus on the extent to which the adoption of mayoral control over schools affects a city's revenues (in total and disaggregated by source) and total expenditures (to be discussed in the next section). We use data drawn from four files. The first three datasets were collected by the National Center for Education Statistics: the School District Fiscal-Nonfiscal Detail File, Fiscal Years 1990–2005 (FNFD); the Common Core of Data Local Education Agency Survey; and the Common Core of Data School Universe Survey (CCD) for each school year between 1991 and 2002. We also obtained city-level data from the Geostat City Data Book, 2000 edition (a compilation of selected Census Bureau information from the University of Virginia's Geospatial and Statistical Data Center).[52]

50. Wong and others (2007).

51. There are a number of suspected explanations for these conflicting results. For the purposes of this study, we classified districts as "mayoral control" or "nonmayoral control," while Wong and others focused on the distinctions between different types of mayoral control by including governance characteristics, such as whether the mayor appoints the majority of the board and whether the mayor has the power to appoint the superintendent. Although a nuanced understanding of mayoral involvement in education is important, the small number of mayoral control cities presents a risk of overspecifying the model by including more parameters than can be uniquely estimated from available data. Furthermore, although Wong and his colleagues utilized multiple controls related to school districts' governance structures, they did not include city-level controls that may have influenced their findings. Finally, we used a slightly different sampling approach than that used by Wong and colleagues by including the 200 largest school districts as defined by the National Center for Education Statistics. We will be exploring this matter more fully in subsequent studies.

52. The FNFD contains school district finance data collected annually from the 15,181 regular school districts open for at least one year beginning in 1992. These data include district geographic region, district size, government type (that is, state dependent, county dependent, city dependent, township dependent, independent), total district revenue, detailed district revenue amounts categorized by their source (for example, federal, state, local), total district expenditures, detailed expenditure allocations by function (for example, instruction, administration, capital outlay), and median household income and median household value for each district's geographic area from the 1999 census. The CCD surveys collect data from each public elementary and secondary education agency and all public elementary and secondary schools in the United States, including district staffing information, and student demographics that can be aggregated to the district level. The Geostat City Data Book includes city population in total and disaggregated by racial and ethnic group and age, the percent change of the population and nonfamily households from 1990 to 2000, and the unemployment rate in 2000.

Our sample included the 200 largest school districts in the school district universe as defined by NCES, which includes 11 districts under some form of mayoral governance.[53] Four outcome variables relate to school district revenues: total revenue per pupil, federal revenue per pupil, state revenue per pupil, and local revenue per pupil. Also included are total expenditures per pupil. All fiscal variables are adjusted for inflation to 2002 constant dollars and are in a dollars-per-pupil metric. The predictor of special focus is a dichotomous indicator of mayoral control (0 = no mayoral control, 1 = mayoral control). These models account for the fact that mayoral control in these cities began (and, in the case of Detroit, ended) at different times within the eleven-year period of study.

Our study employs growth-curve analysis within a hierarchical linear model-ing (HLM) framework; specifically, our analyses entail two-level models that nest revenue and expenditure patterns over time within school districts (2,200 indicators of annual per-pupil revenues and expenditures nested within 200 school districts).[54] HLM is a widely used tool in the social sciences—particularly in education, public health, and criminology—because it recognizes and accom-modates the nested nature of data such as ours, thereby eliminating aggregation bias and misestimated standard errors resulting from violations of assumptions regarding the independence of error terms. Several characteristics of our data and questions suggest using HLM. First, we analyze expenditures across an eleven-year period. Rather than collapsing these data and constructing tradi-tional gain-score or analysis of covariance models, we chose to maintain the con-siderable variability present within these revenue and expenditure trajectories to yield more robust estimates of change. Second, the introduction of mayoral control varied across time among these school districts, so our models had to allow cities to experience differential exposure to the "treatment" of mayoral control. Third, many sociodemographic characteristics of these districts them-selves varied over time. By including some district characteristics as time-varying covariates, we can avoid spurious attributions of revenue and expenditure changes resulting from shifting enrollment patterns to mayoral control.

A major benefit of using HLM within our current study is that it partitions the variance in fiscal patterns into its within- and between-district components. Our approach allows us then to *simultaneously* model the variability in revenue and expenditures that exists at each of these distinct analytic levels. Within dis-tricts (level 1), we examine the extent to which average changes in fiscal trajecto-ries are associated with the introduction of mayoral control. These estimates are adjusted for district characteristics that vary over time, including total district

53. Baltimore, Boston, Chicago, Cleveland, Detroit, Jackson, New York, Oakland, Philadelphia, Providence, Washington, D.C.
54. Raudenbush and Bryk (2002).

enrollment and minority and low-income enrollments. Between districts (level 2), we investigate how these revenue and expenditure patterns vary as functions of district and local characteristics that are more stable over time, including median household income, unemployment rate, region, and district funding source.[55] As a result, the coefficients we present can be interpreted as the average effect of mayoral control *within districts*, adjusted for the characteristics of districts that are both time varying and constant.

As figure 3-1 illustrates, the average district revenue for an average-size district, without a high-minority or high-poverty student population and absent mayoral control, was about $7,587 per pupil between 1990 and 2002; with mayoral control, districts took in an average of $1,142 more per pupil in total revenues.[56] This amount varied according to enrollment and student demographics, but of the district characteristics included in the model, the presence of mayoral control had the largest effect on per-pupil revenue. Districts in which mayoral control was in effect received an average of $247 more per pupil in federal aid and $651 more per pupil from state sources than those districts where it was not (see figure 3-2). Overall, the presence of mayoral control was associated with greater total revenues and additional intergovernmental aid, but it did not have a significant relationship with local revenues.

Although increasing revenues from intergovernmental sources might be in the cities' (and mayors') best interests, one might question why gaining some type of formal governing authority over the local school district would enhance a mayor's success at securing these funds. One possibility is that big city mayors are well situated to engage in the politics of grantsmanship, such as when the mayors of Boston, New York, Chicago, and Los Angeles formed a coalition to lobby for additional federal education dollars in 2001.[57] The mayors who have

55. Median household income for 1999 (in 2002 constant dollars) and unemployment rate for 2000 are included to control for the fiscal capacity of local government; see Morgan and Pelissero (1989); Stein and Hamm (1987). District funding source, whether the district has its own fundraising authority or is dependent on a specific parent government, is captured by two dummy variables (city dependent and independent compared with county dependent and state dependent). Three dummy-coded regional variables (Midwest, Northeast, and South compared with the West) help address issues of regional cost variation and city age. Median household income and unemployment rate may not adequately capture the full variation that actually exists in the sample districts because of cases where school district boundaries are not coterminous with one specific city. These cases are virtually limited to the Deep South where there is one district for the county that encapsulates both a city and its surrounding suburbs. This issue will be explored in future work, but for immediate purposes, the benefits of including local characteristics outweighed their imperfect application to a limited number of cases.

56. See table 3-1 for detailed results. We also include a table of variance components in table 3-2.

57. Elizabeth Mehren, "Riordon Enlists 3 Colleagues for School Lobby," *Los Angeles Times*, February 16, 2002, p. B3.

Figure 3-1. *Total Revenues and Expenditures per Pupil*[a]

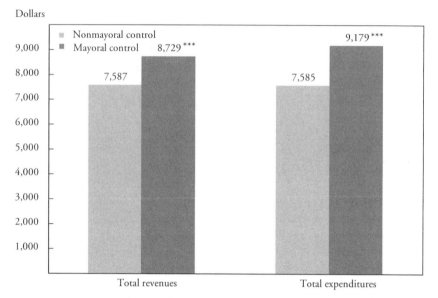

Source: National Center for Education Statistics datasets: the School District Fiscal-Nonfiscal Detail File, Fiscal Years 1990–2002 (FNFD) and the Common Core of Data School Universe Survey (CCD) for each school year between 1990 and 2002; census data from the Geostat City Data Book 2000.

***Statistically significant at the 0.001 level.

a. Estimates in this figure are adjusted for the full complement of covariates from table 3A-1. Estimates are in a dollars-per-pupil metric and are adjusted for inflation to 2002 dollars (*n* = 2,200, 200 districts × 11 years).

been granted some form of mayoral control over their local school system tend to be those with a national profile who wield more power than their less high-profile counterparts and more influence than local school boards. Moreover, during the time period of this dataset, all districts were experiencing the first generation of mayoral involvement, meaning that the mayors who initially gained some form of governing authority over their school districts were still in power. These particular mayors were granted mayoral control by their state government, city voters, or both, which suggests they are able to forge the necessary relationships and to lobby successfully for increased authority over city matters, which bodes well for their ability to secure funds from intergovernmental sources. Furthermore, since states were willing to grant control to these mayors, it is not surprising that they were also willing to make a financial investment in the governance reform. It is not difficult to imagine that in large cities, such as

Figure 3-2. *Per-Pupil Revenues, by Source*

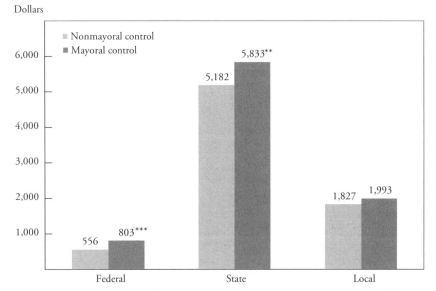

Dollars

Source: National Center for Education Statistics datasets: the School District Fiscal-Nonfiscal Detail File, Fiscal Years 1990–2002 (FNFD) and the Common Core of Data School Universe Survey (CCD) for each school year between 1990 and 2002; census data from the Geostat City Data Book 2000.
***Statistically significant at the 0.001 level; **statistically significant at the 0.01 level.
a. Estimates in this figure are adjusted for the full complement of covariates from table 3A-1. Estimates are in a dollars-per-pupil metric and are adjusted for inflation to 2002 dollars (*n* = 2,200, 200 districts × 11 years).

New York, Boston, and Chicago, state governments, and even the federal government, would have a stake in the success of their education system.

While mayoral control is associated with more external funding, we do not find that it is related to funding from locally generated revenues. In one sense, this seems unsurprising. Raising external funds, after all, makes it possible to substitute these for internally generated support, and the ability to do so without increasing the local tax burden is highly desirable to all mayors. But at least some enthusiasts have argued that one of the most important contributions that mayors can make is using their political skills to broaden local constituency support for investment in public education; from that standpoint, simply shifting the funding burden to higher levels of government may be seen as falling short of expectations. If school improvement is not seen quickly enough, mayors may have to make the strategic choice to direct more local funds toward education or risk losing mayoral control over schools. Time will tell whether the increase in federal and state revenues represents a short-term increase in funds to smooth the transition to mayoral control or a longer-term investment in districts by federal and state sources, as well as the degree to which mayors are willing to deploy their political capital to augment possibly unreliable external support.

Expenditures

Wong and colleagues expected to find that mayoral control cities would spend more per student, especially on direct instruction, student support services, and school administration services, the areas they argue that most directly affect teaching and learning. They also expected to see evidence that mayoral control would be associated with reallocation of spending to provide more staff at the school and classroom level and less on central administration. Some of their results supported their expectations and some did not. Mayors with formal authority over the schools did not seem to be able to convert their position into added funds for schooling; if anything the relationship was a negative one. Funding was driven far more by factors relating to the character of the students (race, ethnicity, poverty, special needs, for example), the size of the district, and competitive pressure from private schools. Again, our results differed from those of Wong and colleagues; as figure 3-1 illustrates, mayoral control was associated with an average of $1,594 in additional spending per pupil.

While Wong and colleagues did not find that mayoral control cities were spending more, they did find that cities were spending differently. There is some evidence that mayoral control may lead to less administrative spending, some shift toward greater instructional support, and a decline in outstanding debt.[58] There is, however, little evidence that they can substantially alter staffing patterns, and, despite the relatively positive interpretation Wong and others offer, the bottom line at this point remains rather murky. Overall, it appears that mayoral control, if it systematically leads to greater administrative efficiency, does so modestly and slowly and in ways that are not easily captured by the kinds of simple budgetary accounting systems we have available to monitor such things across places and over time.

Democracy and Public Involvement

Commonly, school district policy is in the hands of five to seven school board members elected on a nonpartisan ballot to serve three- or four-year terms.[59] Although the school boards must work within the framework of increasing federal and state guidelines, most boards have the task of setting district regulatory

58. Wong and others (2007, table 7.2).
59. Wirt and Kirst (2001). Very large districts may be atypical in these respects.

policies, adopting an annual operating budget, placing levies or bonds before voters, and hiring (or firing) a superintendent. Contrary to the idealized notion that school board elections are instruments of local democracy, in most cases they are more representative of voter apathy and the disproportionate influence of a few entrenched interest groups. School board elections are notorious for low voter turnout, attributable in part to Progressive era reforms meant to depoliticize education, such as making school board elections nonpartisan and holding them in off years without big ticket races to encourage participation. Not only is the general electorate unlikely to vote in school board elections, in many communities it is difficult to find individuals to run.[60] The National School Boards Association reported the results of a survey by its New York State affiliate, which found that almost one-third of school board candidates in New York State ran unopposed.[61]

In communities where school board elections are outside of most citizens' realms of interest, a mobilized constituency can have a dramatic impact on the outcome of an election. The most commonly mobilized interest group in school board elections is not parents as one might expect, but the local teachers union. This makes sense when you consider that the school board often engages in contract negotiations with the union, covering everything from class size to teacher salaries and seniority and transfer rules. It is in the union's best interest to ensure that sympathetic board members are elected and remain in office. One of the purported benefits of mayoral control is that it broadens the constituency for education beyond the usual suspects involved in board elections, engaging the wider public in debates about education.[62] Although this may in fact be true, structuring an appointed school board is equally as political as, if different from, the standard school board election process. The composition of appointed boards, their general operations, and how they interact with the public tend to vary from those of elected boards, often engendering complaints from particular segments of the population.

Board Composition and Operations

Recalling Chester Finn's description of dysfunctional elected board members paints a picture of the divisive and fractious nature of many urban school boards. When analyzing board behavior pre– and post–mayoral control in Boston, Portz

60. Frederick Hess (2008) describes a 2002 election in Dallas where only 4 percent of registered voters turned out for a vote to replace six school board members.
61. Carol Chmelynski, "In Some Communities, Fewer People Are Willing to Run for the School Board" (Alexandria, Va.: NSBA, August 12, 2003) (www.nsba.org/MainMenu/Governance/WhySchoolBoards/Insomecommunitiesfewerpeoplearewillingtorunfortheschoolboard.aspx).
62. Meier (2004).

and Schwartz contrasted the extended meetings and divided votes that were common under the elected board with meetings that were half as long and votes that were 98 percent unanimous just two and three years after the switch to mayoral control.[63] They also point to a more recent news article from the *Boston Globe* that reported all but less than 1 percent of nonprocedural votes between 2004 and 2005 were unanimous.[64] The same experience can be found in other mayoral control cities. In Cleveland, for instance, almost all votes are unanimous and are preceded by very little discussion. The board's chairman explains, "It's because we work just like a corporation. We don't argue in public. When we have disagreements, we deal with them in-house. . . .We've already made our decision."[65] New York City's newly appointed school board was dubbed a "study in blandness and efficiency" by the *New York Times* after its first meeting stood in marked contrast to the often raucous and dramatic meetings of the past.[66]

The business-like efficiency with which appointed boards seem to function may reflect the backgrounds of board members. Whereas elected board members, by virtue of their route to office, have to be adept at managing interest group dynamics and constituency concerns, appointed board members are more likely to come from a professional, even corporate, background. In describing the seven board members he appoints, John DeStefano, mayor of New Haven, said, "I'm able to appoint people who, I guarantee you, would not typically run for public office because it's just not their thing. They are leaders in their field. I think that's the opportunity."[67] Most appointed boards are composed of business executives, university professors, and civic-minded professionals who are unlikely to be seeking any sort of notoriety from the experience. If not a desire to further a potential political career or resolve a beef with the district, what does guide their decisions then?

There is evidence that appointed board members are guided at least in part by the wishes of the mayor who appointed them. This is somewhat expected since a mayor is unlikely to appoint an individual whose opinions do not reflect or resemble the mayor's own. In Chicago, board members under the decentralized system that preceded mayoral control were accountable to a wide variety of interest groups, forcing them to engage in community outreach. In contrast, the

63. Portz and Schwartz (2009).

64. Tracy Jan, "Where NAY Is Rarely Heard: Is Boston School Committee Working for You?" *Boston Globe*, October 9, 2005, p. B1.

65. Jane Elizabeth, "In Shambles, Cleveland Schools Turned to Mayor," *Pittsburgh Post-Gazette*, April 28, 2003, p. A1.

66. Abby Goodnough, "A New Sort of School Board, Bland and Calm," *New York Times*, September 24, 2002.

67. Carmen J. Lee and Eleanor Chute, "Will City Join in Trend to Give More Control over Board Members?" *Pittsburgh Post-Gazette*, April 27, 2003, p. A1.

post–mayoral control board, although it professes also to feel accountable to parents and the community, appears to feel most directly accountable to Mayor Daley.[68] Perhaps an instance in New York City illustrates the most obvious reason appointed board members might feel a sense of accountability to the mayor. Upon being granted control over the New York City school district, Mayor Bloomberg handpicked eight of thirteen members to sit on a Panel for Educational Policy. Meetings were quick and votes were harmonious until Bloomberg introduced a contentious proposal to end "social promotion," by retaining third graders who did not meet promotion requirements. Three of Bloomberg's panel members were opposed to the policy and intended to vote against it, at which point Bloomberg dismissed them and filled the vacant seats with individuals whose votes would align with his policy agenda. Bloomberg's unapologetic explanation for his act of power was, "In the olden days, we had a board that was answerable to nobody. And the Legislature said it was just not working, and they gave the mayor control. Mayoral control means mayoral control, thank you very much. They are my representatives, and they are going to vote for things that I believe in."[69]

It is worth pointing out that the mere fact that board members feel a sense of accountability to a particular person or group is not negative in and of itself. Accountability is lauded as a noble goal as much as lack of accountability is faulted for numerous educational failings. In fact, an underlying premise of mayoral control is that the public will be able to hold one person, the mayor, electorally accountable for the state of the school system. Whether the process by which individuals are held accountable and to whom they are held accountable is considered reasonable may depend more on which interest groups are privileged in and which are frozen out of educational decisions under a particular governance structure than on an objective assumption of fairness.

Public Perception

A major complaint asserted by critics of mayoral control is a lack of access to the education policy decisionmaking process. It is interesting that the charge that elected boards are inefficient and slow to respond to citizen demands may be due to the extent that they make themselves available to the community through public meetings and informal conversations with community members.[70] Appointed boards may be efficient and decisive in their actions but potentially at the expense of their interactions with the public. The decreased

68. Chambers (2006, p. 143).

69. David M. Herszenhorn, "Leaders of Parent Councils Form School Association," *New York Times*, December 9, 2004.

70. Chambers (2006).

controversy and debate at board meetings reflects less transparency in the decisionmaking process and contributes to a sense of diminished access from formerly active interest groups. Predictably, the most vocal complaints about decreasing access come from those groups that had gained traction under previous regimes, such as racial minorities, or those that have long been privileged in educational policymaking (for example, teachers and parents).

Concerns about limited opportunities for public participation intersect with issues relating to race. Despite being presented in race-neutral language, mayoral control has sparked racially defined responses in a number of cities. There are several reasons for this. Public schools and school systems have played an important historical role in the economic, social, and political advancement of African American families and communities. Jobs, including good jobs, opened to blacks within public schools during periods in which discrimination ran rampant in the private sector and other public bureaucracies. As large urban centers began to experience black in-migration and white suburbanization, blacks made political inroads by gaining positions on school boards and at the upper reaches of school administration earlier than they did, say, in the police and fire departments.[71] This historical role gives added emotional and symbolic importance to the issue of governance in schools. Giving immediacy and a more concrete manifestation to these theoretical and symbolically based concerns is the belief among many in the African American community that mayoral control is a precursor to the imposition of a cluster of specific policies—school closings, contracting out to private providers, erosion of tenure and other protections to teacher independence, and institution of special programs designed to attract white and wealthier households—that they believe will be implemented in a way that will hit directly at their jobs and valued community institutions.[72]

It is not immediately obvious whether these concerns are warranted; there is not an obvious pattern in how racial representation and influence changes under mayoral control. Stefanie Chambers looked specifically at racial representation in Chicago and Cleveland, interviewing forty-six community activists, parents, school and city officials, and researchers in Chicago between 1998 and 2002 and thirty-seven in Cleveland from 2000 to 2002.[73] Although she did find that parent and community activists believed they had lost access overall, the results differed between the cities. Chicago had experienced a major decentralizing reform in 1988 in which Chicago's minority community gained considerable power through a more racially and occupationally diverse school board and through local school councils. Upon the adoption of mayoral control, board

71. Henig and others (2000); Orr (2000).
72. Henig (2004); Henig and others (2000).
73. Chambers (2006).

members were less likely to share racial, economic, or occupational characteristics with the majority of the families served by Chicago Public Schools. Since 1981 an African American had served as the chief executive in the school system, but someone white was then appointed to fill this position; and the powers of local school councils were severely constrained as more decisions were pushed to the district level. The most significant change was for the lowest-performing schools, whose boards were essentially stripped of all authority. Understandably, community members, particularly racial minorities, felt they had lost their recently gained power and influence, but many simultaneously believed that the new management team was doing a good job.[74]

Unlike Chicago, Cleveland had not experienced a decentralizing reform effort before mayoral control. Mayor White initially faced criticisms from the National Association for the Advancement of Colored People (and the local teachers union), but those died down when he appointed Barbara Byrd-Bennett, an educator, administrator, and African American woman, as CEO. Furthermore, the racial composition of the appointed board more closely mirrors the community it serves than does the board in Chicago.[75] Ultimately, Cleveland residents appear to have become more comfortable with mayoral control over time since they voted to retain it in 2002.

Other cities have exhibited racially defined voting patterns in response to mayoral control. Despite an overwhelming margin of victory for retaining mayoral control in Boston in 1996, two of the city's politically active, predominantly black wards voted to return to the elected board. Moreover, opposition across all precincts was strongly correlated with the size of the black and white populations.[76] When the adoption of a partially appointed board was being considered in a referendum in Washington, D.C., in June 2000, one of the authors found that precincts with a majority white population supported increased mayoral control at rates more than two-and-a-half times greater than those in majority African American precincts.[77]

In addition to race, another point of cleavage has tended to arise between mayoral control regimes, on the one side, and teacher and parent activists on the other. Two years after New York City adopted mayoral control, Diane Ravitch, an education historian, and Randi Weingarten, president of the United Federation of Teachers, wrote an editorial titled "Public Schools, Minus the Public" for the *New York Times*.[78] In it, they decried the nonexistent role of the public under

74. Chambers (2006).
75. Chambers (2006).
76. Portz (2004).
77. Henig (2004).
78. Diane Ravitch and Randi Weingarten, "Public Schools, Minus the Public," *New York Times*, March 18, 2004, p. A33.

the new governing regime and advocated for a stronger and more independent board with members appointed for fixed terms and not subject to removal at the pleasure of the mayor. It may be that the tensions stemming from diminished access at the city board level are exacerbated when other venues for local involvement are curtailed under mayoral control. In New York City, formerly influential community school boards were replaced with largely ineffectual parent councils, sparking complaints that parents were being "shut out."[79] Similarly, in Chicago, community members did not object to the effectiveness of the specific reforms as much they did to the diminished role in these reforms played by the local school councils, composed of parents, teachers, and local community members as opposed to the elites serving on the school board.

Whether the decreased access of formerly privileged groups results from the inclusion of a broader range of legitimate stakeholders or the marginalization of those groups that do not fit within the mayor's electoral coalition remains to be seen. If these groups truly are being marginalized, it raises questions about the legitimacy of mayoral control as a governing approach. The idea that restraining the influence of these traditional stakeholders is the price we have to pay for clear progress would be compelling if there were strong evidence that mayoral control leads to significantly better results for students. With the currently mixed results—mayoral control sometimes being associated with clear gains, but certain mayors without formal control fostering improvements that lead to gains as well—it is more difficult to dismiss the concerns of important stakeholders.

What Difference Does It Make? Education Levels and Gaps

In this era of accountability, schools and districts are judged first and foremost on the basis of their achievement test scores, particularly in reading and mathematics. Their success or failure is dependent on measurements of achievement gains and determinations of whether educational gaps (between poor and nonpoor and between racial and ethnic minorities and white students) are widening or narrowing. The standards-based reform movement, which has been growing steadily over the past twenty-five years, culminated in the 2001 enactment of the federal No Child Left Behind legislation, under which schools and districts must demonstrate that they are making adequate yearly progress (AYP) toward the goal of universal proficiency by 2014. Extended failure to show progress results in sanctions ranging from a designation of "in need of improvement" to school restructuring or, in the most extreme cases, to district takeover. While

79. David Herszenhorn, "Leaders of Parent Councils Form School Association," *New York Times*, December 9, 2004, p. B5.

other measures of improvement exist and might enrich our understanding of the teaching and learning taking place in a school or district, none draw so much public attention or invite as many rewards or sanctions as test scores.

This unyielding focus on achievement scores may present an objective measure with which to determine the effectiveness of school or district interventions like mayoral control, but it is not without limitations. One significant issue is that we cannot say with certainty how long it should take for a governance reform to translate to achievement gains. Two years? Five years? Enough years for a cohort of students to move through all grade levels under the reform? It is an expectation of immediate gains in the face of reform that has been blamed for the problem of "spinning wheels" or "policy churn," whereby school districts place reform on top of reform without giving any the time to take root.[80]

There are at least two ways in which our lack of a clear sense of when demonstrable results reasonably should be expected can contribute to misestimating the effect of mayoral control on student achievement. First, if achievement gains are not visible immediately, but citizens and policymakers expect them to be, districts risk making a premature assumption about the ineffectiveness of mayoral control and abandoning it before it reasonably could be expected to demonstrate results. Second, if gains are visible immediately, but mayoral control actually takes, say, five years to result in achievement gains, citizens and policymakers, in an effort to validate their reform, may inaccurately attribute gains to mayoral control instead of earlier reforms. In New York City, for instance, students demonstrated gains between the 2001–02 and 2002–03 school years. Proponents of mayoral control point to the gains achieved during the 2002–03 school year as a product of mayoral governance (not as a continuation of the 2001–02 upward trend) since the governance change was adopted by the state legislature in June 2002.[81] Others claim that it makes no sense to attribute those gains to mayoral control because the Bloomberg and Klein reforms were not implemented until the 2003–04 school year.[82] Whether or not the 2002–03 school year is included in the assessment of mayoral control has a substantial impact on its perceived effectiveness. When gains are measured between 2002 and 2007, scores increased by 12 percent in reading and 19 percent in math, but if gains are measured between 2003 and 2007, they appear more moderate at 6.4 percent in reading and 4.2 percent in math.[83]

To estimate the relationship between mayoral control and test scores in New York City, we conducted a time series cross-sectional analysis using English Lan-

---

80. Hess (1998).
81. Meyer (2008).
82. Diane Ravitch, "Why I Resigned," *New York Sun*, February 15, 2008.
83. Meyer (2008).

guage Arts (ELA) achievement test results (both mean test scores and percent proficient) from 1999 to 2008 (see results in table 3-4).[84] Test results and the percentage of students meeting proficiency standards (a grade of 3 or 4 on the ELA exam) were aggregated to the grade level within each school for the universe of New York City public schools.[85] Our variable of interest is mayoral control, a dichotomous variable indicating whether mayoral control was in effect for that school year. In the first two models, the effect of mayoral control is assumed to be manifested during the 2002–03 school year, reflecting the year Bloomberg and Klein were granted control over the New York City school system. The second two models incorporate a two-year lag, which means the effects of mayoral control are not measured until the 2004–05 school year, giving the Bloomberg and Klein reforms two years of implementation before assessing their relationship to test scores.[86] Given that all test scores within a single year conceivably would be affected by citywide policies, scores within a single year are not independent of one another; therefore, the standard errors in each model are clustered by year.[87]

These models are intentionally underspecified to reflect the reality of the data used by policymakers and the public to gauge the effectiveness of mayoral control in New York City. In addition to mayoral control, there are undoubtedly other forces influencing the achievement scores of New York City schools during the time period of study (for instance, the implementation of NCLB's accountability requirements took place during the same period), but those are being left out of the debate about whether to renew mayoral control in 2009. Consequently, our models only control for the grade for which the test score was reported and a mayoral control–grade interaction term. The inclusion of

84. The authors thank Miya Hirabayashi for her help in this analysis of New York City test scores.

85. Thus, our sample sizes reflect the number of grades within schools included in the analysis.

86. As we mentioned earlier, it may take years for successful reforms to contribute to measurable gains on achievement tests. That said, it is not unreasonable to expect that there might be a small, but immediately noticeable, increase in test scores with the introduction of a districtwide intervention such as mayoral control. The specter of increased accountability and its associated consequences may be enough to stimulate improvements at the school or classroom level or to focus attention on student preparation for the annual achievement test. We include both sets of models for the sake of comparison but focus our attention on the models where mayoral control takes effect for the 2002–03 school year rather than arbitrarily choose a number of lag years.

87. These models do not include year fixed effects because of a problem of multicollinearity between year dummy variables and the mayoral control year dummy variable. However, the robust standard errors are clustered by year. A fixed effects model would certainly be more effective for showing trends over time; however, this analysis approach more closely mimics the way data are used by policymakers and the media.

Table 3-4. *Associations between Mayoral Control and English Language Arts (ELA) Achievement Test Scores and Proficiency Levels in New York City, 1999–2008*[a]

| | Immediate mayoral control | | Lagged mayoral control | |
	ELA scores N = 34,252	Percent proficient N = 34,252	ELA scores N = 34,264	Percent proficient N = 34,264
Item				
Mayoral control year	19.65*	9.46**		
Mayoral control year[b] (lagged)			25.00**	11.33***
Grade 4[c]	14.68***	–2.29	19.29***	0.80
Grade 5	28.84***	2.67	30.62***	4.37*
Grade 6	37.95***	–8.57	35.62***	–11.54**
Grade 7	44.23***	–10.98***	44.37***	–10.90***
Grade 8	66.08***	–10.53***	64.78***	–12.24***
Mayoral control*Grade 4	–2.53	4.76	–12.48	0.58
Mayoral control*Grade 5	–9.51	2.91	–16.63	0.73
Mayoral control*Grade 6	–22.51	–3.56	–27.09	0.71
Mayoral control*Grade 7	–26.31	2.60	–34.75*	1.10
Mayoral control*Grade 8	–41.06*	–6.38	–53.24*	–5.76
Constant	617.03***	41.065***	618.14***	41.96***
R^2	0.21	0.13	0.24	0.14

Source: New York City Department of Education (http://schools.nyc.gov/).

***Significant at the 0.001 level; **significant at the 0.01 level; *significant at the 0.05 level.

a. These models have robust standard errors that are clustered by year.

b. "Lagged mayoral control year" refers to models in which mayoral control takes place after the 2004 test.

c. Compared with grade 3.

the interaction term is meant to reflect that the relationship between mayoral control and ELA achievement during this time period may vary by grade.

As seen in table 3-4, our results indicate that on average, third grade ELA test scores under mayoral control were 19.65 points (or 3 percent) higher than in pre–mayoral control years. When we control for grade and mayoral control–grade interactions, mayoral control years were associated with 9.5 percent more students meeting proficiency levels in third grade in a given school than during pre–mayoral control years. When we look for an effect of mayoral control beginning in the 2004–05 school year, this percentage rises to about 11 percent. The mayoral control–grade interaction terms demonstrate that the magnitude of the association between mayoral control years and test scores declines in eighth grade. Furthermore, in the lagged model, the association is weakened in the seventh and eighth grades. This suggests that for older students, the test score gains are smaller than those of younger students in years with mayoral control. The trend of smaller gains on standardized tests in later grades can be seen nationwide, suggesting this may be an issue of test reliability. It is possible that this testing issue is becoming more pronounced over time—which explains why it appears to coincide with mayoral control—or that Bloomberg and Klein have focused their energies on securing gains in the early years opposed to gains in later grades.

Although the relationship between mayoral control years and achievement test scores varies by grade, the difference in the percentage of students deemed proficient during mayoral control years compared with the percentage during nonmayoral control years is uniform across grades (as indicated by the non-significant interaction terms). Mean test scores in the later grades during mayoral control years rose only slightly. (In the lagged model, third through sixth graders, on average, scored 25 points higher under mayoral control, but seventh graders scored only ten points higher, and eighth graders scored only slightly more than 11.5 points higher); however, the percentage of students deemed proficient in the later grades did not differ from that of the lower grades.

The finding that gains appear more substantial and reliable when one looks at proficiency levels rather than scale scores is consistent with the possibility—raised in some of the literature—that under the high stakes of the NCLB regime, schools engage in a form of triage in which they tactically focus on boosting the scores of students just below and just above the proficiency cut points, possibly to the exclusion of those who already are advanced or well below the bar.[88] In the case of New York City, our finding is consistent with the possibility that this is especially prevalent in the later grades.

Compared with the assertions of those who suggest that the Bloomberg and Klein administration's claims of great success rest entirely on their problematic choice of a start date, our findings show only small differences in the apparent effectiveness of mayoral control based on whether one looks for results immediately or two years later. One reason for this may be that our models include more recent scores, for the 2007–08 school year, a year in which the New York Department of Education reported historic gains for all grades but eighth. This, along with slow growth during the 2002–05 school years, may explain why the coefficients of the lagged model are larger than those of the nonlagged model. Though test scores have risen since 2002, the rate of improvement has not been constant; instead, schools have, on average, shown greater improvements in more recent years. Logically, then, the lagged model would show a larger coefficient for mayoral control, as the lagged variable encompasses the years with the greatest amount of growth. As some critics of New York City's mayoral control have noted, however, the historic gains of the 2007–08 school year were paral-

88. Booher-Jennings (2005); Koretz (2008).

leled by equal or greater gains in a number of other districts in New York State, leaving some questions at least about whether the test may have been easier. Although the debate about to what extent Bloomberg and Klein can take credit for these early results will wage on as mayoral control approaches reauthorization in 2009, it may prove unimportant as long as the upward trend of test scores and proficiency levels continues to be maintained.

Focusing on those districts that have had mayoral control in place for a longer time than New York City is one way to avoid the debate about when to begin looking for effects from the reform. Excluding those districts that have been governed historically by the mayor, the early adopters, such as Boston and Chicago, have been under mayoral control for well over a decade. Unfortunately, analyses focused on these districts present their own limitations because of issues of availability and validity of existing data for the purposes of judging the effectiveness of mayoral control. Before the implementation of NCLB, states' approaches to achievement testing and data systems varied wildly, with the vast majority lacking standardized testing regimes. Even when testing regimes were in place, most states have made substantial changes to their assessment tools or scaling systems since NCLB's implementation, creating problems for assessing growth over time. Comparing across states is similarly difficult because each state uses a different test and scaling system. As time passes, the quality of data available with which to address the effect of mayoral control on achievement will only improve. In cities like New York, high-quality data systems have existed from the inception of mayoral control.

Using achievement results from the National Assessment of Educational Progress's (NAEP) Trial Urban District Assessment (TUDA) is one way of handling the disadvantages of extant district and state data. The districts that take part in this assessment were not specifically chosen for the purpose of evaluating mayoral control, but they do provide a chance to compare—using the same test instrument—five districts with full or partial (at the time, Washington, D.C.) mayoral control with six districts that have more traditional governance arrangements.[89] One of the authors used these data to compare test scores in mayoral control with those in traditionally governed districts.[90] He found that of the five mayoral control districts included in TUDA, only Boston and New York scored in the top three on more than one of the ten measures used. Chicago and Wash-

89. The eleven cities studied were Charlotte; Austin; New York City; San Diego; Boston; Atlanta; Houston; Chicago; Cleveland; Washington, D.C.; and Los Angeles. Participation in TUDA is voluntary, but the selection criteria require that each district have a general population of 250,000 or more, be able to support a three-subject assessment cycle for NAEP, and have a majority of students who either are of African American or Hispanic descent or are eligible for participation in the free and reduced price lunch program.

90. Henig (2009).

ington, D.C., performed poorly across the board. Cleveland, another mayor-controlled city, was in the top three on the equity measure (a smaller gap between the performance of high- and low-achieving students), but only because its top students are doing so poorly (not, as would be desirable, because its lower-achieving students are doing unusually well). In comparison, the traditionally governed districts do better. Much of this pattern is explained by socioeconomic factors, not governance structures. Austin, Charlotte, and San Diego, traditionally governed districts, have the highest family incomes among TUDA districts, while Cleveland has the lowest. That said, income differences do not tell the full story of the lackluster achievement in mayoral control districts. When we predicted test scores according to the cities' income level, some cities did better than would be expected by family income alone and some did worse. Although New York City's reading scores fall in the middle of the pack, it is actually doing better than would be predicted on the basis of its median family income; Washington, D.C., and Chicago, however, are doing much worse.

Wong and others have conducted the most systematic analysis of the relationship between mayoral control and student achievement, which is not to say that their results warrant a definitive statement on the matter.[91] Using data from the National Longitudinal School-Level State Assessment Score Database (NLSLASD), they analyzed changes in performance during the period 1999–2003 for 101 districts, 10 of which were under some type of mayoral governance for all or part of the time period.[92] They use these data to create a value added model controlling for student enrollment characteristics (size, poverty, race, special education), funding (per-pupil expenditures, percentage of revenue from the state), previous test scores, and other contextual factors.[93]

Wong and others offer an initially upbeat assessment of their results. "Does mayoral control help to raise student achievement?" they ask. "The answer, simply put, is *yes*."[94] This is because their overall mayoral control measure is positively correlated with reading and math score gains when calculated with a two-year lag. As they move on to provide an "answer expressed with more nuance," however, the story gets quite a bit murkier. Giving mayors power to appoint the majority of the school board is associated with gains, but giving the mayor even *more* power (the power to appoint board members without oversight from a nominating committee) actually has a negative effect. More important, when

91. Wong and others (2007).
92. Baltimore, Boston, Chicago, Cleveland, Detroit, Jackson, New Haven, Oakland, New York, and Providence.
93. To account for the different tests used across states and the revisions made to state assessments throughout the time period of study, they standardized district achievement relative to other districts in the state using a Z score of the district, for a given year.
94. Wong and others (2007, p. 83).

they looked at the test scores in high-performing relative to low-performing schools, they found evidence that mayoral control is associated with an expansion of the achievement gap.[95] "One way of interpreting the finding that mayors and achievement status are positively linked," they speculate, "is that mayors, facing competition from both the suburbs and private schools, may need to invest resources into high-performing schools to stem 'brain drain.'"[96] Additionally, it "may also be the case that the mayors see a greater need to initially establish stronger schools for middle-class residents before tackling the problem of turning around the school district's worst schools."[97] This interpretation may be consistent with our own finding that New York City may be triaging: focusing the most attention on students just below the proficiency cutoff. Both of these speculations suggest the possibility that, when faced with a choice between focusing on families with greater need and those with greater economic and political resources, mayors may be more likely than elected school boards to aim at the high end, at least initially. Overall, Wong and others found that other factors that mayors inherit—including composition of student body, previous achievement level, private school competition—all weigh more heavily in determining performance than does the simple switching on or off of the mayoral control option.

Concluding Thoughts: What We Do and Do Not Know (Putting Formal Structure in Its Place)

The existing literature on mayoral control is green around the edges. Key terms are vaguely defined, the underlying theory of change is mostly inferential, analysis to date is largely limited to first-generation regimes, and early findings show only small effects, with some differences depending on the data employed, definitions, time frame, and model specification. Mayoral control has been discussed and evaluated critically as if a change in formal governance structure is analogous to the initiation of a new program or a discrete shift in policy.

In terms of future research, recent attention to mayoral control mimics and can learn from an earlier wave of attention to the role of formal governance structures in defining urban politics and policies. Beginning in the late 1960s and continuing with reasonable fervor into the 1980s, urbanists engaged in a spate of quantitative analyses attempting to isolate the independent effects of municipal structures—ward or at-large elections, cities with a city manager or a strong mayor, partisan as opposed to nonpartisan elections—on the electability of minorities and the translation of political interests and values into decisions

95. Wong and others (2007, p. 109).
96. Wong and others (2007, p. 110).
97. Wong and others (2007, p. 112).

about taxation, hiring, and substantive policies. Debates about whether political ethos determined political structure or vice versa were heated at times.[98]

The energy eventually ran out of the "do urban governance structures matter?" debate, arguably less because questions were satisfactorily answered than because the discussion and analyses started to seem stale. But the debate left a trove of solid research and, viewed in retrospect and some steps removed from the heated controversies, provides some insights that seem relevant to the issue at hand. Institutional structures do matter, but indirectly, in combination with other factors likely of greater import and with variant consequences depending on economic, social, and political context.

Rather than determining outcomes, governance institutions act like the rules of a sporting game that set the diameter of the three-point arc in basketball, permission to assign a designated batter to hit in place of a baseball team's pitcher, or the conditions under which coaches are allowed to substitute for players during the course of a game. Variations in these rules make some attributes and combinations of personnel more or less valuable—the value of strong shooters as opposed to high jumpers, of home run hitters with weak fielding skills, of players who are versatile and with great endurance or of those with highly specialized skills.

The rules of the game, however, are only rarely determinative. Variable factors such as how fast a pitcher can throw, whether a team works well together, or who has a hot night are what determines outcomes on any given day. Over time, too, a wealthy team can always reconfigure its personnel to meet the new parameters, making core resources and capacity the more critical determinants. A change from ward-based to at-large elections, similarly, can benefit spatially concentrated minority groups that have been blocked from electoral success by a majority that votes consistently along racial lines. But informal and variable factors such as demographic shifts, levels of political information and acculturation of various groups, charismatic leadership, and the intervention of external actors interact with structural changes to make predictions about consequences in any one city problematic.

This is in keeping with the state of current knowledge about mayoral control as we have sketched it above. The theoretical rationales for why mayoral control might lead to more comprehensive, coordinated, focused, and responsive education policies are more compelling, at this point, than is the evidence to support them. That the movement is as strong as it seems to be may reflect then less

---

98. The literature is too extensive to review here, but see Morgan and Pelissero (1980) for one. For a taste of the testy debates sometimes occasioned, see Lineberry and Fowler (1967), and the communications that followed Wolfinger and others (1968).

upon the existing evidence base of broad collective benefits than on narrower and nearer-term advantages perceived by various stakeholders.

What does this mean for cities that might be considering mayoral control as an option? In assessing the implications, it is important first to acknowledge how much researchers still do not know. One thing we do not know is how the existing experiments with mayoral control will play out over time. Mayoral control tends to emerge in districts with certain characteristics: central city, high poverty, substantial minority population, struggling schools, a dysfunctional school board, a mobilized and concerned business community, an attentive state legislature. And, almost always, mayoral control has been initiated when a mayor who has run as a reformer, who has identified schools as a transcendent priority, and who has the confidence of civic leaders and state officials leads a city. But what happens in a mayoral control city when the stars are differently aligned? What happens if key stakeholders become complacent, if the state is hostile, if the sitting mayor's interests lie in other policy matters, or if the mayor is under pressure from constituencies more interested in downtown development, cutting taxes, building tourism, fighting terrorism, fighting crime?

The nation's experience with the new manifestations of mayoral control is almost exclusively with first-generation mayors who may not be emblematic of all mayors to come. Boston, Chicago, and New York City—the most visible and influential examples of mayoral control—provide almost no insights into the issue of succession. Boston's mayoral control initiative originated with Mayor Raymond Flynn; Flynn, though, was quickly succeeded by Mayor Thomas Menino, who was elected in 1993 and is currently serving in his fourth term. Chicago's experience with mayoral control has been exclusively under Mayor Richard M. Daley, who has been serving since 1989. New York City's experience to date is limited to the Mayor Bloomberg and Joel Klein regime. As one of us has detailed elsewhere, places like Detroit, Cleveland, and Baltimore, where mayoral control has extended beyond the first generation, offer a mixed picture at best.[99]

Second, also unclear, is whether mayoral control is better understood as a manifestation of a broader phenomenon rather than a discrete policy intervention. There has been, over recent decades, an increased focus on "education governors" and the "education president," suggesting that there is something at play across the levels of the U.S. federal system. With greater involvement by elected chief executives may come greater involvement, also, from legislatures and the courts. What society may be witnessing is the erosion of the special status that education decisionmaking historically has enjoyed and its reintegration into general purpose politics. If that is the case, the consequences will depend on

99. Henig (2009).

matters such as the interaction between mayors and strong governors, mayors and the White House and executive agencies, and mayors and attentive city councils. There has been, to date, almost no consideration of these types of interactions or what they might imply.

A third limitation, alluded to earlier, has to do with the fundamental lack of research evidence, at this point, regarding whether some *forms* of mayoral control have substantially different consequences than others. In many policy contexts, the devil is in the details, and if that is the case here, there may be important lessons still to be gleaned about differences in whether mayors appoint some or all of the boards, whether mayors directly appoint superintendents, whether schools retain earmarked revenues, whether parent input mechanisms are grafted onto the mayoral control structure, and so on.

Finally, our review suggests that the existing literature has failed to disentangle the independent effects of formal governance change from the effects of the political environments that bring them about. If the existence and form of reform coalitions is what matters, central city school districts may need first and foremost strong, cross-sector and sustainable constituencies willing and able to keep education support and effectiveness high on the agenda even in the face of competing demands.[100] If such a genuine reform constituency is beginning to come together but is being held in check by existing structures, then a shift in the formal institutions of governance can spark positive change. But a spark on wet wood gets no response. If the real reason that things are stagnant is that the potential reform constituency is disorganized, unfocused, with individual families caught between the idea of contributing to reform or the idea of moving out to the suburbs or to a private school, then changing the rules of the game is not likely to bring much change at all.

100. Stone and others (2001).

Appendix

Table 3A-1. *Estimates of the Effect of Mayoral Control on School District Revenues and Expenditures per Pupil, 1991–2002*

Item	Total revenue	Federal revenue	State revenue	Local revenue	Expenditures
Level 1 (time varying)					
Mayoral control[a]	1,142***[b]	247***	651**	166	1,594***
District enrollment (10,000 students)	21	3*	11	32	26**
High-minority enrollment	744***	136***	429***	220**	843***
High-poverty enrollment	−299*	−9	−229**	−68	−334*
Level 2					
Median household income	.01	−.01***	−.03***	.05***	.02*
Unemployment rate (percent)	2.08	17***	73*	−97*	4
Region[c]					
Midwest	1,850***	36	−282	2,093***	1,794***
Northeast	2,771***	87	−54	2,437**	2,799***
South	−25	−77**	−1,261***	1,315***	62
District funding source[d]					
City financed	−291	71	−877	495	−172
Independently financed[d]	−663*	1	−1,078***	456	−606*
n = 2,200 (200 districts × 11 years)					
Intercept	7,587***	556***	5,182***	1,827***	7,585***

Source: National Center for Education Statistics datasets: the School District Fiscal-Nonfiscal Detail File, Fiscal Years 1990–2002 (FNFD) and the Common Core of Data School Universe Survey (CCD) for each school year between 1990 and 2002; census data from the Geostat City Data Book 2000.

***Statistically significant at the 0.001 level; **statistically significant at the 0.01 level; *statistically significant at the 0.05 level.

a. "Mayoral control" is uncentered. All other predictors are grand mean centered.

b. HLM estimates are in a dollars-per-pupil metric and are inflation adjusted to 2002 dollars.

c. Compared with the West region.

d. Compared to county- and state-dependent school districts.

Table 3A-2. *Between-District Variance Components for Random Effects, Based on Full Models*

Item	Total revenue[a]	Federal revenue	State revenue	Local revenue	Expenditures
Between-district variance	1,088,207	21,530	837,035	1,810,190	1,159,281
Between-district std. dev.	1,043	147	915	1,345	1,077
Degrees of freedom	193	193		193	193
Chi-square	3,531***	3,082***	5,392***	13,063***	3,027***
n = 2,200 (200 districts × 11 years)					

Source: National Center for Education Statistics datasets: the School District Fiscal-Nonfiscal Detail File, Fiscal Years 1990–2002 (FNFD) and the Common Core of Data School Universe Survey (CCD) for each school year between 1990 and 2002; census data from the Geostat City Data Book 2000.

***Statistically significant at the 0.001 level.

a. Dollars.

References

Booher-Jennings, Jennifer. 2005. "Below the Bubble: 'Education Triage' and the Texas Accountability System." *American Educational Research Journal* 42, no. 2: 231–60.

Bowles, Samuel, and Herbert Gintis. 1976. *Schooling in Capitalist America: Educational Reform and the Contradictions of Economic Life.* New York: Basic Books.

Bryk, Anthony S., and others. 1998. *Charting Chicago School Reform: Democratic Localism as a Lever for Change.* Boulder, Colo.: Westview.

Chambers, Stefanie. 2006. *Mayors and Schools: Minority Voices and Democratic Tensions in Urban Education.* Temple University Press.

Council of the Great City Schools. 2006. "Urban School Superintendents: Characteristics, Tenure, and Salary, Fifth Survey and Report." *Urban Indicator* 8, no. 1.

Farkas, Steve. 1992. *Educational Reform: The Players and the Politics.* New York: Public Agenda Foundation.

Finn, Chester. 2003. "Who Needs School Boards?" *Education Gadfly* 3, no. 37 (October 23).

Gill, Brian, and others. 2007. *State Takeover, School Restructuring, Private Management, and Student Achievement in Philadelphia.* Santa Monica, Calif.: RAND Corporation.

Gittell, Marilyn, and others. 1980. *Limits to Citizen Participation.* Berkeley, Calif.: Sage Publications.

Henig, Jeffrey R. 2004. "Washington DC: Race, Issue Definition, and School Board Restructuring." In *Mayors in the Middle: Politics, Race, and Mayoral Control of Urban Schools,* edited by Jeffrey R. Henig and Wilbur C. Rich, chapter 7. Princeton University Press.

———. 2007. "The Political Economy of Supplemental Education Services." In *No Remedy Left Behind: Lessons from a Half-Decade of NCLB,* edited by F. M. Hess and C. E. Finn, chapter 3. Washington: AEI Press.

———. 2008. *Spin Cycle: How Research Is Used in Policy Debates: The Case of Charter Schools.* New York: Russell Sage Foundation and Century Foundation.

———. 2009. "Mayoral Control: What We Can and Cannot Learn from Other Cities." In *When Mayors Take Charge: School Governance in the City,* edited by J. P. Viteritti, chapter 2. Brookings.

Henig, Jeffrey R., Thomas T. Holyoke, Natalie Lacireno-Paquet, and Michele M. Moser. 2003. "Privatization, Politics, and Urban Services: The Political Behavior of Charter Schools." *Journal of Urban Affairs* 25, no. 1.

Henig, Jeffrey R., Richard C. Hula, Marion Orr, and Desiree S. Pedescleaux. 2000. *The Color of School Reform.* Princeton University Press.

Henig, Jeffrey R., and Wilbur C. Rich, eds. 2004. *Mayors in the Middle: Politics, Race, and Mayoral Control of Urban Schools.* Princeton University Press.

Hess, Frederick M. 1998. *Spinning Wheels: The Politics of Urban School Reform.* Brookings.

———. 2008. "Assessing the Case for Mayoral Control of Urban School Systems." AEI Education Outlook, August 25 (www.aei.org/publications/pubID.28511/pub_detail.asp).

Howell, William G., ed. 2005. *Besieged: School Boards and the Future of Education Politics.* Brookings.

Katznelson, Ira, and Margaret Weir. 1985. *Schooling for All: Class, Race, and the Decline of the Democratic Ideal.* New York: Basic Books.

Kirst, Michael, and Katrina Bulkley. 2000. "'New, Improved' Mayors Take Over City Schools." *Phi Delta Kappan* 80: 538–46.

Kirst, Michael W., and Fritz Edelstein. 2006. "The Maturing Mayoral Role in Education." *Harvard Educational Review* 76, no. 2: 152–63.

Koretz, Daniel. 2008. *Measuring Up: What Educational Testing Really Tells Us.* Harvard University Press.

Lineberry, Robert L., and Edmund P. Fowler. 1967. "Reformism and Public Policies in American Cities." *American Political Science Review* 61:701–16.

McGuinn, Patrick. 2006. *No Child Left Behind and the Transformation of Federal Education Policy 1965–2005.* University Press of Kansas.

Meier, Kenneth J. 2004. "Structure, Politics, and Policy: The Logic of Mayoral Control." In *Mayors in the Middle: Politics, Race, and Mayoral Control of Urban Schools,* edited by Henig and Rich, chapter 8. Princeton University Press.

Meyer, Peter. 2008. "New York City's Education Battles." *Education Next* 8, no. 2 (www.hoover.org/publications/ednext/15548227.html).

Miller, Matt. 2008. "First, Kill All the School Boards." *Atlantic Monthly* (January–February) (www.theatlantic.com/doc/200801/miller-education).

Mirel, Jeffrey. 2004. "Detroit: 'There Is Still a Long Road to Travel, and Success Is Far from Assured.'" In *Mayors in the Middle: Politics, Race, and Mayoral Control of Urban Schools,* edited by Henig and Rich, chapter 5. Princeton University Press.

Morgan, David R., and John P. Pelissero. 1980. "Urban Policy: Does Political Structure Matter?" *American Political Science Review* 74, no. 4: 999–1006.

———. 1989. "Interstate Variation in the Allocation of State Aid to Local Schools." *Publius: The Journal of Federalism* 19, no. 2: 113–26.

O'Connell, Brian. 1999. *Civil Society: The Underpinnings of American Democracy.* Tufts University and University Press of New England.

Orr, Marion. 2000. *Black Social Capital: The Politics of School Reform in Baltimore, 1986–1998.* University Press of Kansas.

———. 2004. "Baltimore: The Limits of Mayoral Control." In *Mayors in the Middle: Politics, Race, and Mayoral Control of Urban Schools,* edited by Henig and Rich, chapter 2. Princeton University Press.

Peterson, Paul E. 1981. *City Limits.* University of Chicago Press.

Portz, John. 2004. "Boston: Agenda Setting and School Reform in a Mayor-Centric City." In *Mayors in the Middle: Politics, Race, and Mayoral Control of Urban Schools,* edited by Henig and Rich, chapter 4. Princeton University Press.

Portz, John, and Robert Schwartz. 2009. "Governing the Boston Public Schools: Lessons in Mayoral Control." In *When Mayors Take Charge: School Governance in the City,* edited by J. P. Viteritti, chapter 5. Brookings.

Raudenbush, Stephen W., and Anthony S. Bryk. 2002. *Hierarchical Linear Models: Applications and Data Analysis Methods.* Thousand Oaks, Calif.: Sage Publications.

Reckhow, Sarah 2008. "A Shadow Bureaucracy: How Foundations Circumvent Politics to Reform Schools." Paper presented at the annual meeting of the American Political Science Association. Boston, August 28–30.

Rich, Wilbur C., and Stefanie Chambers. 2004. "Cleveland: Takeovers and Makeovers Are Not the Same." In *Mayors in the Middle: Politics, Race, and Mayoral Control of Urban Schools,* edited by Henig and Rich, chapter 6. Princeton University Press.

Shipps, Dorothy. 2004. "Chicago: The National 'Model' Reexamined." In *Mayors in the Middle: Politics, Race, and Mayoral Control of Urban Schools,* edited by Henig and Rich, chapter 3. Princeton University Press.

————. 2006. *School Reform, Corporate Style: Chicago 1880–2000.* University Press of Kansas.

Stein, Robert M., and Keith E. Hamm. 1987. "A Comparative Analysis of the Targeting Capacity of State and Federal Intergovernmental Aid Allocations: 1977, 1982." *Social Science Quarterly* 68: 447–65.

Stone, Clarence, and others. 2001. *Building Civic Capacity: Toward a New Politics of Urban School Reform.* University Press of Kansas.

Tiebout, Charles. 1956. "A Pure Theory of Local Expenditures." *Journal of Political Economy* 64, no. 5: 416–24.

Toch, Thomas. 2006. "Margins of Error: The Education Testing Industry in the No Child Left Behind Era." Washington: Education Sector (www.educationsector.org/research/research_show.htm?doc_id=346734).

Wolfinger, Raymond E., and others. 1968. "Communications." *American Political Science Review* 62, no. 1: 227–32.

Weir, Margaret, Harold Wolman, and Todd Swanstrom. 2005. "The Calculus of Coalitions: Cities, Suburbs, and the Metropolitan Agenda." *Urban Affairs Review* 40, no. 6: 730–60.

Wirt, Frederick M., and Michael W. Kirst. 2001. *The Political Dynamics of American Education.* 2nd ed. Richmond, Calif.: McCutchan Publishing.

Wong, Kenneth K., and Francis X. Shen. 2001. "Does School District Takeover Work? Assessing the Effectiveness of City and State Takeover as a Reform Strategy." Paper presented at the annual meeting of the American Political Science Association. San Francisco, August 29–September 2.

————. 2003. "Measuring the Effectiveness of City and State Takeover as a School Reform Strategy." *Peabody Journal of Education* 78, no. 4: 89–119.

Wong, Kenneth K., and others. 2007. *The Education Mayor: Improving America's Schools.* Georgetown University Press.

4

The Education Gospel and the Metropolis: The Multiple Roles of Community Colleges in Workforce and Economic Development

W. NORTON GRUBB

A n orthodoxy about education has developed in this country—indeed, in many countries and in many international agencies seeking to increase prosperity and growth. The view I call the *Education Gospel* places its faith in the power of education, especially in education that is focused on preparation for occupations, to solve all manner of individual and social problems, from individual desires for upward mobility to the equity issues of low-income and minority groups to the social problems of competitiveness and growth. Usually the proponents of the Education Gospel invoke the knowledge revolution (or new technologies or globalization) to stress that the nature of work is changing, away from jobs rooted in the industrial revolution toward occupations requiring greater knowledge—the "skills of the twenty-first century" such as problem solving and communications skills—and, in a society like ours where skills acquisition takes place largely in educational institutions rather than at work or in apprenticeship mechanisms, more formal schooling. In addition to the rhetoric, the developments associated with the Education Gospel include the transformation of the high school, a shift in two- and four-year colleges toward increasingly occupational (or professional) programs, the expansion of professional education in many forms, the transformation of adult education, the development of job training and other short-term training, and narrower conceptions about the purposes of education.[1]

This paper has benefited from comments at the 2008 Conference on Urban and Regional Policy and Its Effects, especially those of Stephanie Cellini, Amy-Ellen Duke, and Nancy Pindus. In addition, Kevin Dougherty, Evelyn Ganzglas, Kevin Hollenbeck, and Jim Jacobs provided helpful comments on an earlier draft.
    1. See Grubb and Lazerson (2004) for this argument.

The Education Gospel also characterizes some of the discussion at metropolitan and regional levels. In their efforts to enhance economic development, localities and states invariably turn to education and training from among the incentives they can provide. As the Bluegrass State Skills Corporation declared,

> The importance of workforce training has never been greater. As companies think globally, it's imperative that Kentucky's workforce be the very best it can be to remain competitive and provide good jobs for its citizens.[2]

A report from the Education Commission of the States began with similar claims:

> Confronted with the challenge of developing globally competitive regional economies, policymakers have taken a renewed interest in the role of postsecondary education in state economic development strategies. The rhetoric around the importance of investing in postsecondary education to support regional economic needs is consistent across the nation.[3]

So education, and occupational education in particular, has become one of the tools of local or metropolitan economic development, promising a well-prepared labor force for employers and better employment and economic growth for the region.

Often, responsibilities for occupationally related education and training are given to community colleges and their occupationally focused cousins, the technical institutes, since these are explicitly community-serving institutions where most vocational education now takes place. In this chapter, then, I examine the role of community colleges in providing education and training to urban communities and metropolitan areas. Although the claims of the Education Gospel are often exaggerated, skill shortages or occupational shortages would certainly hamper the development of a locality or region—especially because the middle-skilled labor force that community colleges serve is usually quite local. In addition, given the size of the middle-skilled labor market—which accounts for perhaps three-fifths of the labor force—there is every reason to be concerned about whether public and private institutions provide sufficient human capital to this particular corner of the labor market.[4]

---

2. Kentucky Cabinet for Economic Development, "Workforce Training" (www.thinkkentucky.com/bssc).

3. Zaleski (2007).

4. See Grubb (1996b) for an effort to define the mid-skilled labor market. If the mid-skilled labor market is defined as all those who have at least a high school education but less than a degree, then according to the latest figures from the Current Population Survey for 2006, 58.9 percent of all wage earners fall into this category. Of course, at the edges there may be some substitution between those with less than a baccalaureate degree and those with B.A.s, so equating mid-level *skills* with particular levels of *schooling* may not be accurate.

In the first section, then, I investigate the various forms in which community colleges supply education and training and whatever evidence is available on their responsiveness to demand. The second section examines the employer's perspective and the specific characteristics of demand in the middle-skilled labor market. The third section takes a policy perspective on these issues, raising a question that is rarely explored in discussions on workforce and economic development: what justifies public subsidies for education and training, especially for employer-specific training? The fourth section raises the issue of effectiveness, a difficult subject because there is very little evidence about the effectiveness of many forms of workforce and economic development. Therefore, many of the recommendations in the final section about reforms must rest on indirect evidence. In particular, the faith in the Education Gospel has often rested on exaggerated claims and assumptions, implying that the rhetoric around education and training needs to be moderated.

What Community Colleges Provide: The Supply Side

Over time community colleges have adopted a larger number of roles beyond the academic preparation for transfer to four-year colleges that they started with. After World War II, occupational courses and programs became increasingly important at community colleges, now often called career and technical education (CTE), while workforce and economic development programs that were developed to upgrade the skills of the existing labor force grew during the 1960s and 1970s. The dismal state of high school preparation has required community colleges to take on an increasing role in remediation, also known as basic skills instruction or developmental education, and many serve as community centers as well, providing a variety of theater, athletic facilities, civic forums, and avocational courses. Debates over the purpose or missions of community colleges have been contentious, although community colleges acting in entrepreneurial ways continue to expand their offerings regardless of such debates.

It is useful to divide the occupational offerings of community colleges into *initial preparation*, for those who have not yet entered the adult labor force; *upgrade training*, for those who need to improve their skills as jobs change or as they are promoted; *retraining*, for individuals changing jobs for any of a number of reasons; and *remedial training*, for those, like welfare recipients or the long-term unemployed, whose position in the labor market is precarious.[5] The manifestos of the Education Gospel often stress the greater need for upgrade training and retraining as jobs change in dynamic labor markets. It is also crucial to rec-

5. See Grubb and Ryan (1999) for this conceptualization of occupational training from an international perspective.

ognize the distinction between *education*—which usually connotes longer periods of preparation, with some academic or conceptual content, and is usually provided through long-established educational institutions—and *training*, more likely to be shorter, less concerned with academic underpinnings, often more job specific, often provided by programs that open and close rather than those that persist and develop. In practice, it is difficult to maintain the distinctiveness of the two because individuals and employers may use "education" programs for short-term "training" purposes.

Community colleges provide occupational preparation in many distinct forms.

Credit Programs

These programs generally lead to associate degrees and one-year certificates and can be counted toward baccalaureate degrees. Most community colleges offer a wide variety of degree programs, usually incorporating a progression of vocational courses; related academic coursework, especially in associate programs; and general education requirements. While credit *programs* are usually coherent amalgamations of related courses, students may take individual *courses* from any credit sequence to meet specific needs. Indeed, community colleges often look like two institutions under one roof: daytime programs for (relatively) full-time students of conventional age (say, 18 to 24 years old) pursuing transfer or associate programs and evening programs with older students taking one or two courses for upgrade training or retraining. Furthermore, the specific needs of employers may be met through regular credit programs when employers subsidize the tuition.

Over the past forty years the nature of occupational programs in community colleges has changed significantly, away from the occupations usually associated with traditional vocational education (for example, agriculture, home economics, marketing, trade and industry, which now make up only 12 percent of all enrollments) to a variety of so-called modern occupations that are more dependent on various academic competencies in such fields as business (about 29 percent of postsecondary occupational education), health occupations (22 percent), engineering and science technologies (12 percent), computers and data processing (5 percent), with new fields such as biotechnology emerging all the time.[6] In this sense, community colleges have kept up with changes in labor markets, and employers can usually find in them programs that will prepare their workforce for a variety of new or emerging occupations.

---

6. See Grubb (2002c) for these data.

Noncredit Programs

Virtually all colleges provide noncredit courses, which do not count toward the award of baccalaureate degrees.[7] Noncredit programs are usually easier to establish because they need not be reviewed by as many academic bodies (for example, academic senates) and state agencies; they therefore play a crucial role in colleges' responses to local demands. Noncredit programs are usually cheaper for students and are usually reimbursed by states at lower rates than is credit education. Some community colleges have developed enormous noncredit programs, most of them focusing on upgrade training and retraining, though a few of them emphasize developmental or remedial education for low-skilled adults. Unfortunately, it is impossible to determine the magnitude of noncredit occupational education for the country as a whole, or even for most states, because noncredit programs are often uncounted in institutional surveys, and because the intensity of such courses (that is, contact hours) is so much lower than that of credit programs. With the development of noncredit courses, community college offerings shade from *education* into *training*.

Customized or Contract Training

Most community colleges—reportedly 90 percent—offer customized training for specific employers, tailored to their specific needs and often called *contract training* because it involves a contract with a particular firm. According to a survey of firms by the federal Manufacturing Extension Partnership (MEP) program, 85.5 percent of community colleges offered training specialized for the needs of employers through credit courses and 95.3 percent through noncredit courses.[8] Customized training is therefore a way to respond to employers, including those with firm-specific needs such as training on particular machines or software systems, for example, or on procedures that other employers do not follow.

The funding of customized training varies enormously. Some is supported entirely by employers. In some states, contract training is funded from credit or noncredit education, which is subsidized by the state, and most states have established programs to subsidize customized or employer-specific training (described in the following section). The MEP report found contracts with firms to be the largest source of funding, followed by state funding for customized training, and then various sources of conventional college funding such

7. For a recent review of noncredit practices, see Van Noy and others (2008).
8. See "Supporting Economic Development: Community College Support for 'Specialized Training'" (Washington: Center for Regional Economic Competitiveness for the National Institute of Standards and Technology, MEP) (www.mep.nist.gov/documents/pdf/about-mep/reports-studies/ccsurvey.pdf). See also Dougherty and Bakia (2000).

as continuing education and support for credit courses. As is the case for non-credit education, the division of funding and enrollment numbers in contract training are impossible to determine from institutional surveys; the only studies available have examined small and purposive samples of such programs. It is therefore impossible to know in general what fraction of costs is borne by employers rather than by government subsidies. However, the amount of contract training varies greatly among community colleges, from nothing at all to programs for just a few firms, to substantial programs whose full-time equivalent enrollments are perhaps 15 percent of enrollments in regular credit programs. There is substantially more customized training in metropolitan areas and in large community colleges, and the amounts also vary by sector. Often customized training is provided by a separate department, rather than by the regular departments providing for-credit occupational education. The departments promoting customized training are usually described as more aggressive and entrepreneurial than the rest of the community colleges.[9] Overall, the patterns of customized training indicate that community colleges tend to specialize in certain missions, with only a few specializing in customized training but many more providing some of it.

Economic Development

It is useful to refer to occupational preparation in response to employer demands as *workforce development*, which includes both noncredit education and customized training as well as credit education used for upgrade training or retraining. When community colleges engage in *economic development*, however, they are trying to influence demand as well as supply. (In practice, community colleges often use these two terms interchangeably.) Examples of economic development undertaken by community colleges include participating in the convening of industry clusters, particularly to help clarify their training needs; engaging in technology transfer or establishing Small Business Development Centers and in turn helping small and medium-sized firms understand new technologies and then providing training in these technologies; participating in local or regional economic development committees including those trying to attract employers to a locale; and engaging in media and public relations efforts. Community colleges vary in the intensity of their participation in economic development. Some of them are determined to be one-stop shops for education and training, and they participate in every community and economic organiza-

---

9. For a series of studies of customized training, see Lynch, Palmer, and Grubb (1991); Doucette (1993); Grubb and others (1997); Dougherty and Bakia (2000); Dougherty (2003).

tion around. At the other extreme, some focus on academic preparation for transfer and ignore workforce and economic development.[10]

Remedial Education and Training

In addition to their roles in initial preparation, upgrade training, and retraining, community colleges have always played relatively active roles in remedial training, although they are constrained by the limits that federal programs impose. Community colleges were active participants in the Job Training Partnership Act (JTPA), providing short-term training that could lead to credit courses in the community college. Similarly many community colleges have participated in welfare-to-work programs. (Any census that would allow researchers to know precisely how common such practices have been is unavailable.) Unfortunately, the Workforce Investment Act (WIA), which was enacted to replace JTPA, and welfare reform of 1996, have made these efforts more difficult for community colleges to participate in. However, community colleges often develop new ways of organizing forms of remedial education and training. For example, the Breaking Through project, with projects in twenty-six community colleges, intends to return low-skilled adults to the labor force by providing basic skills instruction, financial aid, and better contacts between community colleges and local employers.[11] Typically such efforts provide academic or basic skills as well as occupational skills.

Efforts by community college to engage in remedial education and training have always seemed more effective than those of other providers since community colleges provide a greater variety of academic and occupational offerings, they offer a potential pathway through credit courses leading to associate degrees and then to the baccalaureate, and they have at least some student services in place. If such efforts were able to markedly reduce poverty and increase incomes among the low-skilled population, then they might contribute to metropolitan economic growth and development in that way. However, such programs are usually quite small and are dependent on uncertain outside funding. They also face the challenges of educating students who are badly underprepared and—since many of their students are black and Latino—who potentially will be confronted with employer discrimination, thereby reducing their success rates when conventional measures are used. Furthermore, remedial education and training have usually been disconnected from economic development efforts. Indeed, some community colleges that are highly committed to working with employers, valuing this relationship as a high-status mission, have neglected remedial education, a very low-status mission for them. In general, the

---

10. See Grubb and others (1997) for conceptions of economic development.
11. For more on the Breaking Through project, see Duke and Strawn (2008).

efforts to integrate low-skilled adults into the labor force probably contribute relatively little to economic development.

The Advantages of Community Colleges

Overall, most community colleges provide a wide variety of occupationally focused courses, and in practice many of their offerings—credit courses, non-credit courses, and customized training—are close substitutes for one another. After some debate among researchers, it has become clear that community colleges allow more individuals to attend postsecondary education ("educational advancement"), rather than being institutions that simply divert students from four-year to two-year colleges ("educational diversion"), and the availability of evening, weekend, noncredit, and other nonstandard courses reinforces this benefit.[12] Community colleges also provide a great deal of remedial education, both through basic skills instruction and ESL (English as a Second Language) courses for immigrants, although (as previously noted and as I will discuss below) changes in federal policy have limited these possibilities. Community colleges' connection to pedagogical issues means that some of these programs have developed innovative approaches to this difficult instruction. The possibility of linking remedial preparation with credit courses means that community colleges can create pathways or career ladders helping individuals out of poverty. Noncredit courses and customized training enable community colleges to be especially responsive to local demand. In addition, community colleges usually have advisory committees so that they can contact and update local employers about their credit programs, although the effectiveness of these committees varies.

Perhaps the most important question for economic development is how responsive are community colleges to local labor market conditions. Duane Leigh and Andrew Gill have devised a metric to measure the responsiveness of community colleges to local employment needs that is based on the differences between the percentage of credits in specific occupational fields and the percentage of projected new jobs in the same occupation. For 106 community colleges in California, they calculated a mean responsiveness of 60.1 percent (in which 100 percent would indicate perfect matches between supply and demand for all occupations). Although it is difficult to know whether 60 percent is high or low, some examples suggest this is relatively high, especially considering the number of occupations for which community colleges offer programs.[13] However, this

---

12. On the debate over *educational advancement* as opposed to *cooling out* or *democracy* in contrast to *diversion*, see Grubb (1996b); Rouse (1995, 1998); Dougherty (1994). On the structure and effectiveness of advisory committees, see Grubb (1996b).

13. See Leigh and Gill (2007). These results also confirm some findings from Jacobson, Yudd Feldman, and Petta (2005).

responsiveness index varies between 32.4 percent and 81.7 percent, and a figure in the range of 30–40 percent is surely too low to be considered responsive. Aside from confirming once again the enormous variation among community colleges, the results indicate that the most responsive community colleges are mid-sized to large; have high proportions of local revenue, indicating an incentive to establish a better relationship with the local community; tend to be located in prosperous suburban regions rather than in central cities or rural areas; and have substantial reputations for their transfer programs that may spill over to occupational programs. The results also suggest that community colleges choosing to specialize in occupational education are not more or less responsive than community colleges that specialize in transfer education. Not surprisingly, competent administration is a prerequisite for responsiveness, since some of the lowest-ranked community colleges are known to have troubled administrations. Finally, if anything, the results understate the extent of responsiveness, since they do not include noncredit and customized training, arguably the most responsive offerings of workforce training.

Now, there are good reasons to believe that community colleges are less responsive than *high-quality* private trade schools. James Rosenbaum, Regina Deil-Amen, and Ann Person have compared a random sampling of community colleges in Illinois with relatively elite, high-cost private occupational colleges, like DeVry University.[14] The privates are able to specialize in a few occupational areas, whereas public community colleges are under pressure to provide broad offerings for all employers and students. Because the private trade schools in this sample spend a great deal more than public colleges do—perhaps three times as much, according to my rough estimates—private institutions are able to engage in more extensive interactions with employers as well as to better provide guidance and counseling and other student services. But the range of quality in the private sector is much greater than that in the public sector, and the worst private trade schools provide little flexibility (since they offer courses in only one or two occupations), are much more expensive, and yield no benefits for students.[15]

However, the multiple missions of public colleges, which limit their ability to specialize as much as some private trade schools do, provide other advantages. Community colleges, with their academic offerings, are much better able to provide a greater breadth of preparation, which may be more important to the skills

14. Rosenbaum, Deil-Amen, and Person (2006).

15. For some evidence on private trade schools compared with community colleges, which shows that returns are generally lower for privates and that private trade schools specialize in shorter-term certificates, see Grubb (1994), based on the National Longitudinal Study of the Class of 1972 data.

of the twenty-first century and to flexible preparation for long-run outcomes. For example, community colleges usually embed short and employer-specific credentials—like the information technology (IT) certificates that proliferated during the 1990s—into broader certificate and associate degree programs.[16] Community colleges can also provide the academic foundations necessary in most modern occupations; they often provide basic skills and ESL courses linked with academic or occupational content, which is a more motivating approach to instruction. Finally, many employers have called on community colleges, with their vast array of remedial or basic skills courses, to provide remedial education and ESL to their employees.

In addition, community colleges have a cost advantage over private providers because of their public subsidies, which support the institutional infrastructure of community colleges, if not the marginal costs of particular courses. This is one reason why many state programs supporting customized training turn to community colleges rather than to private providers.

There are also, not surprisingly, some barriers to responsiveness on the part of community colleges. One is the demand on community colleges to serve a variety of constituencies, which prevents them from specializing. Another is the funding procedures established in most states, often conducted specifically using formulas that weight all students equally—rather than providing higher amounts for students in higher-cost occupational programs. Community colleges have become expert at determining the marginal benefits (from additional revenue and tuition) in relation to the marginal costs of operating courses and programs, and this means that high-cost, low-enrollment programs—in nursing, for example, that have limits on the number of students per instructor or in engineering technologies or in courses with high equipment costs—are less likely to be offered, or are offered with fewer sections, than are low-cost, high-enrollment courses such as regular, credit English and ESL. Community colleges often follow a "portfolio" strategy in which low-cost programs subsidize small numbers of higher-cost programs, but this kind of cross-subsidization always limits the extent of high-cost programs.

The Skills of the Twenty-First Century and Pedagogical Issues

Community colleges have yet another potential advantage over other providers. As educational institutions they are involved in discussions of pedagogical approaches. Indeed, community colleges have long prided themselves on being teaching institutions, more concerned with the quality of instruction than are four-year colleges and universities. Certainly community colleges have distinct

16. See Jacobs and Grubb (2006).

advantages over community-based organizations, job training programs, adult education, and other training providers, which are disconnected from pedagogical issues and usually teach in the most traditional and behaviorist ways.[17] More sophisticated and constructivist (or balanced) approaches to instruction are particularly important in teaching the skills needed for the twenty-first century, which are promoted by many disciples of the Educational Gospel, such as problem solving, communications with different audiences, creativity, and innovation. Very few proponents of these skills have ever clarified how to teach such abilities, although problem-based and project-based methods—that is, conceptual rather than routinized approaches or what I have called *systems* rather than *skills* approaches—and other forms of teaching in context are important to develop such competencies.[18]

Innovative pedagogical approaches are particularly important in occupational education, since teaching such subjects is more difficult than teaching academic subjects. There are more settings in career and technical education, including workshops and often settings at the job site, as well as classrooms. There are more competencies to consider, including nonstandard forms of academic competencies; instructors must balance the needs of students for preparation over the long run and the desire of employers for short-term preparation; and occupational instructors are usually relatively isolated, without the discussions about teaching methods that take place in subjects like English or math. But while some community colleges take the improvement of instruction seriously, use a number of institutional mechanisms to promote better teaching, and develop initiatives like learning communities and the integration of academic content into occupational programs, others ignore this dimension almost entirely.[19] Pedagogical issues are usually missing from policy discussions as well, so there has been little systemic attempt to improve the quality of teaching in occupational and workforce development. The result is that occupational competencies, and particularly the more sophisticated skills of the twenty-first century, are often less well taught than they could be, even in community colleges.

The Spatial Distribution of Community Colleges

One final advantage of community colleges is that they are ubiquitous. There are about 1,000 community colleges spread around the country. As any map of them will show, community colleges are distributed according to the population. In large central cities, there are usually several community colleges, or several branch campuses within a college district, providing prospective students

---

17. Grubb and Kalman (1994).
18. Grubb and Associates (1999); Achtenhagen and Grubb (2001).
19. Achtenhagen and Grubb (2001); Grubb and Associates (1999); Grubb (2008a).

(and employers) with some choice. Such cities are also the places where the largest number of community-based organizations and other private training providers are located, so again competition among providers of training is likely to be more intense. In major suburbs, there is usually a single, dominant community college and less competition—except that suburban community colleges may compete with some nearby central city community colleges. Suburban community colleges often have the strongest reputations, though that may be because their middle-class students are more likely to complete programs and to transfer to four-year colleges than the low-income, racial minority, and immigrant students of large central cities. Many suburban community colleges, as well as community colleges in smaller metropolitan areas, have worked hard to provide a wide variety of education, training, and community services so that they become "the only game in town"—the dominant supplier of every form of human capital as well as a ubiquitous player in every community activity and planning effort. Only in the rural areas of the country is there a more limited number of community colleges.

In contrast, other providers of education and training—certainly four-year colleges and universities, community-based organizations with their concentrations in large central cities, and private trade schools concentrated in employment centers—are not as spatially distributed as community colleges are. The only other ubiquitous provider is adult education offered by most K–12 school districts, but it generally provides remedial or basic skills instruction and ESL but very little else, and adult education does not lead to credit programs and higher credentials. As a result, community colleges are better prepared to offer a great variety of upgrade training, retraining, and remedial training, as well as initial preparation for the workforce, to a wide range of the population.

The View from Employers: The Demand Side of the Middle-Skilled Labor Market

Just as it is difficult to ascertain the supply of workforce development, it is difficult to know what overall demand has been. According to one survey, 81 percent of all establishments offer formal training, and 97 percent offer informal training (which may mean as little as an orientation session).[20] Apparently about 30 percent of businesses that have more than twenty employees use community colleges for specialized training, although this percentage varies enormously: the use of community colleges is more prevalent in urban areas, among larger

20. Lynch and Black (1996). The results from the 1993 and 1995 Bureau of Labor Statistics Survey of Employer-Provided Training are roughly similar; see Frazis, Herz, and Horrigan (1995); Frazis and others (1998).

employers, and by sector, with greater use of community colleges in the fields of health care, manufacturing, transportation, and communications.[21] However, these training efforts can range from tiny to substantial, of course, so by another measure, the contribution of community colleges to employer training is not that large: the Manufacturing Extension Partnership program estimated that community colleges invested about $1 billion in specialized training in 2005, but the magazine *Training* estimated in 2006 that firms spent about $50 billion to $60 billion on training—so by this measure community colleges account for only a small fraction of overall training. Of course, community college training is crucial for some purposes, and certainly Small Business Development Centers and technology transfer programs can be central to improving the productivity of small and medium-sized enterprises (SMEs). But the extent of community college participation in overall workforce development is still relatively small.

On the demand side of these markets for education and training, a number of special issues arise. One is that community colleges operate in what I have called the middle-skilled labor market, preparing for occupations that require some skills but less than a baccalaureate degree that often signifies professional employment. These middle-skilled labor markets have some special characteristics, including spatial limitations that are similar to those of community colleges, that is, employers first search locally for employees and only broaden the spatial scope of their search if there are shortages of qualified workers. In addition, employers are simultaneously demanders of training from community colleges and other providers and suppliers of training because they sometimes provide direct training for their employees. Finally, I disentangle the meaning of *shortages* in the middle-skilled labor markets, because claims of shortages are often misleading.

Characteristics of the Middle-Skilled Labor Market

The middle-skilled labor market has some distinct characteristics that influence employer demand and their interaction with suppliers of education and training:[22]

—The subbaccalaureate labor market is almost entirely local. Firms generally advertise locally, rather than regionally or statewide; if they establish relationships with any educational providers, they do so with local community colleges or area vocational schools. Community colleges target local employers as well, and instructors report that students search locally for education and for employ-

---

21. Dougherty and Bakia (2000).

22. This section is based largely on Grubb (1996b), who investigated six middle-skilled occupations in four labor markets. See also Rosenbaum, Deil-Amen, and Person (2006), who also examined aspects of the labor markets in which community colleges and private trade schools operate.

ment. The exceptions are cases of highly specialized skills and periods of skill shortages during which employers may have to expand their search beyond the local area.

One consequence is that local shortages and surpluses may persist because it is difficult for wage mechanisms to lure trained workers into or from other areas; neither workers nor employers are actively searching in other locales until skill imbalances become too great. In addition, the reputations of providers of occupational education and training are likely to be local rather than regional or statewide, so that the value of credentials may be spatially limited.[23] (This is likely to be a particular problem for noncredit education, for which there is no regularized system of credentials.)[24] While no one has tested this hypothesis, the substantial effort to improve the portability of credentials (for example, the failed effort of the National Skills Standards Board) indicates that the issue of regional validity of credentials has been a real concern. And because finding a job that is related to a student's field of study is crucial to realizing the economic benefits of a credential, the links between community colleges and local employers may be as important as the content of the education program.[25]

—Hiring in middle-skilled labor markets is strongly cyclical, increasing during good times but almost vanishing during downturns. Higher-level professionals and managers with advanced degrees are better protected over the business cycle because of their greater firm-specific skills and their control over production, hiring, and firing. A common pattern in recessions is to lay off less-educated workers who have less specific training and substitute better-educated managers and technicians for them.

—The middle-skilled labor market, particularly in entry-level positions, is dominated by smaller firms. Individuals initially entering these markets tend to be hired by smaller employers; then, the path upward requires them to move to larger firms. There is often a sense among small employers that labor supply is chaotic and fragmented, since they face applicants from a variety of job training programs, community colleges with different credit and noncredit programs, private trade schools, and adult schools. These small employers are often unable to evaluate the strengths and weaknesses of various education providers.

—Partly because of the small size of many employers and the infrequency of hiring, hiring practices are relatively informal. Employment policies and criteria

23. See also Rosenbaum, Deil-Amen, and Person (2006), who investigated the problem of colleges' developing charters with employers to get their credentials recognized, particularly through advisory boards, career services, and job placement—all of which are likely to be local.
24. Van Noy and others (2008).
25. Grubb (1997).

are rarely written down, and hiring procedures are also informal. Some employers may prefer applicants with community college qualifications, but this is rarely written into hiring requirements, and there is often a trade-off between experience and education.

—The reorganization of work by employers has blurrred the lines among occupations, as individuals on the job perform a wider variety of tasks. This means that the occupations as defined in postsecondary occupational programs may be too narrow, since they provide only a subset of the skills now required on the job. One solution has been for employers to work with community colleges to devise programs with a wider range of competencies. If this does not happen, the only solution is to hire individuals with experience in addition to subbaccalaureate credentials.

Overall, the picture that emerges of the middle-skilled labor market is one that is much more fragmented and chaotic than the market for professionals and managers, one that is much more spatially limited, one in which information about suppliers of education and training is harder to find, and conversely one in which job requirements are not always clear. In the third section where I examine the justifications for government intervention, the chaotic and under-informed state of the middle-skilled labor market provides one rationale for government action.

Firm-Based Training

Of course, firms do not rely solely on external providers to provide education and training to their employees, and for upgrade training in particular. Firms themselves sponsor a large amount of training for their employees, sometimes subsidizing their employees to go to community colleges and other providers, sometimes contracting with community colleges to provide customized training, and sometimes creating their own training establishments (which usually happens only in large firms). Reportedly about 30 percent of all firms providing training use community colleges; the remainder of the training programs comes from training programs conducted by outside firms: a vast network of community-based organizations, private trade schools, and private training firms. The estimates of this kind of employer training run between $50 billion and $60 billion, and we will see that these figures dwarf the kinds of subsidies provided in most public job training efforts.[26] In general, such firm-provided training is biased toward those higher up in the firm's hierarchy so that "skill begets skill"—those with high levels of schooling and skills are more likely to receive firm-based training, and presumably the distribution of skills grows

26. *Training* (2006).

more unequal over time. In addition, a great deal of firm-provided training either is firm specific or has important firm-specific components to it—for example, when basic skills or ESL classes also contain some kinds of socialization to employer culture and to the kinds of reading and writing required in a particular firm. As a result, most firm-sponsored training confirms the distinctions set out by economist Gary Becker: firm-specific training ought to be provided by the employers who benefit, general education and training ought to be provided either by government or by the individuals who will benefit, and general education is unlikely to be provided by firms because they are likely to lose their investments if trained individuals are hired away by other employers (so-called poaching of employees).[27]

In this country, there has been a relatively constant concern that firms provide too little training for their workers, particularly for their lower-level workers.[28] Such claims are consistent with the Education Gospel and its demands for the enhancement of skills as the solution to problems of productivity and competitiveness. Some of these claims rest on the observation that U.S. firms provide less training than do European firms. The reasons given for this underprovision range from shortsightedness and short time horizons imposed by an impatient stock market, to ignorance about the productivity effects of training, to a fundamentally different approach exemplified most clearly by the distinction between the German or Austrian systems with their high levels of apprenticeship training compared with the American or British system of poorly trained workers producing highly standardized outputs while using less flexible technology.[29] As a result many of the policy efforts profiled in the third section represent efforts to increase the amount of training provided by firms, either directly or indirectly through customized training.

However, the assumption of underprovision is difficult to evaluate. On the one hand, the few evaluations of specific training programs have usually shown positive effects on earnings and employment stability, consistent with what should happen if those who are trained capture at least some of the productivity benefits.[30] However, the use of customized training and other firm-based training will be limited if firms are unaware of the applications and advantages of new technology. Technology transfer programs and Small Business Development Centers have been created to remedy such problems. On the other hand, the outcome studies are unavoidably imperfectly designed.[31] There are not

27. Becker (1993).
28. See, for example, Lynch (1994); Lynch and Black (1996); Hollenbeck (2008).
29. Bierhoff and Prais (1997).
30. Moore and others (2003).
31. In particular, given the fact that firms tend to provide training to their best-educated workers, there is a powerful selection bias operating in the choice of who receives training.

enough of such studies to make a convincing case for employer-sponsored training, and for every anecdote about a firm that benefits from a training subsidy, there is another about a subsidy that supports firm-specific training or zero-sum "smokestack chasing." So the case for and against more firm-based training is still unsettled.

If the claims that firms are underproviding training and relatively firm-specific training in particular were true, then it would reveal an odd twist in the demand for education and training in the United States. Rather than the under-education feared by the Education Gospel, the dominant evidence suggests that overeducation is a problem in many developed countries.[32] But a combination of *overeducation* and *undertraining* suggests that firms have substituted more education for less training, relying on the substantial subsidies in the U.S. education system rather than providing more firm-specific training from their own pockets. From this perspective, it seems fortunate that publicly subsidized training programs in this country are so small (as I will argue in the next section), since the combination of overeducation and overtraining would involve the worst of both worlds, as well as unwarranted subsidies to employers. For the moment, however, the debates about the extent of firm-based training involve larger issues about the appropriate amounts of both education and training that are difficult to resolve.

The Nature of Shortages

A final issue to confront from the employer side is the claim of periodic shortages—persistent in some occupations such as nursing, sporadic in others such as IT workers and machinists. The normal response to shortages in a free-market system is to increase wages or improve working conditions. This might induce supply responses, but with a lag, if education requirements take a long time (as they do with scientists and engineers, for example). But for most occupations with shorter preparation times, response should be relatively quick *unless* there are rigidities in supply—for example, if community colleges are unresponsive to labor market signals (as some of them surely are, according to the calculations of Leigh and Gill described above).

However, the case of nursing suggests that economists' conceptions of shortages—demand exceeding supply *at a given wage*—are not necessarily the

---

32. See Daly, Büchel, and Duncan (2000, table 1); Hartog (2000, especially tables 1 and 2); *Economics of Education Review*, vol. 19, no. 2 (2000), the special issue on overschooling. Grubb and Lazerson (2004) present the argument for overeducation in greater detail, describing it as a consequence of the separation of the preparation for work from the work itself. See Grubb and Lazerson (2004, ch. 6); Wolf (2002); Grubb (2008b) on the weakness of the relationship between education and economic growth, even in the math and science areas where it is often invoked.

conventional conceptions of shortages, which usually refer to demand exceeding supply at a suboptimal or prevailing wage. In the case of nursing, for example, difficult working conditions and the lack of opportunities for advancement cause large numbers of nurses to leave the occupation, so shortages cannot be remedied by supply-side solutions alone, except at great cost. Viable solutions must include demand-side changes, such as increased wages, fewer patients per nurse, increased opportunities for advancement, and other improvements in working conditions. In other places, employers have complained about short-ages of hospitality workers, mining workers, agricultural workers, or military recruits—all groups with poor pay and difficult working conditions. Still other shortages—such as the shortage of IT workers in the bubble of the late 1990s or the demand for aerospace workers in the defense and aerospace boom during the Reagan administration—represent sudden, sharp increases in demand that virtually no education or training system could respond to quickly.

So we should be skeptical about claims of shortages. Some of these claims are efforts by employers to get public providers of education and training to increase supply so that wages need not increase, and these should be ignored. If, however, there is evidence that education and training providers are unresponsive to labor markets, then that may require some intervention, under one of the market failure justifications developed in the third section. A number of policy instruments exist to do this. For example, Florida has required that all occupational programs have at least 70 percent placement rates, to ensure that programs avoid low-demand occupations in favor of high-demand areas. Many states require advisory committees for occupational programs to ensure that community colleges receive information about demand, although the seriousness of these committees varies a great deal.[33] Cooperative education programs, for which employers and community colleges jointly devise programs of classroom-based and firm-based instruction, are excellent vehicles for employers and community colleges to establish strong linkages (similar to the dual system in Germany and Austria), although these are comparatively rare.[34] So, there are several ways to make community colleges and training providers more responsive to employer demand.

The View from Government: Policy Initiatives and Public Justifications

In response to the needs for education and training, governments at various levels have responded with different initiatives, which largely take the form of con-

---

33. Grubb (1996b).
34. Grubb (1996b, chapter 7); Villeneuve and Grubb (1996).

strained subsidies—that is, subsidies allocated for particular types of education and training. There are too many of these subsidies to cover adequately in a relatively short chapter, but I review four of the most prominent forms.

When public funding is involved, some justification is necessary, at least from an economist's perspective and from theories of public goods. The second part of this section, therefore, presents potential justifications for government support of education and training. Many examples of public subsidies violate these precepts, however, and the field of workforce and economic development has usually been unclear about what justifies public involvement.

Government Initiatives for Workforce Development

The largest subsidies for postsecondary occupational education come through community college systems. Public two-year colleges had about $40 billion in total revenue during the 2003–04 period, and a rough estimate is that perhaps 40 to 50 percent went to various forms of career and technical education. State policy and funding drive these programs: nationwide, community colleges received 32.9 percent of their funding from state governments, 20.1 percent from local governments, and only 12.1 percent from the federal government— although these figures vary widely from state to state. On average, 16 percent of community college budgets comes from tuition, although again these amounts vary widely from state to state. However, these figures cover only credit education. No one has compiled state figures on noncredit education, and indeed these data would be difficult to aggregate because of the variation from state to state in how noncredit education is defined. Similarly, figures on contract and customized training have never been aggregated, and again, conceptual issues would make their compilation difficult. However, the findings from research on specific community colleges—that only a few community colleges have truly substantial customized training—and noncredit divisions indicate that the public subsidies for credit courses represent the lion's share of what community colleges do.

In addition, almost every state has created a program to fund customized training or employer-based training.[35] Some of these are intended to fund customized training in community colleges only; others allow a broader variety of providers to compete for grants. A few unusual funding mechanisms have developed. California provides funding for its Employment Training Panel through an additional unemployment insurance tax, and several other states have mimicked this funding mechanism. Iowa allows community colleges to offer bonds supporting customized training, with the bonds retired through earmarks on

35. See, for example, Ducha and Graves (2007), the most recent in a series of reports; Creticos and Sheets (1992); Regional Technology Strategies (1999).

corporate taxes. Some states restrict these subsidies to manufacturing or to sectors of the economy that arguably could be lured into the state from elsewhere, while other states have no such restrictions. The total amount of state funding in fiscal year 2006 was about $570 million, down from around $720 million seven years earlier.[36] But these amounts are trivial compared to the billions spent by states on community colleges or the amounts of perhaps $50 billion to $60 billion spent by firms on employee training.[37] These state training programs are good examples of symbolic programs and piddle policy, in which trifling sums are provided for specific purposes to signal a state's good intentions, but which, in practice, amount to very little.[38]

The federal counterpart to state funding for community colleges is the Carl Perkins Act, which provides funding for secondary and postsecondary occupational education. This legislation has a long history, dating back to 1918 and the early efforts to support secondary vocational education, although about half of revenues now go to postsecondary CTE. The Perkins legislation has also tried to direct CTE, first to underserved populations (like low-performing and minority students and students with disabilities), then to the integration of academic education into occupational education. By and large, however, high schools and community colleges use these funds for relatively routine expenditures for updating curricula, buying equipment, and paying for remedial education, rather than for enacting real reform.

The federal government has supported a series of job training programs since the Manpower Development and Training Act of 1962. The current version, the Workforce Investment Act of 1998, has redirected funding away from the variety of training supported under its predecessor, the Job Training Partnership Act of 1982, and toward a series of One-Stop Centers providing information about local job training programs. Short-term job training programs under JTPA were on the whole ineffective, although the program did fund some promising youth programs in cooperation with high schools and a series of innovative collaborations between community colleges and job training agencies.[39] Furthermore, under JTPA, some states were beginning to move toward more coherent programs integrating education, training, and economic development. However, the shift from JTPA to WIA has had several negative effects: the amount of training has diminished markedly, supplanted by funding for One-Stop Centers

36. Ducha and Graves (2007). Hollenbeck (2008) reports similar results based on a survey of thirty states.

37. *Training* (2006).

38. Thanks to Lorraine McDonnell for this vivid phrase, intended to denigrate well-intended programs that have too little spending to have much effect. The area of education and training has many examples of piddle policy.

39. LaLonde (1995); Grubb (1996a).

that provide information about job training opportunities; the participation of community colleges in WIA has diminished because of rigid requirements for accountability; and the efforts to coordinate job training and education have been made much more difficult. The shift from JTPA to WIA seemed to signal an exhaustion of federal ideas about job training, and it has left the country with a job training policy that reflects not only piddle policy but also enhances barriers to cooperation among federal programs.[40]

In addition, the federal government has been the principal sponsor for welfare in its narrowest sense, funding programs supporting low-income families (mostly families headed by women) and their children: first, Aid to Dependent Children; then, Aid to Families with Dependent Children; and now, the Personal Responsibility and Work Opportunity Reconciliation Act (PRWORA) of 1996. The 1960s and its *services strategy*, providing supportive services like child care so welfare mothers could work, has over time expanded into education and training and Welfare-to-Work programs so that welfare mothers could find improved higher-paying employment through better education and thereby work themselves out of welfare. Community colleges have always participated in such welfare-related programs and have developed some of the best Welfare-to-Work programs, linking them to regular credit programs, thus creating a pathway or career ladder for unskilled individuals to move into skilled work— something that independent training efforts and community-based organizations cannot do. Under PRWORA, however, the doctrine of Work First has come to dominate, with the idea that dependent individuals should be put to work as a way of returning them to employment *rather than* providing them with additional education and training. Access to serious educational opportunities has diminished drastically as a consequence.[41] In both job training and welfare, then, the federal government limited its support for remedial occupational education and in the process made it more difficult for community colleges to participate in such efforts.

Finally, the federal government has provided a number of tax credits for education and training. The Hope Tax Credit was intended to provide a maximum of $1,500 for each of the first two years of college; it is being modified in the American Opportunity Tax Credit, which makes several changes to the credit and makes 30 percent of it refundable. The Lifelong Learning Tax Credit has provided a credit of up to $2,000 for any form of education or training, including forms of workforce development, and tuition and fees up to $4,000 at virtually all accredited postsecondary institutions can be deducted.[42] Although the

40. Grubb and others (1999); Lafer (2002); Grubb and Lazerson (2004).
41. See Shaw, Goldrick-Rab, and Mazzeo (2006) on the consequences of Work First.
42. National Association of Student Financial Aid Administrators, "Understanding the

Lifelong Learning Tax Credit seems designed to support workforce development, political observers usually attribute the enactment of both tax credits to the desire of the Clinton administration to provide a middle-class tax cut. Since only part of the American Opportunity Tax Credit is refundable, these credits are unlikely to benefit low-income families that cannot qualify because they pay too little tax.

It is difficult to know how much subsidy these tax expenditures provide for workforce education and training. Even more difficult questions concern the distributive effects of tax expenditures and the extent to which they increase the amount of education and training rather than simply providing windfall gains to individuals who would have purchased education and training anyway. Finally, it is impossible to target tax credits on specific types of education and training—for example, the types for which there are good justifications for public support. As with other tax expenditures, the various tax credits and deductions for education and training are poor instruments of policy, even though they are politically attractive.

Overall, then, the bulk of total government support for workforce development comes through community colleges and the state and then local revenues that support them. State support of customized training is small and largely symbolic. Federal policy is trifling in its amounts, except potentially for tax expenditures, and incoherent in its effects.

Justifications for Public Spending: Normative Principles

While a number of public subsidies exist for workforce and economic development, the justification for these subsidies has rarely been examined.[43] There are at least two different normative questions to raise. The first is whether there is justification for public spending on education and training, rather than requiring individuals and employers to bear the costs. The second involves the conditions under which education and training might lead to economic development—that is, to increased productivity, earnings, income per person, or some other measure of economic well-being in a locale. A number of normative principles can be derived to respond to these questions, including Becker's distinction between general and specific training, macroeconomic principles, and microeconomic principles based on market failures. However, these have almost never been applied in policymaking.

Lifetime Learning Tax Credit" (Washington, updated January 10, 2009) (www.nasfaa.org/AnnualPubs/TaxBenefitsGuide.html#lifetime).

43. The exception is Grubb and others (1993), from which this section is drawn and which was an effort to develop recommendations for California's Employment Training Panel concerning which state subsidies for customized training would be justified and which would not. See also Hollenbeck (2008).

Gary Becker has made a widely recognized distinction between *general education*—education that enhances productivity for all employers, like basic literacy and numeracy—and *specific education*, which in the extreme case benefits only one employer.[44] Specific training should not lead to wage increases because the wage that other employers would pay does not increase, unless the employer pays a small premium to be sure that the employee does not leave. The employer captures all the benefits and, therefore, should pay for the costs of specific training. Conversely, general education should be funded either by individuals who benefit from higher productivity and therefore earnings or by governments if there are public purposes for education (such as civic goals or redistribution). In practice the distinction between specific training and general education is not absolute, since employers sometimes provide what looks like general education (basic skills instruction, for example) that is combined with firm-specific socialization or business procedures. But the distinction is still a worthwhile one, and it leads to concern that customized training may subsidize specific training that employers themselves should support.

A second consideration comes from macroeconomic perspectives. One of the most common justifications for activities labeled economic development is that they will foster the growth of sectors that will then produce exports from a region, increasing the regional product or, less often, that they will reduce the need to import goods and services from other regions.[45] Often, for example, community colleges and other training providers join with economic development agencies to create a package of inducements for manufacturing firms to locate a new plant in a region. If the region involved suffers from high unemployment or low wages, as some rural areas and central cities do, then there are obvious equity justifications as well. But then there remain several normative issues to consider. The first is whether the inducements provided are important in the location decisions of employers or whether employers make decisions on other grounds—such as on considerations of wage or transportation costs or union conditions, for example—but then pressure local governments for subsidies that do not affect their decisions. A second is whether such a location is zero-sum from the perspective of a larger unit of government—the state, for example, if the decision is to locate a plant in one community rather than in another one within the state. Finally, there is a benefit-cost calculation to be carried out: whether the benefits, in terms of local benefits, outweigh the costs of inducements. So the burden of proof for justifying this form of economic development is quite substantial. Indeed, this kind of activity, often labeled *smokestack chasing*, seems to have fallen out of favor, perhaps as states have come to

44. Becker (1993).
45. Bartik (2002).

realize that competition among local and state governments for capital relocation is often ineffective or zero-sum.[46] Several states preclude using workforce development funds for employers—for example, for those in retail trade and professional services—that are unlikely to move in response to subsidies or whose location is likely to be zero-sum.

A third category of justifications for public subsidies relies on potential market failures. If these market failures take place, then training (including firm-specific training) will be underprovided—consistent with the fear that U.S. firms engage in too little employee training on their own. Several different justifications emerge from examining case studies of training:

—Sometimes workforce development efforts support training that is relatively transferable—in statistical process control, total quality management techniques, or relatively general computer skills—which employees can use in other types of employment and which employers would presumably underprovide.

—Some firms may not be able to obtain loans for skill development, particularly small firms, new firms, firms attempting to reorganize and provide the training necessary to shift to higher-performance production, and firms trying to provide countercyclical training during a recession. The inability to find capital for education and training, because of the uncertainty of economic returns and the impossibility of providing collateral, applies to certain types of in-house training provided by the firm as well.

—Under some conditions, true shortages exist, which require governments to intervene to resolve the situation. For example, regional shortages in the middle-skilled labor market may not be corrected by wage movements because of the local nature of employers and prospective employees (that is, community college students searching for employment locally). Highly specialized skills may be in short supply because so few workers are required that either a public or a private training program cannot be justified. The incentives for education and training providers to offer certain kinds of skill development may be weak, particularly (for community colleges) in cases of high training costs in states with uniform subsidies per student. Finally, the period of time for markets to respond to increased training needs may be too long, either because information is poor or because the period required for training is long. All these are examples in which shortages are caused by market failures, on the demand or supply side, and for which government interventions may be appropriate.

—In many cases, employers have poor information about the value of training or about the value of production innovations that require training— particularly because of their small size and the costs of acquiring better information. They often view training as costly, because it interrupts their production,

46. Markusen (2007).

and underestimate (or do not know how to estimate) the gains in productivity. In this case, government provision of information, and of training itself, may be necessary to correct these information problems. Examples of such efforts are the Small Business Development Centers run by some community colleges, which help SMEs with specific production problems—the choice among alternative computer-based systems, for example, or the use of various manufacturing technologies—and also provide the training necessary for technological improvements. Technology transfer programs are similar, helping small firms adopt new and more productive technology that they may not learn about on their own. In the Manufacturing Extension Partnership program's survey, about a third of community colleges reported that they provided specialized training for crosscutting technologies like biosciences and biotechnology, nanotechnology, alternative energy, or geospatial technologies and geographic information systems.[47]

—Under certain conditions, expanding employment in high-wage, high-productivity sectors in particular may benefit the local economy as a whole, particularly as workers move from low-wage to high-wage jobs, because the benefits of education may spill over to other employers or to the public sector.[48] If there are such externalities, then firms may underprovide additional education and training, and public support may be justified. However, it is important to examine the specific forms of education or training to see whether spillovers are likely. For example, training Safeway workers on new checkout registers is unlikely to benefit other employers, and the civic benefits of narrow firm-specific training are scant. The corollary of this principle is that, contrary to common practice, public programs should probably not subsidize training in low-wage and low-productivity occupations such as those in hospitality, retail trade, agriculture, or personal services like cosmetology where externalities are unlikely.

—Training related to urban renewal and other social benefits can be justified by the positive externalities created and by distributional effects. As one example, the Department of Housing and Urban Development has funded a job training program called YouthBuild, which provides low-income individuals with training in construction skills while they rebuild housing in blighted neighborhoods. The general training in construction skills can then help them to move to better-paid employment, and the renovated housing helps improve inner-city conditions.

---

47. Center for Regional Economic Competitiveness, "Supporting Economic Development: Community College Support for 'Specialized Training'" (Washington: U.S. National Institute of Standards and Technology, MEP) (www.mep.nist.gov/documents/pdf/about-mep/reports-studies/ccsurvey.pdf).

48. Dickens (1992); Moretti (2003).

—Education and training for low-skilled individuals who have high unemployment rates and earn low wages can always be justified on equity grounds. This is, of course, the impulse behind remedial training: to get welfare recipients, the long-term unemployed, and others with skill barriers to employment back into the labor force. However, the success of short-term training through JTPA was limited at best, and in customized training programs, employers are often reluctant to work with such individuals.[49] An alternative is therefore to use community colleges, with additional student support services, to provide longer-term programs for such individuals.

—Since research and development often generate public goods and will be underprovided in conventional markets, government programs might subsidize training for individuals working in R&D.

—The markets—really, quasi-markets—for education and training are often poorly organized, particularly when SMEs are faced with a variety of small education and training providers. In such cases, the transaction costs of forming organizations to represent the interests of employers are too high, and training needs may go unmet. Similarly, the sources of training may be unknown to small employers unless there is a dominant institution—like a community college—in the region. Under these conditions, any efforts to organize these quasi-markets with public funding can be justified as a way of overcoming high transaction costs with small employers and providers. Indeed, when community colleges participate in economic development efforts to assess training needs in a region, or when One-Stop Centers provide information on the variety of education and training options, they are in effect trying to overcome these kinds of market imperfections. Another example is the convening of local businesses, education providers, and workforce development agencies by the Michigan Regional Skills Alliances or a demonstration project of the Department of Labor in funding thirty-nine Workforce Investment Boards to convene key stakeholders to see which services different participants might provide.[50]

There are, then, many different market-failure justifications for public support of education and training. Unfortunately, public subsidies usually are not justified in these terms, and case studies of publicly funded training (especially of customized training) indicate that many subsidies cannot be justified by any of these rationales.[51] What is necessary for public funding, then, is both evidence that programs are likely to be effective and a well-considered rationale for public support.

49. LaLonde (1995); Grubb (1996a); Lafer (2002).
50. Hollenbeck and Eberts (2006).
51. Grubb and others (1993); Creticos and Sheets (1992).

Evaluation and Effectiveness

A final issue is determining what the effects of workforce and economic development are, particularly those provided by community colleges.[52] In general, there has been a dearth of outcome evaluations, and many of the existing studies suffer from a lack of data. Often, anecdotes about successful programs and individuals are used in place of real evidence; in one report, a researcher noted:

> After an 80-hour general, basic skills class, John [a dependable, hard worker stuck in an entry-level position] blossomed. His supervisor marveled at the change and indicated that John has recently contributed several useful suggestions for improving the work flow.

John may, in fact, have blossomed (despite suspicions that short literacy courses are likely to be ineffective); but cherry-picking heart-warming anecdotes does not constitute strong evidence of general effectiveness. Often, to measure their impact on the local economy, community colleges use their payrolls times a multiplier, forgetting to factor in the opportunity costs of locating a community college elsewhere or the taxes used to support community colleges. Community colleges often evaluate the success of their customized training efforts by measures of employer satisfaction or repeat business. So the quality of many evaluation and claims for success are weak, if not purposely misleading.

The best data that are available look at the effects of credit courses and programs of community colleges. The available studies have increased over time, and a relatively clear set of conclusions can be drawn from them.[53] One is that the returns in terms of higher earnings to associate degrees is substantial—not, of course, as high as the returns to baccalaureate degrees but still on the order of 20 to 30 percent over what high school graduates earn. There are substantial differences in these returns by occupational areas, however, with such fields as business, engineering technologies (for men), and health (for women) having substantially higher returns than those for agriculture, education (which prepares teachers' aides and child care workers), and other low-wage occupations. Finally, I have found substantial differences in the returns to associate (and baccalaureate) degrees between individuals who find employment related to their field of study and those individuals finding work in unrelated occupations.[54] If occupational preparation is relatively job specific, then it should have less value in other

52. There is an analogous issue for private firm–based training, in which the lack of research is complicated by the unwillingness of most firms to release their data. For one such analysis, with some review of the existing research, see Krueger and Rouse (1998).

53. See Grubb (2002a), summarizing a number of studies based on national datasets; Bailey and others (2004), using four datasets.

54. Grubb (1997).

occupations, but this implies that finding the right kind of job may be as important as obtaining the right kind of education.

What is less clear is whether small amounts of education in community colleges provide much benefit. The returns to small numbers of credits without earning a credential are generally quite low—insignificant in most cases, and substantively small (on the order of 5 percent) even when significant. The returns to certificates—which are usually one-year programs with little academic coursework and no general education requirements—are often insignificant, although Thomas Bailey and his colleagues find them significant for women only. However, small samples plague the estimation of these effects. Since there is substantial variation among fields of study, insignificant effects probably average high returns for some kinds of certificates—for example, those for medical technicians—with insignificant or negative returns for others. Davis Jenkins has found a tipping point where community college coursework seems to matter, using data from Washington State: students who had at least two semesters of credits and obtained a certificate or other credential earned substantially more than those who received ten credits or fewer.[55] By and large, then, small amounts of coursework do not lead to economic benefits, although there are surely exceptions for highly specialized certificates.

Finally, several researchers have posed the question whether a credential is worth more than the credits required to earn it. Most results find that there is an additional benefit from completing a credential, above the effects of the equivalent number of credits—sometimes called a *sheepskin effect* to indicate the value of the diploma but perhaps better labeled as a *program effect* since credentials require a coherent program of courses. However, a few studies have not found such program effects, so there remains at least some uncertainty about this pattern.[56]

Several states have developed datasets that link the records of community college students to unemployment insurance (UI) data and have used them to calculate the economic benefits of various courses and credentials. While these datasets tend to contain relatively few descriptors of individuals, they do have information on earnings before entering community college, so in effect, they examine changes in earnings due to community college education. Again, the results are quite consistent: the returns to associate degrees are substantial, although they vary by fields of study, and completing a credential program is worth substantially more than simply taking courses without a credential.[57]

55. Grubb (2002b, table 4); Bailey and others (2004); Jenkins (2008).

56. For reviews confirming program effects, see Grubb (2002a); Bailey and others (2004). Jacobson, LaLonde, and Sullvan (2003) provide an exception.

57. Grubb (2002b).

However, these results say nothing about the benefits of noncredit course-work. The lack of data on noncredit enrollments, the inconsistencies of how *noncredit* is defined, and the difficulties of linking data on noncredit education to earnings data or UI data have precluded any attempts to determine the value of such coursework in the labor market. The heterogeneity of noncredit education also makes this task harder. Remedial or developmental education accounts for a substantial portion of noncredit education in some community colleges, but its effect would be positive only when remedial education students are compared with similarly low-performing students without remedial education, not when a comparison is made with the community college population as a whole. Nevertheless, noncredit courses created in response to demand from employers, for selected individuals slated for advancement, might show substantial gains in earnings, but again the comparison group would have to be carefully chosen and selection effects considered. All in all, very little is known about the labor market effects of noncredit education. Most community colleges, therefore, rely on student satisfaction surveys and on continued enrollment in noncredit courses to justify their continuation.

A few researchers have been able to evaluate state-funded customized training. Richard Moore and his colleagues examined data from the California Employment Training Panel (ETP), combining them with unemployment insurance data, and found positive effects on a wide variety of employment measures including labor force participation, earnings, and unemployment.[58] Unfortunately, ETP creates a number of selection effects—the program selects which firms it funds, and then firms select which employees they enroll—and so the control group may not be comparable with the employees who completed ETP training, a serious problem in all but random assignment studies.[59] In addition, Kevin Hollenbeck made a series of estimates for training programs sponsored by the Massachusetts Workforce Development Board and used a series of assumptions to calculate that the rates of return to workers were 5.4 percent; to firms, 16.6 percent; and to the state itself, 38.9 percent.[60] However, the underlying data were self-reports by employers and workers about whether they experienced improvements in productivity and employment as a result of the grants. The high rates of return therefore reflect the approval among firms and employees of these programs, but these satisfaction ratings are not the same as direct evidence of effects. The existing evaluations are highly positive, but there remain virtually unavoidable methodological problems that undermine their power.

58. Moore and others (2003).
59. For example, in 1988 an ETP report revealed that only 8 percent of those trained were high school dropouts, suggesting considerable creaming.
60. Hollenbeck (2008).

Lou Jacobson, Robert LaLonde, and Daniel Sullivan examined a program for dislocated workers provided by community colleges in Washington State. They found Mincerian returns of about 8 percent for older males and 10 percent for older females.[61] However, the internal rate of return for these investments depended on assumptions about costs. If the opportunity costs of training for older men were assumed to be zero—on the assumption that they would otherwise be unemployed—then the internal rate of return was about 11 percent. If one assumed that they could have found some alternative employment, the rate of return fell to as little as 2 percent for men and 4 percent for women. This research leads to a caution: Mincerian rates of return, the dominant approach to investigating the benefits of workforce development, may not be sufficient in cases of retraining and upgrade training for which there may be substantial opportunity costs.

However, this research has asked only whether public training benefits employees in the form of higher earnings. Although there may be a presumption that increases in productivity will raise wages, this is not necessarily the case for specific skill training, which is often the point of customized training. Tracing increases in productivity captured by employers is much more difficult, and the methods of doing so have usually relied on satisfaction surveys of employers. The results have generally been positive; however, employers receiving subsidized customized training do not have much incentive to question the value of what they have received.[62]

Overall, then, relatively little is known about the effects of occupational education and training, aside from the fact that credit programs lead to degrees and certificates. One underlying problem is that community colleges have not in general developed a "culture of evaluation" that might enable them to try new practices, evaluate and possibly improve them, and move to greater confidence about what they are doing. While some community colleges have institutional researchers, others do not, or they share a researcher with other colleges in a district. Researchers are often charged with generating routine data on enrollments and completion and other information necessary for public relations purposes, and they rarely have time for more analytic work. If there were more time for evaluative research, the priorities in most community colleges would be to concentrate on those issues facing the largest numbers of students—the effectiveness of remedial or developmental courses in helping students progress, for example, or the success of new approaches to instruction like learning commu-

61. Jacobson, LaLonde, and Sullivan (2003). A *Mincerian return* is the percent increase in wages as a result of an additional year of training or schooling, holding work experience and relevant demographic characteristics constant.

62. See Hollenbeck (2008) for results based on satisfaction.

nities, or the reasons that completion rates are so low. Programs with small enrollments—such as noncredit education in particular occupational areas or customized training with a small employer—are always going to be low priorities for institutional research. Unless states or the federal government change their attitudes toward evaluation research, the usual claim—"more research is needed"—will remain true but ineffective in mobilizing resources.

Conclusions and the Limits of the Education Gospel

In developing conclusions and recommendations for the education and skill needs for workforce and economic development, I distinguish issues for education and training providers, especially community colleges; issues for states that are responsible for community college systems as well as other forms of workforce development; and issues for the federal government. In the final section, I discuss some caveats about the claims of the Education Gospel.

Issues for Community Colleges and Other Providers of Education and Training

Community colleges now provide a variety of offerings, both individual courses and complete programs, both training and education, in credit, noncredit, and customized forms for the regions they serve. But these are often offered by different units or departments within community colleges; thus, small employers sometimes find themselves bewildered by the options. The various alternatives are not well integrated with one another—for example, in most community colleges the path from noncredit to credit education is not well marked, and the potential lessons from providing customized training to employers are not used to inform credit programs. Many community colleges could therefore improve the coordination of their various offerings and create more integrated pathways through the institution. This step would benefit both prospective students as well as employers.

In general there seems to be enough education and training provided in most metropolitan areas; only in the few cases of high-demand, high-cost occupations (like nursing and some technical specialties) are there reported to be shortages of places in community colleges. However, Leigh and Gill's research in California shows that community colleges vary widely in their responsiveness to labor market conditions, and at the low end of the distribution, some community colleges seem unresponsive. It is not clear whether this variety of responsiveness is due to different priorities (such as placing an emphasis on transfer programs or large amounts of remedial and developmental education), or to a lack of contact with employers, or to volatile labor markets that are difficult even for employers to forecast. However, greater responsiveness of community colleges would improve the efficiency of the quasi-markets in education and training, and this might mean that the community colleges would participate more actively with employers and local councils of employers and providers of training and education. A combination of data collection (for example, on placement rates, mirroring Florida's requirement of at least 70 percent placement), technical assistance in creating advisory committees, and analytic and diagnostic research of the sort that Leigh and Gill have carried out might support local community colleges' efforts to be more responsive.

Even though the quality of instruction in community colleges is better than it is in community-based organizations (CBOs) or in adult education programs or better than the quality of job training providers, there is still too much conventional and unimaginative teaching, including the kinds of behaviorist teaching that violates all the principles for engagement and motivation.[63] Community colleges have experimented with practices, such as learning communities and efforts to integrate academic content into CTE, with substantial promise. Some have created teaching and learning centers that provide faculty with multiple resources to enhance instruction, and others have used a variety of institutional mechanisms including professional development, coursework in pedagogy, and support for new instructors to encourage more innovative approaches. Some of these mechanisms need to be initiated at the local level, and some of them could be enhanced by state funding and technical assistance. But improved instruction would enhance learning and skill acquisition for all of CTE and workforce development, especially when employers call for higher-order skills and the skills of the twenty-first century. Of course, it would be desirable to have instructional improvements spill over to other providers like CBOs and adult education, but this might require difficult changes in institutional cultures and personnel practices.

The spatial dimensions of community colleges are also important. On the one hand, many of them are committed to being community service institutions, and they provide a wide variety of education, training, and other services according to the needs of the community. On the other hand, the limited boundaries of most community colleges, together with the spatial limitations of employers in the middle-skilled labor market, mean that neither employers nor suppliers may be aware of imbalances elsewhere. The efficiency of local labor markets might be improved if community colleges, as well as associations of employers, were able to participate in regional or even statewide councils—like the local and statewide Workforce Investment Boards that exist under WIA—so

---

63. Grubb and Kalman (1994); Grubb and Associates (1999); NRC (2004).

that they could assess the demand and supply of education and training in neighboring regions.

Finally, community colleges need to assess the effectiveness of workforce development and its opportunity costs. In a few cases, community colleges have embraced workforce development so enthusiastically that other missions of the community college—particularly its equity role in supporting low-performing students needing remedial education or ESL—have suffered. Sometimes community colleges provide overly specific forms of occupational education, and the pressures of employers to hire *turnkey employees*—employees able to be fully productive on the first day of work—contribute to that. Finally, it appears that an intensely occupational approach to education causes students to view their classes in overly instrumental and narrow ways, asking whether every little element of their coursework will help them on the job. Such narrow conceptions of learning, however, turn out to be counterproductive.[64] For a comprehensive community college, then, workforce development must be balanced with other missions.

Issues for States

There are various roles that states can play in strengthening community colleges. However, a crucial caveat is necessary. States have often imposed requirements on educational institutions without giving them the capacity, the resources, or the funding to meet these requirements. State accountability systems for K–12 education and the federal No Child Left Behind legislation are good examples of new requirements outrunning existing capacity.[65] Therefore any new requirements on community colleges or other providers must be carefully matched with methods of enhancing capacity, through funding and technical assistance, including providing information about promising practices.

One of the common state practices that limit workforce development is funding through conventional formulas that do not consider the costs of programs. This type of funding provides incentives for community colleges to overenroll low-cost programs and underenroll high-cost programs in which some of the greatest social benefits may lie.[66] States should, therefore, consider shifting to weighted funding formulas that account for the costs of provision, being careful to ensure that high-cost programs do indeed have social net benefits. This would also conform to the precept given above of investing in high-wage, high-productivity occupations.

64. Grubb and Cox (2005); Cox (2004).
65. Grubb (2008c); Welner and Weitzman (2005).
66. That is, colleges based their decisions on marginal *institutional* costs and benefits and only by accident will these be aligned with marginal *social* costs and benefits.

States have subsidized a certain amount of customized training, though the amounts are small relative to what employers provide (and so the room for serious error is correspondingly small). However, there is almost no notice taken of what conditions justify public support and what forms of training should be supported by employers themselves. Therefore, state programs ought to articulate a set of consistent rationales for support of training, especially relatively specific training, so that they do not simply subsidize what firms should be doing on their own. Of course, the politics of such a shift might be difficult, particularly when employers claim a right to tax-generated revenues.

Finally, for many states the vision of an integrated system of education, training, and workforce development remains distant. Community colleges are, in fact if not in principle, the mainstay of such systems, simply because they provide the greatest amount of education, in the greatest variety, to many different groups. But the linkages to WIA have become weaker because of a variety of factors:

—Accountability standards are too rigid.

—The connections to adult education are often poor.

—The role of community colleges in state-funded workforce development programs varies among states (sometimes intentionally so).

—The function of statewide and then local planning councils that could incorporate economic development planning, workforce development, short-term training, and longer-run education is uneven at best.

Some states were beginning to move toward such coherent systems during the 1990s, and some particularly active states with strong leadership, such as Washington, Oregon, and Kentucky, continue to develop such systems. In addition, establishing career pathways that align a sequence of education and training programs in one occupational area is another way that several providers have collaborated with one another. However, the efforts to develop coherent systems seem to have slowed, partly because of shifts in WIA. Resuming the effort to develop coherent workforce development systems remains a worthy goal and is a policy that only the states can undertake.

The Federal Role

The federal government funds at least forty-four employment and training programs, and their variety is simply bewildering.[67] In the past, many observers have called on the federal government to create a coherent workforce policy from its complex of small programs. Indeed, in 1996 there was a movement to replace the Job Training Partnership Act with legislation that would have combined a wide variety of occupational education and training funds into a block grant, which would then have gone to the states to allocate according to state plans. When this

67. GAO (2004).

failed to pass, the WIA legislation that emerged in 1998 returned to much more categorical uses of federal funds. Unfortunately, there seems little hope at the moment of creating any coherent policy at the federal level, so states in all likelihood will have to continue to live with disconnected federal programs and will have to generate coherent state policies as best they can.

Nonetheless, several important training goals exist that the federal government can fulfill better than any other level of government. One is the provision of remedial training for those who have low skills and are on the margin of the labor force, such as welfare-to-work programs and adult education programs—this is one of the redistributive functions of central government. But these are now scattered in different programs in different agencies. The sums involved are often trivial, and the coordination with community colleges is poor. Many of these programs would benefit from being transferred to community colleges, because of their closer connections to instructional improvement and their automatic connection to a variety of other occupational and credit courses. A system in which individuals could enter remedial training or adult education and then progress into subsequent forms of education as the conditions of their lives allow—in current terms, a *system of career pathways*—would be a vast improvement over the current complex of short-term, dead-end training that now prevails.[68]

Similarly, the federal government engages in redistribution through grants and loans for postsecondary education. This funding can be used in community colleges and proprietary trade schools as well as in four-year colleges and universities, and indeed the utilization rate is especially high in private trade schools. But eligible community college students often do not use such federal support, partly because many of them may not make their college plans that far in advance, partly because the process is complex, and partly because the quality of financial aid offices varies.[69] And federal financial aid intended for colleges and universities does not extend to shorter-term training, so most of the workforce development efforts reviewed here are not supported by such aid.

A third commonly recommended activity for federal action is research. As I have illustrated, research about a wide variety of short-term education and training programs is missing; most of the evidence we have focuses on longer-term and credential-oriented programs of education. However, there is a great deal of short-term education and training, as well as a great deal of dropping out of community colleges and four-year colleges, creating what are in effect short-

68. On career pathways see Jenkins (2006) or the Career Pathways Toolkit developed by the Workforce Strategy Center. I have made the argument about the centrality of community colleges in creating such pathways many times; see, for example, Grubb (1996a, 1996b) for a much fuller argument.
69. Grubb and Tuma (1991). These patterns, analyzed for the 1986 National Postsecondary Student Aid Study data, continue to hold in the more recent data.

term education programs. Understanding the labor market effects of such short-term programs, and of local economic development policies more generally, would be a valuable role for the federal government.[70]

Other federal initiatives require some agreement about what problems persist in local and regional labor markets that state policy cannot correct. If there are regional shortages and surpluses of skilled labor, because of the local focus of middle-skilled labor markets, a federal program of relocation or retraining—like the existing dislocated worker training—would be justified, again one that might be better carried out in conjunction with community colleges. If there were a consensus on underinvestment by employers in workforce training, then a national workforce training program would be appropriate. But because federal policy is now a hodgepodge of little programs—each meeting some disparate need, each satisfying a particular constituency—the need for more coherence is great.

Two other recommendations seem in order. One is to avoid tax expenditures as instruments of federal (or state) policy. These are almost never made refundable, so they cannot benefit low- and moderate-income groups. They tend to benefit middle-class families who would have supported education or training anyway, so they are inefficient as well as inequitable. When tax credits are aimed at employers, they tend to be used haphazardly and inefficiently, as the experience with the Targeted Jobs Tax Credit shows. Finally, tax expenditures are poor vehicles for creating any coherent policy system or for integrating different providers into a system. Again, the politics of eliminating middle-class tax benefits are difficult, but still, tax expenditures should play no role in a carefully crafted workforce development policy.

Finally, the federal government has begun traveling down the path of accountability, and here there are many dangers to be avoided. The rigid accountability standards in WIA have caused many community colleges to drop out of the program. In the realm of postsecondary education, Margaret Spellings, President George W. Bush's secretary of education, proposed a "robust system of accountability and transparency" by developing new data and measures of outcomes—and presumably, as with No Child Left Behind (NCLB), attaching punitive consequences to such outcomes. However, the record of state and federal accountability so far is abysmal. The complex accountability system for elementary and secondary education under NCLB has had dreadful effects in stampeding underperforming schools to use ineffective curricula that they hope will yield quick results, but that in the long run are sure to be counterproductive.[71] As many have pointed out, NCLB imposed additional requirements

70. See Bartik (2002) for more detail.
71. See Grubb and others (2008) for a study of twelve schools, one of many such studies.

on schools but without enhancing their capacities to meet these requirements. The obvious lesson is that accountability cannot work unless it is matched with the resources to enhance capacity at the local level. And given the complexity of postsecondary programs, any simple system of accountability is sure to backfire in unpredictable ways. Unless these issues can be resolved, any federal efforts to impose accountability in the realm of postsecondary programs should be viewed with alarm

The Exaggerations of the Education Gospel

Finally, I return to the claims of the Education Gospel. Much of the rhetoric underlying the need for skill development of all kinds in the United States comes back to the faith that enhancing educating and training can enhance growth and competitiveness, at the national level but also at local and regional levels. But while the benefits of additional education (though not the benefits of shorter-term training) for individuals are well-known as one compares poorly educated and well-educated individuals *at one point in time*, the benefits for the nation or for regions are much more difficult to establish. Consistently, advocates of the Education Gospel use cross-sectional evidence of benefits, such as the voluminous literature on the individual and social benefits of education, to claim that increasing average levels of education over time would have the same benefits. However, rather than facing a gross problem of undereducation, this country and other developed countries suffer from extensive *over*education, particularly at the top of the skill distribution, so one should be careful of claims that there is a need for many more well-educated workers. This is not so true at the bottom of the skill distribution, where individuals leave formal schooling still reading at the elementary school level and without any job-specific skills to enable them to escape unskilled work. This implies that remedial education—whether for incumbent workers or for the unemployed—is one of the most important priorities, but not education and training at the top or the middle of the skills distribution. In addition, the forecasts of employment in this country suggests that education requirements grow only slowly and that the largest numbers of job openings are still in relatively unskilled positions—as waitresses, clerical workers, personal service workers, and other occupations not requiring any college at all. So further education and higher-order skills may be necessary for individual mobility, but their effects on the economy as a whole are much less clear.[72]

The first evaluation of Reading First has shown no effects on reading comprehension (Gamse and others 2008), and similarly, other evidence from National Assessment of Educational Progress tests has shown no improvements (Fuller and others 2007).

72. For the arguments about overeducation, see the sources cited in note 32. On forecasts of skill requirements, see Hecker (2001) and the biennial forecasts in the November issue of the *Monthly Labor Review*.

Furthermore, when researchers follow a microeconomic approach to growth and development, rather than a macroeconomic perspective focusing only on a few measurable variables, then dozens of factors influence growth—state and local governance; the sociopolitical climate including its stability; tax policies; local or regional institutions including financial, legal, and corporate institutions; structural and supportive policies including education, labor relations, and science and technology policy; and regulatory and environmental policies. In addition, there may be factors specific to particular industries that help explain their growth or stagnation, as well as company-specific issues. So education is only one of the multiple factors affecting the growth of a region. The lack of skills can certainly hamper growth, if there is no response to increasing demand, but education and training cannot by themselves stimulate growth.[73]

This in turn leads to two conclusions. One is simply that the rhetoric around the Education Gospel, and its claims about education and economic growth, should be moderated at the national and the local or regional levels. A second is that the real role of educational institutions, aside from responding to demand in labor markets, is to participate in wider economic development efforts like those described in the first section, in which community colleges participate with local or regional development councils to put together the combination of factors necessary for growth and development. Such cooperation, in effect, invites community colleges to participate in creating the demand for skilled labor, as well as giving them opportunities to provide additional education and training, but it does not pretend that education and training are the most important factors in local growth.

Overall, then, there are many sources of human capital development in this country, especially in metropolitan areas. Despite periodic complaints about shortages, very few of them seem to persist, and many apparent shortages are really demand-side problems. Community colleges are among the most important providers, offering a variety of education and training in many formats including noncredit and customized training that can be highly responsive to employers. Community colleges have many advantages over other providers such as spatial breadth, a variety of offerings, and some commitment to instructional improvement. Some community colleges may need to be more responsive to employers, and many more could make instructional improvement a higher priority, but the variation in the quality of community colleges is surely less than that of private providers.

---

73. This argument is more fully developed in Grubb and Lazerson (2004). See also Wolf (2002). For an example of the micro approach to growth, see Landau, Taylor, and Wright (1996).

Elsewhere in the workforce development system, the subsidies for workforce development and customized training seek to fill some potential gaps in provision. But the state and federal programs that support such programs are trivial, compared with the efforts of community colleges and employers, and many of these programs have failed to consider why public funding for private training is justified. There are many potential market failures that can lead to undertraining, particularly in small and medium-sized firms. However, identifying and responding to these specific opportunities to create training programs—rather than providing across-the-board training subsidies—would require more careful state decisions than most states have been able to make. Finally, the goal of creating coherent systems of workforce development remains elusive, although states and the federal government could help in creating such systems if only both put their will to it.

References

Achtenhagen, Frank, and W. Norton Grubb. 2001. "Vocational and Occupational Education: Pedagogical Complexity, Institutional Indifference." In *Handbook of Research on Teaching*, edited by V. Richardson, 4th ed., pp 176–206. Washington: American Educational Research Association.

Bailey, Thomas, Gregory Kienzl, and David Marcotte. 2004. "Who Benefits from Postsecondary Occupational Education? Findings from the 1980s and 1990s." CCRC Brief 23. Columbia University, Teachers College, Community College Research Center.

Bartik, Timothy. 2002. "Evaluating the Impacts of Local Economic Development Policies on Local Economic Outcomes: What Has Been Done and What Is Doable?" Staff Working Paper 03-89. Kalamazoo, Mich.: W. E. Upjohn Institute for Employment.

Becker, Gary. 1993. *Human Capital: A Theoretical and Empirical Analysis with Special Reference to Education*, 3rd ed. University of Chicago Press. (Original 1964).

Bierhoff, Helvia, and S. J. Prais. 1997. *From School to Productive Work: Britain and Switzerland Compared*. Cambridge University Press.

Cox, Rebecca. 2004. *Navigating Community College Demands: Contradictory Goals, Expectations, and Outcomes in Composition*. Ph.D. dissertation, University of California–Berkeley, School of Education.

Creticos, Peter, and Robert Sheets. 1992. *Evaluating State-Financed, Workplace-Based Retraining Programs: Case Studies of Retraining Projects*. Research Report 91-05. Washington: National Commission for Employment Policy.

Daly, Mary C., Felix Büchel, and Gregory J. Duncan. 2000. "Premiums and Penalties for Surplus and Deficit Education: Evidence from the United States and Germany." *Economics of Education Review* 19: 169–78.

Dickens, William T. 1992. "Good Jobs: Increasing Worker Productivity with Trade and Industrial Policy." University of California–Berkeley, Department of Economics.

Doucette, Don. 1993. *Community College Workforce Training Programs for Employees of Business, Industry, Labor, and Government: A Status Report*. Mission Viejo, Calif.: League for Innovation in the Community College.

Dougherty, Kevin J. 1994. *The Contradictory College: The Conflicting Origins, Impacts, and Futures of the Community College*. State University of New York Press.

———. 2003. "The Uneven Distribution of Employee Training by Community Colleges: Description and Explanation." *Annals of the American Academy of Political and Social Science* 586, no. 1: 62–91.

Dougherty, Kevin J., and Marianne Bakia. 2000. "Community Colleges and Contract Training: Content, Origins, and Impact." *Teachers College Record* 102, no. 1: 197–243.

Ducha, Steven, and William Graves. 2007. "The Employer as the Client: State-Finance Customized Training, 2006." ETAOP 2007-14. Washington: U.S. Department of Labor, Employment and Training Administration.

Duke, Amy-Ellen, and Julie Strawn. 2008. *Overcoming Obstacles, Optimizing Opportunities: State Policies to Increase Postsecondary Attainment for Low-Skills Adults*. Boston: Jobs for the Future.

Frazis, Harley, and others. 1998. "Results from the 1995 Survey of Employer-Provided Training." *Monthly Labor Review* 121, no. 6: 3–13.

Frazis, Harley, Diane Herz, and Michael Horrigan. 1995. "Employer-Provided Training: Results from a New Survey." *Monthly Labor Review* 118, no.5: 3–17.

Fuller, Bruce, Joseph Wright, Karen Gesicki, and Erin Kang. 2007. "Gauging Growth: How to Judge No Child Left Behind?" *Educational Researcher* 36, no. 5: 268–78.

Gamse, B., and others. 2008. "Reading First Impact Study: Interim Report." U.S. Department of Education, National Center for Education Evaluation and Regional Assistance.

General Accounting Office (GAO). 2004. *Workforce Training: Almost Half of States Fund Employment Placement and Training through Employers' Taxes and Most Coordinate with Federally Funded Programs.* GAO-04-282. Washington: General Accounting Office.

Grubb, W. Norton. 1994. "The Long-Run Effects of Proprietary Schools: Corrections." *Educational Evaluation and Policy Analysis* 16, no. 3: 351–56

———. 1996a. *Learning to Work: The Case for Reintegrating Job Training and Education.* New York: Russell Sage.

———. 1996b. *Working in the Middle: Strengthening Education and Training for the Mid-Skilled Labor Force.* San Francisco: Jossey-Bass.

———. 1997. "The Returns to Education in the Sub-Baccalaureate Labor Market, 1984–1990." *Economics of Education Review* 16, no. 3: 231–46.

———.2002a. "Learning and Earning in the Middle, Part I: National Studies of Pre-Baccalaureate Education." *Economics of Education Review* 21, no. 4: 299–321.

———. 2002b. "Learning and Earning in the Middle, Part II: State and Local Studies of Pre-Baccalaureate Education." *Economics of Education Review* 21, no. 5: 401–14.

———. 2002c. "Occupational Education." In *Higher Education in the United States: An Encyclopedia,* edited by James Forest and Kevin Kinser. Santa Barbara, Calif.: ABC-CLIO.

———. 2008a. "The Complexities of Instruction in Career-Technical Education: The Issues in Community Colleges." Paper prepared for the National Community College Symposium, U.S. Department of Education.

———. 2008b. "Linking Learning Science Theories and Measures to Economic Growth Models." Prepared for SRI International, Menlo Park, Calif.

———. 2009. *The Money Myth: School Resources, Outcomes and Equity.* New York: Russell Sage Foundation.

Grubb, W. Norton, and Associates. 1999. *Honored but Invisible: An Inside Look at Teaching in Community Colleges.* New York and London: Routledge.

Grubb, W. Norton, Norena Badway, Denise Bell, Debra Bragg, and Marilyn Russmann. 1997. *Workforce, Economic, and Community Development: The Changing Landscape of the Entrepreneurial Community College.* Mission Viejo, Calif.: League for Innovation in the Community College.

Grubb, W. Norton, Norena Badway, William Dickens, Neil Finkelstein, Hilary Hoynes, and David Stern. 1993. *Choosing Wisely for California: Targeting the Resources of the Employment Training Panel.* Berkeley, Calif.: National Center for Research in Vocational Education and Center for Labor Research and Education.

Grubb, W. Norton, and Rebecca Cox. 2005. "Pedagogical Alignment and Curricular Consistency: The Challenges for Developmental Education." In special issue *Responding to the Challenges of Developmental Education,* edited by Carol Kozerecki. *New Directions for Community Colleges* 129 (Spring): 93–103.

Grubb, W. Norton, and Judith Kalman. 1994. "Relearning to Earn: The Role of Remediation in Vocational Education and Job Training." *American Journal of Education* 103, no. 1: 54–93.

Grubb, W. Norton, Heather Kinlaw, Linn Posey, and Katharine Young. 2008. "Dynamic Inequality: Exploring What Schools Do for Low-Performing Students." University of

California–Berkeley, School of Education (April). Also, in *The Money Myth: School Resources, Outcomes and Equity*, edited by W. Norton Grubb, chapter 8, Russell Sage Foundation (2009).

Grubb, W. Norton, and Marvin Lazerson. 2004. *The Education Gospel: The Economic Power of Schooling*. Harvard University Press.

Grubb, W. Norton, and Paul Ryan. 1999. *The Role of Evaluation for Vocational Education and Training: Plain Talk on the Field of Dreams*. London: Kogan Page and Geneva: International Labour Office.

Grubb, W. Norton, and John Tuma. 1991. "Who Gets Student Aid? Variations in Access to Aid." *Review of Higher Education* 14, no.3: 359–82.

Grubb, W. Norton, and others. 1999. *Toward Order from Chaos: State Efforts to Reform Workforce Development Systems*. MDS-1249. Berkeley, Calif.: National Center for Research in Vocational Education.

Hartog, Joop. 2000. "Over-Education and Earnings: Where Are We, Where Should We Go? *Economics of Education Review* 19, no. 2: 131–47.

Hecker, Daniel. 2001. "Occupational Employment Projections to 2010. *Monthly Labor Review* 124, no. 11: 57–84.

Hollenbeck, Kevin. 2008. "Is There a Role for Public Support of Incumbent Worker On-the-Job Training?" Working Paper 08-138. Kalamazoo, Mich.: W. E. Upjohn Institute for Employment Research.

Hollenbeck, Kevin, and Robert Eberts. 2006. *An Evaluation of Michigan Regional Skills Alliances (MiRSAs)*. Kalamazoo, Mich.: W. E. Upjohn Institute for Employment Research.

Jacobs, James, and W. Norton Grubb. 2006. "The Limits of 'Training for Now': Lessons from Information Technology Certification." In *Defending the Community College Equity Agenda*, edited by Thomas Bailey and Vanessa Smith Morest, pp. 132–54. Johns Hopkins Press.

Jacobson, Lou, Robert LaLonde, and Daniel Sullivan. 2003. "Should We Teach Old Dogs New Tricks? The Impact of Community College Retraining on Older Displaced Workers." WP 2003-25. Federal Reserve Bank of Chicago.

Jacobson, Lou, Regina Yudd Feldman, and Ian Petta. 2005. *The 21st Century Community College: A Strategic Guide for Maximizing Responsiveness. Research Appendices*. Washington: U.S. Department of Education.

Jenkins, Davis. 2006. "Career Pathways: Aligning Public Resources to Support Individual and Regional Economic Advancement in the Knowledge Economy." New York: Workforce Strategy Center.

————. 2008. "A Short Guide to 'Tipping Point' Analyses of Community College Student Labor Market Outcomes." *CCRC Research Tools* 3. New York: Community College Research Center.

Krueger, Alan, and Cecilia Rouse. 1998. "The Effect of Workplace Education on Earnings, Turnovers, and Job Performance." *Journal of Labor Economics* 16, no. 1: 61–94.

Lafer, Gordon. 2002. *The Job Training Charade*. Cornell University Press.

LaLonde, Robert. 1995. "The Promise of Public Sector-Sponsored Training Programs." *Journal of Economic Perspectives* 9, no. 2: 149–68.

Landau, Ralph T., Timothy Taylor, and Gavin Wright. 1996. *The Mosaic of Economic Growth*. Stanford University Press.

Leigh, Duane, and Andrew Gill. 2007. *Do Community Colleges Respond to Local Needs? Evidence from California*. Kalamazoo, Mich.: W. E. Upjohn Institute for Employment Security.

Lynch, Lisa. 1994. *Training and the Private Sector: International Comparisons.* University of Chicago Press.

Lynch, Lisa, and Sandra Black. 1996. *Beyond the Incidence of Training: Evidence from a National Employers Survey.* Philadelphia: National Center on the Education Quality of the Workforce.

Lynch, Richard, James Palmer, and W. Norton Grubb. 1991. *Community College Involvement in Contract Training and Other Economic Development Activities.* Berkeley, Calif.: National Center for Research in Vocational Education.

Markusen, Ann. 2007. *Reining in the Competition for Capital.* Kalamazoo, Mich.: W. E. Upjohn Institute for Employment Research.

Moore, Richard, and others. 2003. *Training That Works: Lessons from California's Employment Training Panel.* Kalamazoo, Mich.: W. E. Upjohn Institute for Employment Research.

Moretti, Enrico. 2003. "Human Capital Externalities in Cities." Working Paper 9641. Cambridge, Mass.: National Bureau of Economic Research.

National Research Council (NRC). 2004. *Engaging Schools: Fostering High School Students' Motivation to Learn.* Washington: National Academy Press, NRC, Committee on Increasing High School Students' Engagement and Motivation to Learn.

Regional Technology Strategies. 1999. "A Comprehensive Look at State-Funded, Employer-Focused Job Training Programs." Washington: National Governors' Association.

Rosenbaum, James, Regina Deil-Amen, and Ann Person. 2006. *After Admission: From College Access to College Success.* New York: Russell Sage Foundation.

Rouse, Cecilia. 1995. "Democratization or Diversion: The Effect of Community Colleges on Educational Attainment." *Journal of Business and Economic Statistics* 13, no. 2: 217–24.

———. 1998. "Do Two-Year Colleges Increase Overall Educational Attainment? Evidence from the States." *Journal of Policy Analysis and Management* 17: 595–620.

Shaw, Kathleen, Sara Goldrick-Rab, and Christopher Mazzeo. 2006. *Putting Poor People to Work: How the Work-First Idea Eroded College Access for the Poor.* New York: Russell Sage Foundation.

Training. 2006. "2006 Industry Report." *Training* 43, no. 12: 20–32.

Van Noy, Michelle, and others. 2008. "The Landscape of Noncredit Workforce Education: State Policies and Community College Practice." Brief 38. New York: Community College Research Center, Teachers College.

Villeneuve, Jennifer, and W. Norton Grubb. 1996. *Indigenous School-to-Work Programs: Lessons from Cincinnati's Co-op Education.* Berkeley, Calif.: National Center for Research in Vocational Education.

Welner, Kevin, and Don Weitzman. 2005. "The Soft Bigotry of Low Expenditures." *Equity and Excellence in Education* 38, no. 3: 242–48.

Wolf, Alison. 2002. *Does Education Matter? Myths about Education and Economic Growth.* London: Penguin Books.

Zaleski, A. 2007. "Policies to Engage Postsecondary Education in State Economic Development." *ecs StateNotes*: Economic Development. Denver: Education Commission of the States.

5

Living Wage Laws:
How Much Do (Can) They Matter?

HARRY J. HOLZER

Living wage laws are "local ordinances requiring private businesses that benefit from public money" to pay above-market wages and benefits to their workers.[1] These laws have been passed and implemented in many municipalities and counties nationwide. They are widely viewed as efforts to aid the working poor and address labor market inequality, particularly as other institutions that have traditionally done so (such as minimum wage laws and collective bargaining) have eroded over time.

But how effective are these laws at helping the working poor? Do they have unintended, and perhaps negative, consequences—such as a drop in employment rates of the working poor? Do they affect enough workers to matter one way or another? And, if not, could they potentially be more effective than they are to date?

In this chapter I explore this set of issues. I begin by reviewing some facts about living wage laws—such as where and how they have been implemented, whom they cover, and so forth. I also outline their potential impacts, both positive and negative, on employment and other urban outcomes. Then I review the literature on the impacts of living wage laws before concluding with some final thoughts.

I am grateful to Igor Kheyfets for excellent research assistance. I also benefited from helpful comments made by Doug Wissoker, Howard Wial, and other participants in the 2008 Conference on Urban and Regional Policy and Its Effects.
1. Living Wage Resource Center, "The Living Wage Movement: Building Power in Our Workplaces and Neighborhoods" (www.livingwagecampaign.org/index.php?id=2071 [2006]).

Living Wage Laws: The Facts

Campaigns to pass living wage ordinances have become increasingly frequent in U.S. cities during the past two decades. In addition to the basic goal of trying to raise wages among low earners, campaign organizers and sponsors have often had other goals in mind as well—such as preventing the outsourcing of municipal work to lower-wage providers, supporting union organizing, limiting local governments' use of economic development subsidies to attract large firms, mobilizing a broader social movement to combat low wages and inequality, and even making a symbolic statement about fair wage levels and the appropriateness of government efforts to raise low wages. These efforts began to grow in a context of dramatically widening income inequality in the United States at a time when other policies and institutions that had traditionally been used in efforts to limit such inequality—such as minimum wage laws and unions—have been used less aggressively and are becoming scarcer in the private sector.[2]

The first living wage law in a major U.S. city was passed in Baltimore in 1994. As of May 2006, about 140 municipalities and counties around the country had implemented them—including such large cities as Boston, Chicago, Cleveland, Detroit, Los Angeles, Milwaukee, and San Francisco.[3] A list of these localities and the characteristics of their living wage laws appears in the appendix. Campaigns to introduce new ordinances are under way in dozens of more cities, usually under the active leadership of the community organizing group known as ACORN (Association of Community Organizations for Reform Now) and involving local labor and religious organizations, among others.

Figure 5-1 maps the metropolitan areas in which the living wage municipalities and counties are located. It shows that living wage laws are unevenly distributed among metropolitan areas. The largest concentrations of these laws are found in the metropolitan areas of the San Francisco Bay Area, southern California, southeastern Michigan, and, to a somewhat lesser extent, south Florida, Connecticut, New York City, and Washington, D.C. Metropolitan areas in the Southeast (except for south Florida) have few localities with living wage laws.

In general, these laws apply to the employees of private firms in one or both of the following categories: those that have service contracts with the municipality or county with dollar values above some defined minimum level and those

2. Until the most recent rounds of increases in the federal minimum wage that were implemented in 2007 and 2008, the statutory minimum had fallen to only about 30 percent of the mean wage in the private sector—its lowest level in five decades. The fraction of private sector workers organized into unions, at less than 8 percent, has also fallen to a fifty-year low. See Mishel, Bernstein, and Shierholz (2006).

3. Living Wage Resource Center, "The Living Wage Movement: Building Power in Our Workplaces and Neighborhoods."

Figure 5-1. *Distribution of U.S. Living Wage Ordinances, by Metropolitan and Micropolitan Area*

- • Municipality/County (living wage ordinance in effect)
- ▨ Municipality/County (living wage ordinance repealed)
- ▨ Metropolitan/Micropolitan Area

that receive other kinds of financial assistance from the municipal government, in the form of grants, loans, tax abatements, bond financing, or other forms of local economic development policies. In some limited cases, workers at publicly owned but privately operated facilities (like airports or marinas) are also covered.

These firms are required to pay wages to their workers that are well above those specified by federal or state minimum wage laws.[4] The wage levels are usually set with the goal of lifting the incomes of year-round, full-time workers above the official federal poverty line for a family of four. Since the poverty line is now at about $21,000 per year, this requires an hourly wage of $10 to $11, which is a bit below the average wage mandated in these laws.[5] Although only a few such laws require that health or other benefits be provided to all workers in

4. The federal minimum wage is $6.55 and is scheduled to rise to $7.25 in July 2009. Nearly thirty states currently have minimum wage laws exceeding the federal level. See Economic Policy Institute (2007).

5. Some cities instead use the poverty rate for a family of three, at roughly $18,000, as a guideline in setting their required wage levels. The official poverty lines rise annually with the rate of inflation (as measured by the consumer price index), although the locally required wages do not always rise as well. But comparisons of annual incomes based on year-round, full-time work at these wage levels with poverty rates assume only one worker per household and no other income supplements, such as the Earned Income Tax Credit, which is available to low-income workers with children. For a discussion of the limits of the current poverty measures, see Blank (2008).

these firms, many stipulate a somewhat lower mandated wage level when such benefits are provided and a higher one when they are not.

Despite these generally shared characteristics, and in addition to differences in the mandated wage and benefit levels specified, living wage laws vary substantially across local jurisdictions, as table 5A-1 also implies. For instance, the scope of coverage varies quite a bit even within the categories of firms defined above—with some laws applying only to full-time workers or limited to specific occupational categories.

The administrative apparatus for implementing these laws varies as well across local areas, with some localities hiring officials explicitly to enforce these laws and making them quite accessible to the public, while others do not.[6] The geographic scope of coverage also varies, as some laws apply to municipalities and others to counties. and even in the case of the former, some cities face a situation in which similar laws are being implemented in contiguous municipalities while many others do not. Finally, some laws also contain provisions that require workers to be hired that live in the covered communities, and some are explicitly superseded by collective bargaining provisions, while others are not. All of these characteristics of the policy context and how the laws are designed and implemented will likely affect their impacts on labor market outcomes.

One other characteristic seems to apply almost universally in these efforts: *local living wage ordinances generally seem to affect very few workers directly.* Most studies imply that, even among workers in the bottom tenth of wage levels, only 2 to 3 percent are covered by these laws, since so few work for firms that benefit from local service contracts or other forms of public financial assistance. Even in larger cities, the absolute number of workers covered will be very modest. For example, consider a city with a total population of 1 million, half of whom are in the workforce.[7] Of the 50,000 workers in the bottom tenth of earnings, if 3 percent are directly covered by living wage ordinances, then only 1,500 workers are affected. In smaller jurisdictions, proportionately fewer workers will be affected.

It is possible that higher wages in these firms spill over onto firms with whom they must compete in local markets, whether in the same or other geographic jurisdictions. It is also possible that these laws could be implemented in other ways that expand their reach. But, at the moment, it is important to recognize the relatively limited scope and impacts of existing laws, as their actual or potential economic effects are considered.

---

6. Luce (2004).

7. On average, only about three-fourths of the U.S. population falls between the ages of 16 and 64, and labor force participation rates for this group generally average 60 to 70 percent.

Living Wage Laws: The Issues

Since living wage ordinances mandate the payment of higher wages and benefits to workers than what might be generated by the labor market, their effects are likely similar to those of minimum wage laws—though the living wage ordinances provide substantially higher wages or benefits or both for a much smaller range of workers.

The general concern that economists have about any attempt by government to mandate higher wage payments by private employers is that it might result in lower employment levels. This potential effect is based on the notion that employer hiring behavior is reflected in a "demand curve"—in which, all else equal, they will hire fewer workers if they are forced to pay more for each of them.

The expected impact of living wage ordinances is depicted in figure 5-2. The figure shows the impact of living wage laws, as a type of "wage floor," on the wages (W) and employment (L) levels (measured on the vertical and horizontal axes, respectively) of covered workers, relative to what might be generated in a "competitive equilibrium" in the labor market. As indicated, economists generally expect that any wage floor will generate a "surplus" in the labor market (as indicated by $L_F^S - L_F^D$), with wages above the market level ($W_F > W^*$) and employment below it ($L_F^D < L^*$).[8]

But, since this floor will generally cover only a small number of firms in the labor market, any surplus of workers in the covered sector might well shift to the uncovered sectors of the economy—perhaps gaining employment but driving down wages in the latter.[9] This implies that the wage gains of some workers might be offset by wage losses among others, although initial employment losses might be offset as well—making it harder to detect impacts on labor market outcomes either way. But, if market rigidities (such as minimum wage laws) make it difficult for the uncovered sectors to absorb the surplus workers, the positive effects on wages and negative effects on employment levels for the covered workers are more likely to be observed in the market overall.

The magnitude of these effects (for any given level of mandated wages and coverage) will also be determined primarily by the "elasticity of labor demand" in the covered sector, which measures the degree to which employer demand for (or hiring of) workers responds to market wages. The more elastic (or flatter)

8. D, S, and F in this diagram represent "demand," "supply," and "wage floor," respectively.
9. The extra jobs in the uncovered sectors are generated because wages are reduced in those sectors to accommodate the workers who move there after losing their jobs in the covered sector, and that creates enough extra jobs to employ them. These are known as "general equilibrium" effects in the labor market. See, for example, Mincer (1976); Johnson and Mieszkowski (1970).

Figure 5-2. *Employment Effects of Wage Floors*

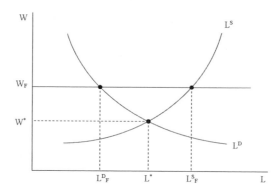

this curve, the greater the responsiveness of employers to wages and the greater the potential negative effect of higher mandated wages on employment levels.

This elasticity, in turn, will be affected by a few characteristics of this labor market. For one thing, firms that supply services to government agencies operate in less competitive "product markets" than most other firms, since public agencies face less competition for the services they provide than does the private sector.[10] All else equal, less competitive product markets generate lower elasticities of labor demand because it is easier for firms to raise prices to cover the higher wages they pay without reducing product demand and employment. Whether this is also true of firms receiving financial assistance from local governments is less clear a priori. Whether or how most local governments can easily absorb the higher costs associated with such labor, in an era of widespread fiscal tightness, is less clear as well.

The size of the jurisdiction covered by these laws could also affect labor demand elasticities. All else equal, firms in larger covered geographic jurisdictions or in those where contiguous municipalities are also covered by similar laws will likely face less competition from other (uncovered) firms than those in smaller areas with fewer covered neighbors, thereby making it easier for the former to raise wages without generating employment losses or displacements. Covered firms might have less incentive to relocate geographically to avoid the higher mandated costs of labor under these circumstances as well.[11]

This, of course, raises the possibility that the laws passed in any particular jurisdiction might create *geographic spillovers* onto other local areas. If the employers directly affected by these laws choose to relocate, this might benefit workers in the

10. Ehrenberg and Smith (2005).

11. This discussion assumes that the covered employers are all located nearby in the same geographic area. For firms with municipal contracts, that might not actually be the case.

uncovered areas (by generating more jobs nearby for them and maybe raising local "wage norms" there) while disadvantaging workers somewhat in the covered area—who now might also face longer commutes to avoid job loss.

Also, the higher wages at these firms might also generate some positive effects on their worker retention rates, job performance, and perhaps even skills, as workers with more ability might now apply for these jobs and try harder to keep them after being hired. These effects are associated with the notion of "efficiency wages" in the economics literature; they suggest that sometimes it is in the interest of employers to pay above-market wages, since the quality of the workers whom they hire and retain might fully or partially offset their higher costs.[12] They also imply that demand for some groups of slightly more skilled workers might actually rise over time, even while those of the least skilled decline.

All else equal, the effects of higher wages on firm costs (and therefore on product prices and employment levels) will be higher if the production process for the firm's goods or services is more labor intensive, and most services provided by municipal contractors are likely quite labor intensive. However, if the numbers of covered workers at these firms are relatively small in comparison to their overall workforces, the effects of the mandate might not be very large, even on the quantities and prices of services provided. Indeed, Robert Pollin and Stephanie Luce argued that living wages in Los Angeles have raised operating costs for contractors by 1 to 2 percent and costs to the city by less than 1 percent.[13]

A few other caveats should be noted that might further reduce the likelihood of adverse employment effects associated with living wage ordinances. For one thing, other imperfections, such as limited market competition, might render the analysis above less valid and concerns about job losses less pressing.[14] If these laws are passed in strong labor markets where job growth has been robust, any fears regarding job loss might also be less of a concern, as job availability might still be ample to provide jobs to most or all who seek them.[15] And even the notion of a well-defined demand curve might be challenged, since local govern-

12. Katz (1986).

13. Pollin and Luce (1998).

14. If, for instance, the labor market is characterized by "monopsony"—in which employers face very little competition for the workers whom they hire—then market forces generate wages below the competitive level, and a government wage mandate could actually raise employment levels as well as wages. See Ehrenberg and Smith (2005). But whether the labor markets in question might really be characterized by monopsony power is quite doubtful, in my view.

15. Even in these cases, there might be job losses relative to what might exist in the absence of the living wage ordinance, but the employment prospects of low-wage workers might not be negatively affected, as the losses are fully offset by other sources of job growth. As an example, when the federal minimum wage was raised in 1996–97, job growth in U.S. labor markets at that time seemed sufficiently strong to offset any losses that might otherwise have been observed.

ments and voters must make choices without any real information about how employers will actually respond to higher mandated wages—though employers will no doubt plead hardship and predict reduced hiring during any such campaign.[16] In this case, the nature of the interaction between public and private actors is more uncertain than the analysis above would indicate.

Finally, the effects of living wage ordinances might also go beyond the labor market outcomes considered above. For example, if higher mandated wages do generate higher costs and prices at contractor firms, local public services might be reduced or taxes might have to rise to offset the higher costs. These developments, in turn, might disproportionately hurt lower-income residents of cities, who are relatively more dependent on these services than are other residents. But if there is already some slack in city budgets, or if the magnitudes of services affected by these higher costs are small, any impacts on the costs or availability of services in urban areas will be mitigated.

In sum, the mandating of higher wages in a very limited sector of the local workforce might reduce employment there, but the magnitudes of these effects will depend on a variety of market factors and might well be offset by a variety of forces in that market.

Evidence on the Effects of Living Wage Laws

How are the effects of living wage laws on outcomes such as wages, employment, family incomes, and poverty rates inferred? The literature can be largely divided into two categories: studies of differences *across* cities that have or have not implemented these laws and studies *within* cities that compare firms and workers covered with those that are not.

In both cases, studies of the effects of these laws are somewhat limited by data availability, especially at the level of the firm. Furthermore, in both cases, major questions exist about identifying comparable workers, from whom the counterfactual wage and employment levels for affected workers in the absence of these laws can then be inferred.

Cross-City Studies

Most of the studies of the effects of living wage laws that are based on evidence across cities have been generated by Scott Adams and David Neumark.[17] Adams

16. Economists might characterize this situation as one of "asymmetric information," in which employers know how they intend to respond to the passage of prospective living wage ordinances, but the public does not and can only speculate about that.

17. Their several papers on this issue are summarized in Adams and Neumark (2004, 2005).

and Neumark used data from the Outgoing Rotation Groups of the Current Population Survey (CPS-ORG) for their analyses. The CPS-ORG is a large monthly survey of about 50,000 households, used by the federal government to calculate monthly employment rates. Since participating households stay in the sample for four months in each of two different time periods (separated by eight months), the ORG sample limits the sample to include only those answering the survey for the last time, thus ensuring they will appear in any statistical analysis only once.

Using CPS-ORG data for the period 1996–2002, Adams and Neumark estimated regression equations to analyze the relationship between the wages, employment levels, and poverty status of individuals and whether or not their city has a living wage law, controlling for many other characteristics of the individuals and where they live. The details of this estimation are provided in the appendix.

Generally, the Adams and Neumark papers showed the following:

—Wages of low-wage workers are modestly higher in cities that have passed living wage ordinances than in those that have not.

—Employment levels of these workers are modestly lower in these cities.

—Poverty rates are lower in these cities as well.

The magnitudes of these estimated effects often differ quite substantially between those in the bottom tenth of workers and those between the tenth and fiftieth percentiles.[18] Furthermore, the estimated effects also differ between laws covering contractors and those covering firms obtaining financial assistance, and they also vary according to the lag imposed on the law's passage.

For example, a 50 percent increase in any type of specified living wage (relative to the minimum wage) raises wages of workers in the bottom tenth by 2 percent after a one-year lag, though this effect is not statistically significant.[19] It raises wages by about 1 percent for those between the tenth and fiftieth percentiles, regardless of how long a time lag is allowed between the effective date of the living wage law and the time at which potential effects of the law are measured (with a six-month lag showing the most significant results). But contractor-only laws generate few significant positive effects on wages at all, while the effects on wages for business assistance laws are more consistently positive and significant for both groups.[20]

18. By definition, 10 percent of workers earn less than the 10th percentile and 90 percent earn more. Half of workers earn less than the 50th percentile and half earn more.

19. Adams and Neumark (2005). Statistical significance is measured at the 0.10 level in this chapter.

20. Specifically, wages rise by about 3 percent for the lowest tenth of workers with a 50 percent increase in the living wage mandated for firms receiving business assistance relative to the minimum wage after a one-year lag; and this type of living wage law raises the wages of

As for employment effects, Adams and Neumark found that a 50 percent increase in the living wage reduces employment 6 percent among those in the bottom tenth of wages, with a one-year lag; the effect is again largest (nearly 9 percent) for business assistance laws and smallest (and insignificant) for contractor laws. No negative employment effects are observed for those in the tenth to fiftieth percentiles of the wage distribution. Regarding poverty, Adams and Neumark estimated that a 50 percent increase in the living wage reduced the number of families below the poverty line by 1 to 2 percent, with much smaller changes for those below subpoverty thresholds.

The last of these findings is quite striking, since it implies that the positive effects of living wage ordinances on wages more than offset their negative effects on employment, even though the estimated magnitudes of the former are not always greater than the latter. This finding is also noteworthy, since it is the opposite of what Neumark found (in his work with William Wascher) on the effects of minimum wage increases at the state or federal levels.[21]

Adams and Neumark attributed their findings on poverty to the apparent fact that employers in covered firms shift employment away from those in the bottom tenth of workers and toward those somewhat higher in the wage distribution, whose skills are presumably stronger and more likely merit the now-higher wages that are mandated. Indeed, this interpretation is consistent with the changes in the relative employment rates of the two groups associated with living wages in their studies.

To bolster this interpretation, Adams and Neumark also showed that poor families are more likely to be included in both categories of lower-wage workers; but that those further below the poverty threshold contain relatively more workers from the lowest tenth of wages, while those nearer the top of the threshold contain relatively more workers between the tenth and fiftieth percentiles.[22] They argued that those in the latter group are more likely to be pushed just over the poverty threshold by living wage laws, while those in the former group were and remain further below that threshold.

Thus, the improvement in poverty rates associated with living wage laws does not necessarily imply uniformly positive effects of these laws on labor market outcomes of the working poor. Rather, Adams and Neumark's estimates suggest somewhat more negative effects for the bottom rung of workers in these cities, whose employment is most reduced by the presence of these laws, and more

---

those in the tenth to fiftieth percentiles by 1 to 2 percent regardless of how long a time lag is allowed.

21. Neumark and Wascher (2006).

22. Of course, very young workers in middle- or upper-income families can also be found in large numbers among those in the bottom tenth or tenth to fiftieth percentiles of the wage distribution.

positive effects for those slightly higher (but still well below the median) in the distribution of workers, who show no negative employment effects associated with these laws.

If correct, this interpretation might also account for why living wage laws appear to reduce poverty in their work, while minimum wage laws seem to increase it. Adams and Neumark speculated that living wage laws affect workers high enough in the skills distribution such that they maintain employment, while those affected by minimum wage laws are more concentrated among the bottom rung of adults whose employment is more negatively affected by either type of law.

A few other findings by Adams and Neumark are noteworthy as well. For one thing, their results suggest that the impacts of living wage laws depend on geographic coverage and implementation. Specifically, they showed that county-wide living wage laws, and those in cities where other nearby cities also have such laws, have the largest positive effects on observed wages of workers in the bottom tenth. In the case of countywide laws, negative effects on employment are also reduced—consistent with the notion mentioned above of more limited competition from other lower-wage firms in these situations. The magnitudes of wage gains and employment losses for these workers are also greater (though not always significantly so) when community hiring is specified, when these laws are superseded by collective bargaining, when contractor coverage is relatively broad, and when enforcement and implementation of the laws are stricter and more aggressive.[23] These findings thus confirm the notion that the context and specific features of how these laws are designed and implemented have important effects on their outcomes.[24]

One troubling aspect of the work by Adams and Neumark is that their results, both positive and negative, seem too large, especially given the small numbers of workers directly affected by these laws. For example, if just 2 to 3 percent of workers in the bottom tenth are directly affected by these laws, then a 50 percent increase in the living wage must generate more than that amount of wage increase for the affected workers to raise their overall wages by 2 percent, as specified above. Since four times as many workers are found in the tenth to fiftieth percentiles as in the bottom tenth, fewer than 1 percent of workers in the former category should be affected by living wage laws. Yet 50 percent increases in the living wage raise wages for this entire category of workers by 1 percent or more in their estimates. The employment declines estimated for

23. See Adams and Neumark (2004, 2005) for exactly how they define each of these characteristics.

24. The effects of other design features, such as the handling of health insurance and other benefits, have not been studied to date.

those in the bottom tenth and noted above (as large as 6 to 9 percent in some cases) also seem too big, especially relative to the wage increases estimated for this group.

Mark Brenner, Jeannette Wicks-Lim, and Robert Pollin also criticized Adams and Neumark's work.[25] Specifically, their criticisms were the following: Adams and Neumark's limiting their samples to workers in the bottom tenth (or even the tenth to fiftieth percentiles) generated sample selection biases; subminimum-wage workers are very unlikely to be covered by living wage ordinances and therefore should not be in the sample; business assistance laws are often enforced very weakly and cannot really generate the kinds of stronger effects that were estimated by Adams and Neumark; and coverage of cities in their sample is heavily tilted toward Los Angeles along with some other very large cities. Indeed, they argued that Adams and Neumark's results were quite sensitive to these specification issues.[26]

In turn, Adams and Neumark responded to many of these criticisms, especially the ones regarding sample selection bias and the reach of business assistance laws.[27] Though I find their arguments more compelling than those of their critics on many of these issues, some concerns over sample sizes and representativeness both within and across their cities remain. And questions about why some cities implement living wage ordinances in the first place, while others do not—even within a sample of cities in which campaigns are attempted—raise concerns about whether treatment and control cities are truly comparable in all other dimensions but the living wage measure.

Studies within Cities

A series of studies has also been done that focuses on specific cities in which living wage ordinances have been implemented. Generally, these studies attempt to define groups of workers or firms that are relatively comparable with one another, except that one group should be affected by the passage of these laws and the other should not be. They then compare wage growth across the two groups of workers or firms after the passage of the living wage ordinance.[28] Of

25. Brenner, Wicks-Lim, and Pollin (2002) actually focus on an earlier paper by Neumark (2002) in their critique. But most features of that paper to which they object have been retained in subsequent analyses by Adams and Neumark.

26. Sample selection biases may occur when statistical estimates are based on a sample (in this case, low-wage workers) that is not representative of the entire population (in this case, all workers regardless of wage level). Such biases may be an especially important problem when, as in Adams and Neumark's work, the dependent variable in the regressions (that is, the wage) is being used to define the sample.

27. Adams and Neumark (2004).

28. In so doing, these studies mostly generate difference-in-difference estimates of the impacts of the ordinances on workers' wages.

course, open to question in virtually every study are several factors; the extent to which the two groups are really comparable, the extent to which the living wage law affects one group but not the other, and the extent to which the living wage law differentially affects the two groups.

For instance, Michael Reich, Peter Hall, and Ken Jacobs analyzed the extension of San Francisco's living wage law in 1999 to cover workers at the San Francisco International Airport.[29] They combined data from establishments at the airport, surveys of workers there, and administrative data. The study found strong positive effects on the lowest-paid workers' wages and on reductions in inequality across worker groups. The positive effects at the bottom of the spectrum generated ripple effects on wages above those levels. They also found evidence of lower turnover and improved morale among workers. Additional costs to employers were estimated to be less than 1 percent of revenue. Finally, they found no evidence of reduced employment between 1998 and 2001. In fact, employment at the airport rose considerably during this time period.

However, it is noteworthy that this study contained no control group at all. A new international terminal was opened at the airport during this time period, and no doubt the terminal contributed importantly to rising employment. Absent the extension of the living wage law, it is impossible to know what the counterfactual level of employment would have been, and whether or how much decline there might have been because of that extension.

David Fairris analyzed the effects of a living wage ordinance in Los Angeles, using data on 75 contractor firms and 210 noncontractors.[30] Controlling for observable characteristics of these firms (size, union status, and profits), he found higher wages for low-wage workers, though no change in benefit levels. He also found reductions in turnover and absenteeism, as well as cuts in overtime hours and job training. And he found modest reduction of employment of 1.6 percent overall at contractor firms relative to noncontractor ones, which presumably was concentrated among (and represents an even higher percentage of) low-wage worker employment.[31] In another study using these data, Fairris and Leon Fernandez Bujanda found that newly hired workers after the passage of the ordinance were older, more educated, and had already been earning higher wages elsewhere, thus offsetting as much as 40 percent of the wage gains generated by the ordinance (in their estimates).[32]

29. Reich, Hall, and Jacobs (2005).
30. Fairris (2005).
31. Indeed, Adams and Neumark claim that the reduction in employment among low-wage workers is likely two to three times as large in magnitude as the 1.6 percent figure suggests, since low-wage workers constitute one-third to one-half of total employment.
32. Fairris and Bujanda (2008).

Finally, Mark Brenner concentrated on the effects of a new living wage law in Boston, by analyzing fifteen service contractor firms that were affected by the law (because they hired low-wage workers) and fifty-one firms unaffected (because they did not).[33] Like the other studies, Brenner found that wages rose among the least-paid workers and that inequality declined at the firms affected by the new law. He found little effect on turnover and absenteeism and a reduction in the fraction of part-time workers. While Brenner claimed that there was no reduction in employment at the affected firms, Adams and Neumark pointed out that employment grew relatively more rapidly (by about 10 percent) at the unaffected firms during the same period.[34]

From these types of studies, it is impossible to infer the broader effects of living wage ordinances on the local labor markets in which they occur and the magnitudes of effects on both wages and employment there. For instance, when employment grows less rapidly at covered firms, we do not know whether or where the workers who otherwise would have worked at these firms become employed, nor at what wages. But the observed reductions in part-time (or overtime) employment and in relative employment at these firms in both the Brenner and Fairris papers are consistent with modest reductions in labor demand and a reallocation of labor across firms, as emphasized in basic economic models of the labor market. Positive effects on turnover and morale are additional benefits that likely offset part of the higher costs to employers, but these do not necessarily offset those costs entirely. Whether or not the affected employers shift their hiring to those with more skills in response to the mandated payments of higher wages, as Adams and Neumark have suggested, has also not been determined in any of these studies.

Conclusion

In this chapter I have reviewed the likely effects of living wage ordinances on employment outcomes, at least according to economic theory, as well as evidence on their actual effects. The evidence includes studies across cities that have or have not implemented these ordinances, using data from the Current Population Survey, as well as several studies focusing on smaller samples of workers or firms or both within specific cities that have passed these ordinances.

Both types of studies have clear limitations. Yet there is some consensus across most of them that wages rise among the least-paid workers, while their employment levels modestly decline (at the covered firms and maybe more broadly) as a result of these laws. There appears to be some evidence of lower turnover and

33. Brenner (2005).
34. Adams and Neumark (2005).

better morale as well, although this might be partly driven by changes in the nature of workers hired as a result of the laws. There is also some evidence of reduced training and reduced use of part-time or overtime work on the part of employers as additional ways of offsetting their now-higher labor costs.

The cross-city work of Adams and Neumark has generated the additional finding that the implementation of living wage laws might be associated with modest reductions in poverty. This stands in sharp contrast to earlier work by Neumark on the effects of minimum wage increases. But Adams and Neumark also suggested that the poverty reductions are likely driven by improved wage and employment outcomes among workers whose wages are below the median but above the bottom tenth. In contrast, their work suggested that employment declines most for those in the bottom group.

Finally, it is clear from all of these studies that any effects of living wage laws—positive and negative—are extremely modest in magnitude, since very few low-wage workers are actually affected by these laws and the impacts per worker are quite modest. The possibility that living wage ordinances on their own might help build a middle class is very remote. Indeed, one might apply a version of Henry Kissinger's description of academic politics to the study of living wage laws—namely, that the politics are so fierce while (or maybe because) the stakes are so very small.

It is not at all clear how the scope of living wage laws might be expanded so that they could affect more workers. But, even if it were known how to do so, their potential negative as well as positive effects might grow in overall magnitude. As such, the usefulness of this particular tool as a means of combating growing labor market inequality will necessarily be limited.

This does not mean, in my view, that living wage laws should not be passed. Generating some very modest net benefits for workers with below-average wages, especially in poor households, is arguably better than generating none at all. In a world where few other tools might realistically be available to directly raise the wages of low earners, perhaps living wage ordinances should be thought of as one of the few policy tools available in a very imperfect and constrained situation for the advocates of low-wage workers. Moreover, perhaps other goals—such as limiting the outsourcing of municipal work and the use of public money to subsidize large companies through economic development—have been accomplished through living wage ordinances as well.

Furthermore, if placed within the context of broader campaigns to improve the wages and benefits of less-skilled workers in the private sector, the living wage battles might play some useful symbolic role and raise awareness of pay disparity issues. Expanding collective bargaining, for example, would likely have far greater impacts, and perhaps living wage campaigns can be part of broader efforts to do so. But living wage campaigns must then be viewed as complements to, not substitutes for, these other efforts.

It seems that a few other lessons might be derived from this work. For one thing, attempts to address labor market inequality through public mandates alone inevitably generate the risks of trade-offs between wage levels and employment. The possibility of trade-offs does not necessarily imply that these mandates have no role—only that they entail potential costs as well as benefits. This notion is also true of higher minimum wages and expanded collective bargaining—especially in a world where new technologies, immigration, and offshoring present employers with many more options for offsetting higher wages than they had in the past. In other words, labor demand has likely grown more elastic (wage sensitive) over time, which results in greater inequality and more serious constraints in the efforts to reverse it through government dictates.

Efforts to reverse wage inequality will likely require a wide range of efforts, including much more education and training, and publicly financed benefits (like health insurance and parental leave) that do not induce employers to respond to higher labor costs with employment reductions. Efforts to support the creation of higher-wage jobs—through tax credits for training or job upgrading, technical assistance, as well as mandates—also need to be part of the equation.[35] Battles to expand social justice by directly raising the wages of a small group of workers might contribute to these broader efforts, but their own limited direct effects should be acknowledged.

35. Holzer (2007).

Appendix

Using Current Population Survey Outgoing Rotation Groups (CPS-ORG) data for the period 1996–2002, Adams and Neumark have estimated equations of the following form:

$$Y_{ikt} = f(LW_{kt}; X_{it}; X_{kt}) + u_{ikt},$$

where Y represents the log of the wage, employment, or poverty status of the individual, i; LW represents the log of the living wage for city k and for month and year t (and is set to zero where no such wage exists); X represents certain control variables for characteristics of people or their cities and states; u is a residual.

The samples are frequently limited to workers aged 16–70 in the bottom tenth of workers in each metro area, or sometimes those between the tenth and fiftieth percentiles. Personal characteristics for which controls are included are generally age, sex, race, education. and marital status. Time and city dummies are included to control for average local unemployment rates and average wages; state-level statutory minimum wages during the relevant period, as well as time trends for cities with and without living wages at any point in time, are included as controls as well.

LW appears either contemporaneously or in lagged form (by six months or one year). Sometimes a single LW variable is used to represent the presence of living wage laws, while in other cases, separate variables are included for cities with provisions covering contractors as opposed to firms receiving city assistance.

Only those cities with at least twenty-five low-wage workers appearing in the sample in any specified month are included in the sample. This condition, along with the fact that the CPS only identifies the larger metropolitan areas to start with, implies that the sample of cities is quite highly skewed toward the largest. Finally, to account for differences in unobserved characteristics between cities that choose to implement living wage laws and those that do not, at least one of Adams and Neumark's papers limits the sample only to those cities that have at least tried to pass a living wage law in a local referendum, either successfully or not.[36]

---

36. Adams and Neumark (2003).

Table 5A-1. *Summary of U.S. Living Wage Ordinances*

Municipality or county	Adoption date	Living wage with health insurance	Coverage without health insurance	Local government employees	Public contracts	Financial assistance	Local minimum wage	Notes
Ventura, CA	May 2006	$9.75	$12.50	Yes	Yes	No	No	
Manchester, CT	April 2006	$11.06	$14.00	No	Yes	Yes	No	
Miami, FL	April 2006	$10.58	$11.83	Yes	Yes	No	No	
Albuquerque, NM	April 2006	n.a.	$7.50	Yes	No	No	No	Final wage level of $7.50 to be phased in by 2009.
Sandia Pueblo, NM	April 2006	n.a.	$8.18	Yes	Yes	Yes	Yes	
Santa Barbara, CA	March 2006	$12.00	$14.00	No	Yes	No	No	Living wage set at $11.00 for employers who provide additional benefits to employees.
Washington, DC	January 2006	n.a.	$11.75	No	Yes	Yes	No	Additionally, a citywide minimum wage is set at $7.00 per hour or $1.00 above the federal minimum wage, whichever is greater.
Nassau County, NY	December 2005	n.a.	$12.50	No	Yes	No	No	Final wage level of $12.50 to be phased in by 2010.
Albany, NY	September 2005	n.a.	$10.25	No	Yes	Yes	No	Living wage level is indexed to rise with the consumer price index.
Brookline, MA	May 2005	n.a.	$10.30	No	Yes	No	No	
Syracuse, NY	May 2005	$10.08	$11.91	No	Yes	No	No	Living wage level is indexed to rise with the consumer price index. Only employees working 30 years or more are covered.
Philadelphia, PA	May 2005	n.a.	$7.73	Yes	Yes	No	No	Living wage level is set to 150 percent of the higher of federal or state minimum wage.
Eau Claire, WI	May 2005	n.a.	$5.65	Yes	Yes	Yes	Yes	Repealed by state law in June 2005.
Lacrosse, WI	April 2005	n.a.	$5.70	Yes	Yes	Yes	Yes	Repealed by state law in June 2005.
Santa Monica, CA	March 2005	n.a.	$12.10	No	Yes	No	No	Previous living wage ordinance passed in 2001, repealed in 2002.
Bloomington, IN	March 2005	$8.50	$10.00	No	Yes	Yes	No	Living wage level is indexed to rise with the consumer price index.
Milwaukee, WI	February 2005	n.a.	$7.98	Yes	Yes	Yes	Yes	Repealed by state law in June 2005.
Sonoma, CA	July 2004	$11.70	$13.20	Yes	Yes	Yes	No	Living wage level is indexed to rise with the consumer price index.

Location	Date							Notes
Durham County, NC	June 2004	n.a.	$10.34	Yes	Yes	No	No	Living wage level is set at 7.5 percent above the federal poverty level for a family of four.
Lincoln, NE	March 2004	$9.62	$10.58	No	Yes	No	No	Living wage level is set at 100 percent (w/health insurance) or 110 percent (w/o health insurance) of the federal poverty level for a family of four.
Sacramento, CA	December 2003	$9.67	$11.17	Yes	Yes	No	No	Living wage level is indexed to rise with the consumer price index.
Sebastopol, CA	December 2003	See notes.	$13.20	Yes	Yes	Yes	No	Employers may deduct health-care costs from the wage level. Living wage level is indexed to rise with the federal cost of living adjustment for the San Francisco area.
Lawrence, KS	October 2003	$11.00	$12.50	No	No	Yes	No	Living wage level is set at 130 percent of the federal poverty level for a family of three.
Port Hueneme, CA	October 2003	$9.00	$11.50	No	Yes	No	No	Employers may deduct health-care costs from the wage level (up to 20 percent of the wage). Living wage level is set at 125 percent of the federal poverty level for a family of four.
Lansing, MI	September 2003	$10.60	$13.25	No	Yes	Yes	No	
Orlando, FL	August 2003	$8.50	$10.20	Yes	Yes	Yes	No	Living wage level is indexed to rise with the consumer price index.
Lakewood, OH	July 2003	$10.28	$11.39	Yes	Yes	Yes	No	
Dayton, OH	July 2003	$9.30	$11.16	No	Yes	No	No	Living wage level is set at 100 percent (w/health insurance) or 120 percent (w/o health insurance) of the federal poverty level for a family of four.
Arlington, VA	June 2003	n.a.	$11.20	No	Yes	No	No	Employers may deduct health-care costs from the wage level (up to 20 percent of the wage). Living wage level is set at 125 percent of the federal poverty level for a family of four.
Ingham County, MI	June 2003	$10.00	$12.50	Yes	Yes	No	No	
Prince George's Co., MD	June 2003	n.a.	$11.25	No	Yes	Yes	No	Living wage level is indexed to rise with the consumer price index.
Palm Beach Co., FL	February 2003	n.a.	$10.39	No	Yes	No	No	Living wage level is indexed to rise with the consumer price index.
Santa Fe, NM	February 2003	n.a.	$10.50	Yes	Yes	Yes	Yes	Living wage level is indexed to rise with the consumer price index.

Table 5A-1. *Summary of U.S. Living Wage Ordinances* (continued)

Municipality or county	Adoption date	Living wage with health insurance	Coverage without health insurance	Local government employees	Public contracts	Financial assistance	Local minimum wage	Notes
Cincinnati, OH	November 2002	$9.23	$10.80	Yes	Yes	No	No	Living wage level is adjusted annually by the percentage increase in the federal poverty guidelines.
Louisville, KY	November 2002	$11.00	n.a.	Yes	Yes	No	No	Health care must be provided on top of the living wage. Living wage level is indexed to rise with the federal cost of living adjustment.
Bellingham, WA	November 2002	$10.81	$12.43	No	Yes	No	No	Living wage level is adjusted annually by the percentage change in the Implicit Price Deflator.
Westchester Co., NY	November 2002	$11.50	$13.00	No	Yes	Yes	No	Living wage level is set at 100 percent (w/health insurance) or 125 percent (w/o health insurance) of the federal poverty level for a family of four.
Taylor, MI	November 2002	$9.67	$12.09	No	Yes	No	No	
Broward County, FL	October 2002	$10.15	$11.48	Yes	Yes	No	No	Living wage level is indexed to rise with the federal cost of living adjustment.
Watsonville, CA	September 2002	$12.43	$13.56	No	Yes	No	No	Living wage level is indexed to rise with the consumer price index.
Fairfax, CA	August 2002	$13.00	$14.75	Yes	Yes	Yes	No	Living wage level is set at 100 percent (w/health insurance) or 125 percent (w/o health insurance) of the federal poverty level for a family of four.
Southfield, MI	July 2002	$10.00	$12.50	No	Yes	Yes	No	
Oxnard, CA	July 2002	n/a	$12.88	No	Yes	No	No	
Montgomery Co., MD	July 2002	n/a	$11.60	No	Yes	No	No	Citywide minimum wage is set at $1.00 above the federal minimum wage.
New Orleans, LA	February 2002	n/a	$6.85	Yes	Yes	Yes	Yes	Repealed in June 2002.
Hazel Park, MI	February 2002	n.a.	n.a.	n.a.	n.a.	n.a.	n.a.	
Marin County, CA	January 2002	$9.50	$10.75	Yes	Yes	No	No	Living wage level is indexed to rise with the consumer price index.
Pima County, AZ	January 2002	$8.60	$9.67	Yes	No	No	No	

Location	Date						Notes
Bozeman, MT	December 2001	$9.00	$10.06	No	Yes	No	Yes	Living wage level is indexed to rise with the consumer price index.
Santa Cruz Co., CA	December 2001	$12.43	$13.56	No	No	Yes	No	Living wage level is indexed to rise with the consumer price index.
New Britain, CT	December 2001	n.a.	$10.97	No	No	Yes	No	Living wage level is set at 118 of the federal poverty level for a family of four.
Cumberland Co., NJ	December 2001	$10.87	$8.50	No	No	Yes	No	Employers who do not provide a pension benefit must add a further $1.25 to the hourly wage.
Camden, NJ	December 2001	$8.00	$9.50	No	No	Yes	No	Repealed in January 2003.
Burlington, VT	November 2001	$12.02	$13.49	No	Yes	Yes	Yes	Living wage level is indexed to rise with the state-level cost of living adjustment.
Charlottesville, VA	November 2001	n.a.	$9.73	No	No	Yes	No	
Richmond, CA	October 2001	$11.42	$12.92	No	Yes	Yes	No	Living wage level is adjusted annually by the percentage increase in wages under citywide employee labor agreements.
Washtenaw Co., MI	October 2001	$9.87	$11.58	No	No	Yes	No	Repealed in December 2001.
Hempstead, NY	October 2001	$9.00	$10.25	No	Yes	Yes	No	Repealed in March 2003.
Monroe Co., MI	October 2001	$8.70	$10.20	No	No	Yes	Yes	
Ashland, OR	September 2001	See notes.	$12.43	No	Yes	Yes	Yes	Employers may deduct health-care costs and other benefits from the wage level. Living wage level is indexed to rise with the consumer price index.
Oyster Bay, NY	August 2001	$9.00	$10.25	No	No	Yes	No	Only employees in janitorial and security jobs are covered.
Gloucester Co., NJ	August 2001	$8.50	$10.87	No	No	Yes	No	Living wage level is set at the greater of $8.50 per hour or the federal poverty level.
Suffolk County, NY	July 2001	$10.02	$11.41	No	Yes	Yes	No	
Pittsburgh, PA	May 2001	$9.12	$10.62	No	Yes	Yes	Yes	Repealed in March 2002.
Ventura County, CA	May 2001	$9.00	$2.00	No	No	Yes	No	
Miami Beach, FL	April 2001	$8.56	$9.81	No	No	Yes	Yes	Living wage level is indexed to rise with the consumer price index.
Pittsfield Twnshp., MI	April 2001	$9.88	$11.58	No	Yes	Yes	No	Living wage level is indexed to rise with the consumer price index.
Eastpointe, MI	March 2001	$10.00	$12.50	No	Yes	Yes	No	Living wage level is set at 100 percent (w/health insurance) or 125 percent (w/o health insurance) of the federal poverty level for a family of four.

Table 5A-1. *Summary of U.S. Living Wage Ordinances (continued)*

Municipality or county	Adoption date	Living wage with health insurance	Coverage without health insurance	Local government employees	Public contracts	Financial assistance	Local minimum wage	Notes
Missoula, MT	March 2001	$9.22	n.a.	No	No	Yes	No	Living wage level is set to at least match the pay of the lowest-paid city full-time employee. Health benefits must also be provided.
Ann Arbor, MI	March 2001	$9.91	$11.48	No	Yes	Yes	No	Living wage level is adjusted annually by the percentage increase in the federal poverty guidelines.
Ferndale, MI	February 2001	$8.50	$9.75	No	Yes	No	No	Living wage level is indexed to rise with the consumer price index.
Rochester, NY	January 2001	$9.68	$10.81	No	Yes	Yes	No	
Salem, OR	January 2001	$9.50	$11.00	Yes	No	No	No	Repealed in January 2003.
Meriden, CT	November 2000	$10.64	See notes.	No	Yes	No	No	Living wage level is set at 110 percent (w/health insurance) of the federal poverty level for a family of four. If health insurance is not provided, the employer must pay an additional hourly sum determined by the city based on average costs of comprehensive health insurance in the state.
Santa Cruz, CA	October 2000	$12.43	$13.56	Yes	Yes	No	No	
Eau Claire Co., WI	September 2000	$7.53	$8.29	No	Yes	No	No	Repealed by state law in June 2005.
San Francisco, CA	August 2000	See notes.	$11.03	No	Yes	No	No	Covered employers must provide health insurance or pay $1.25 per worker per hour into the city's public health system fund. Additionally, a citywide minimum wage is set at $9.36 per hour and is indexed to rise with the consumer price index.
St. Louis, MO	August 2000	$10.31	$13.18	No	Yes	Yes	No	Living wage level is defined as a wage sufficient to lift a family of three above the eligibility level for food stamps.
Berkeley, CA	June 2000	$11.39	$13.28	Yes	Yes	Yes	No	Amended in October 2000 to include all employees at the city marina.
Cleveland, OH	June 2000	n.a.	$10.00	No	Yes	Yes	No	Only employees working at least 30 hours per week are covered.

Location	Date							Notes
Alexandria, VA	June 2000	n.a.	$12.75	No	No	Yes	No	Living wage level is indexed annually to the poverty threshold for a family of four in combination with costs for health insurance.
Toledo, OH	June 2000	$10.57	$12.50	No	Yes	Yes	No	Living wage level is set at 110 percent (w/health insurance) or 130 percent (w/o health insurance) of the federal poverty level for a family of four.
Omaha, NE	April 2000	n.a.	n.a.	Yes	Yes	Yes	No	Repealed in September 2001. Living wage level was set at 100 percent (w/health insurance) or 110 percent (w/o health insurance) of the federal poverty level for a family of four.
San Fernando, CA	April 2000	$7.75	$8.82	No	Yes	Yes	No	Wages are adjusted annually based on changes in the state employment retirement system.
Denver, CO	February 2000	n.a.	$9.62	No	No	Yes	No	Only employees in the following jobs are covered: parking lot attendant, security guard, clerical support worker, childcare worker. Living wage level is set at 100 percent of the federal poverty level for a family of four.
Warren, MI	January 2000	$9.68	$12.09	No	Yes	Yes	No	Living wage level is set at 100 percent (w/health insurance) or 125 percent (w/o health insurance) of the federal poverty level for a family of four.
Corvallis, OR	November 1999	n.a.	$10.47	No	No	Yes	No	Living wage level is indexed to rise with the consumer price index.
Hartford, CT	September 1999	$10.58	$15.39	No	Yes	Yes	No	Living wage level is set at 110 percent (w/health insurance) of the federal poverty level for a family of four.
Tucson, AZ	September 1999	$9.17	$10.32	No	No	Yes	No	Living wage level is indexed to rise with the consumer price index.
Buffalo, NY	August 1999	$9.03	$10.15	No	No	Yes	No	
Los Angeles Co., CA	June 1999	$8.32	$9.46	No	No	Yes	No	
Ypsilanti, MI	June 1999	$8.50	$10.00	No	Yes	Yes	No	
Ypsilanti Twnshp., MI	June 1999	$8.50	$10.00	No	Yes	Yes	No	
Somerville, MA	May 1999	n.a.	$10.51	Yes	No	Yes	No	
Miami-Dade Co., FL	May 1999	$9.81	$11.23	Yes	No	Yes	No	Living wage level is set at 100 percent of the federal poverty level for a family of four.

Table 5A-1. *Summary of U.S. Living Wage Ordinances (continued)*

Municipality or county	Adoption date	Living wage with health insurance	Coverage without health insurance	Local government employees	Public contracts	Financial assistance	Local minimum wage	Notes
Cambridge, MA	May 1999	n.a.	$12.19	Yes	Yes	Yes	No	Living wage level is indexed to rise with the consumer price index.
Hayward, CA	April 1999	$9.71	$11.20	Yes	Yes	No	No	Living wage level is indexed to rise with the area cost of living adjustment.
Madison, WI	March 1999	n.a.	$10.92	Yes	Yes	Yes	No	Living wage level is set at 110 percent of the federal poverty level for a family of four.
Dane County, WI	March 1999	n.a.	$9.31	Yes	Yes	Yes	No	Living wage level is set at 100 percent of the federal poverty level for a family of four.
Hudson County, NJ	January 1999	$7.73	n.a.	No	Yes	No	No	Living wage level is set at 150 percent of the federal minimum wage. Only employees in security, food service, and janitorial jobs working at least 20 hours per week are covered. Health benefits must also be provided.
San Jose, CA	November 1998	$12.20	$13.52	No	Yes	Yes	No	Living wage level is set at 100 percent (w/health insurance) or 125 percent (w/o health insurance) of the federal poverty level for a family of four.
Detroit, MI	November 1998	$10.00	$12.50	No	Yes	Yes	No	
Multnomah Co, OR	October 1998	See notes.	$10.63	No	Yes	No	No	Living wage level is indexed to rise with the consumer price index. Only employees in security, food service, and janitorial jobs are covered. Mandated wage level is the hourly value of the wage and benefits package paid to the employee.
Pasadena, CA	September 1998	$9.16	$10.73	Yes	Yes	No	No	Living wage level is indexed to rise with the consumer price index.
Cook County, IL	September 1998	$9.43	$11.78	No	Yes	No	No	Living wage level is set at 100 percent of the federal poverty level for a family of four.
Chicago, IL	July 1998	n.a.	$10.33	No	Yes	No	No	

City		Date						Notes
San Antonio, TX	n.a.	July 1998	$9.62	No	Yes	Yes	No	Covered employers must also pay at least 70 percent of their workers a higher wage ($11.14 for services involving durable goods and $10.86 for services involving nondurable goods).
Oakland, CA	$10.07	March 1998	$11.58	No	Yes	Yes	No	Living wage level is indexed to rise with the consumer price index.
Durham, NC	n.a.	January 1998	$9.51	Yes	Yes	No	No	Living wage level is set at 105 percent of the federal poverty level.
West Hollywood, CA	$8.67	October 1997	$9.92	No	Yes	Yes	No	Living wage level is set to the higher of 100 percent of the federal poverty level for a family of four or 110 percent of the state minimum wage.
Boston, MA	n.a.	September 1997	$11.95	No	Yes	No	No	
Duluth, MN	$7.61	July 1997	$8.49	No	No	Yes	No	Living wage ordinance mandates that covered employers pay at least 90 percent of their employees the living wage.
Milwaukee County, WI	n.a.	May 1997	$7.88	No	Yes	No	No	Living wage level is indexed to rise with the consumer price index. Only employees in janitorial, security, and parking lot attendant jobs are covered.
New Haven, CT	n.a.	April 1997	$11.50	No	Yes	No	No	Living wage level is set at 120 percent of the federal poverty level for a family of four.
Los Angeles, CA	$9.39	March 1997	$10.64	No	Yes	Yes	No	Wages are adjusted annually based on changes in the benefits paid to the members of the city employees' retirement system.
Minneapolis, MN	n.a.	March 1997	$10.57	No	No	Yes	No	Living wage level is set at 110 percent of the federal poverty level for a family of four.
St. Paul, MN	n.a.	January 1997	$10.57	No	No	Yes	No	Living wage level is set at 110 percent of the federal poverty level for a family of four.
New York City, NY	$10.00	September 1996	$11.10	No	Yes	No	No	Only employees in clerical, food service, janitorial, and security jobs are covered. Health and vacation benefits must also be provided.
Jersey City, NJ	$7.50	June 1996	n.a.	No	Yes	No	No	
Portland, OR	$8.91	June 1996	$10.57	No	Yes	No	No	Only employees in temporary janitorial, parking lot attendant, clerical, and security jobs are covered.

Table 5A-1. *Summary of U.S. Living Wage Ordinances (continued)*

Municipality or County	Adoption date	Living Wage with health insurance	Coverage without health insurance	Local government employees	Public contracts	Financial assistance	Local minimum wage	Notes
Santa Clara Co., CA	October 1995	$10.00	n.a.	No	No	Yes	No	Covered employers must provide health insurance or a suitable alternative to permanent employees.
Baltimore, MD	December 1994	n.a.	$9.30	No	Yes	No	No	
Gary, IN	January 1991	See notes.	n.a.	No	No	Yes	No	Covered employers must pay a prevailing wage and provide a complete health care package to employees working over 25 hours per week.
Des Moines, IA	January 1988	$9.00	n.a.	No	Yes	No	No	Living wage ordinance covers urban renewal projects and mandates an average wage of $9.00 with benefits.

Source: Living Wage Resource Center; websites of respective jurisdictions.
n.a. Not available.

References

Adams, Scott, and David Neumark. 2003. "Living Wage Effects: New and Improved Evidence." Working Paper 9702. Cambridge, Mass.: National Bureau of Economic Research.

————. 2004. "The Economic Effects of Living Wage Laws: A Provisional Review." Working Paper 10562. Cambridge, Mass.: National Bureau of Economic Research.

————. 2005. "A Decade of Living Wages: What Have We Learned?" California Economic Policy Series. San Francisco: Public Policy Institute of California.

Blank, Rebecca. 2008. "How to Improve Poverty Measurement in the United States." *Journal of Policy Analysis and Management* 27, no. 2: 233–54.

Brenner, Mark. 2005. "The Economic Impact of the Boston Living Wage Ordinance." *Industrial Relations* 44, no. 1: 59–83.

Brenner, Mark, Jeannette Wicks-Lim, and Robert Pollin. 2002. "Measuring the Impact of Living Wage Laws: A Critical Appraisal of David Neumark's *How Living Wage Laws Affect Low-Wage Workers and Low-Income Families*." Working Paper 43. Amherst: University of Massachusetts, Political Economy Research Institute.

Economic Policy Institute. 2007. *EPI Issue Guide: Minimum Wage.* Washington.

Ehrenberg, Ronald, and Robert Smith. 2005. *Modern Labor Economics: Theory and Public Policy.* Indianapolis, Ind.: Addison-Wesley.

Fairris, David. 2005. "The Impact of Living Wages on Employers: A Control Group Analysis of the Los Angeles Ordinance." *Industrial Relations* 44, no. 1: 84–105.

Fairris, David, and Leon Fernandez Bujanda. 2008. "The Dissipation of Minimum Wage Gains for Workers through Labor-Labor Substitution: Evidence from the Los Angeles Living Wage Ordinance." *Southern Economic Journal* 75, no. 2: 473–96.

Holzer, Harry J. 2007. "Better Workers for Better Jobs: Improving Worker Advancement in the Low-Wage Labor Market." Brookings.

Johnson, Harry, and Peter Mieszkowski. 1970. "The Effects of Unionization on the Distribution of Income: A General Equilibrium Approach." *Quarterly Journal of Economics* 84, no. 4: 539–61.

Katz, Lawrence. 1986. "Efficiency Wage Theories: A Partial Evaluation." *NBER Macroeconomics Annual* 1: 235–75. MIT Press.

Luce, Stephanie. 2004. *Fighting for a Living Wage.* Cornell University Press.

Mincer, Jacob. 1976. "Unemployment Effects of Minimum Wages." *Journal of Political Economy* 84, no. 4 (pt. 2): S87–S104.

Mishel, Lawrence, Jared Bernstein, and Heidi Shierholz. 2006. *The State of Working America: 2006-07.* Washington: Economic Policy Institute.

Neumark, David. 2002. *How Living Wage Laws Affect Low-Wage Workers and Low-Income Families.* San Francisco: Public Policy Institute of California.

Neumark, David, and William Wascher. 2006. "Minimum Wages and Employment: A Review of Evidence from the New Minimum Wage Research." Working Paper 12663. Cambridge, Mass.: National Bureau of Economic Research.

Pollin, Robert, and Stephanie Luce. 1998. *The Living Wage: Building a Fair Economy.* New York: New Press.

Reich, Michael, Peter Hall, and Ken Jacobs. 2005. "Living Wage Policies at the San Francisco Airport: Impacts on Workers and Businesses." *Industrial Relations* 44, no. 1: 106–38.

6

The Next Move:
Metropolitan Regions and the Transformation of
the Freight Transport and Distribution System

SUSAN CHRISTOPHERSON AND MICHAEL H. BELZER

After a period, beginning in the 1980s, in which freight shipping costs declined in the United States because of cheap fuel and deregulation of freight transport industries, costs began to rise in the first decade of the twenty-first century. Rising costs are linked to volatile fuel prices but also to increasing congestion on roadways. Communities affected by road congestion and the environmental and safety costs associated with truck transport are demanding that freight shipping prices reflect the full cost associated with shipping, including the social costs.

An increase in the cost of moving commodities and semifinished goods has the potential to change the geography of freight transportation in the United States, a geography that has been built around truck transport and, to a lesser extent, air freight, for twenty-five years. A new location-and-transport cost calculus has important implications for shippers and carriers but also for places, particularly the metropolitan hubs in the transport system. An increase in transport costs, including that driven by policies to reflect social costs in total shipping prices, would present firms with a different set of strategic choices about how they ship goods and where they locate production and distribution operations.

An understanding of how rising costs might affect freight shipping and distribution is particularly important to economic development policymakers. Many communities have invested (through tax incentives) in distribution facilities. Others are being lobbied to use public monies to improve highways, air-

The authors would like to thank Jan Vink, Athena Ullah, Andrew Rumbach, and Margaret Cowell for research assistance.

194

ports, and rail infrastructure to eliminate transport bottlenecks and speed the transport of freight. Advocates for these investments point to job growth in the U.S. distribution industries to argue that communities need to do everything possible to support these industries, contending that the jobs produced will replace those lost to global outsourcing.[1]

At the same time, environmentalists are advocating for increased public investment in passenger transportation and decreased investment in infrastructure serving freight carriers.[2] All of these scenarios are likely to render decisions about where to make public investments more difficult, in terms of both equity and efficiency.

What are the alternatives and what is likely to happen to the freight transport and distribution industries if costs rise? Will their strategies and those of the shippers change how freight is shipped and the role and location of distribution centers? How will different metropolitan areas fare in this new world?

In this chapter we examine the current freight transportation and distribution system, how it developed, and what it looks like on the ground. As economic development policymakers look forward, they will have to imagine a different world, one in which investment in people transport takes precedence and freight shippers adopt new strategies. They will also have to conceive of new opportunities, for example, to reconnect the distribution and transport industries to support domestic manufacturing. This chapter is intended to help economic development policymakers in their scenario building process. Our goal is to inform thinking about possible futures by examining the geography of the time-sensitive, trucking-dominated freight transportation system that has emerged in the United States. since the 1980s.

In the next sections, we examine how policy decisions, beginning in the 1980s and continuing through the 1990s, changed the underlying incentive structure that had shaped the freight distribution system for fifty years. While these policy decisions were justified on the basis that they would increase efficiency and thus decrease the cost of goods and services to U.S. consumers, they also had consequences for the organization of production and distribution and, by extension, for regional economies. After reviewing key policies, we examine which metropolitan areas have become national transport hubs in the contemporary time-sensitive, low-cost, trucking-based freight distribution system. We then look at the intrametropolitan location of freight distribution facilities and the signal importance of very large distribution centers at the metropolitan periphery. Finally, we speculate on how this intensive truck transport system and its network of hubs might change with higher transport costs, greater demand

1. Joel Kotkin, "The Myth of Deindustrialization," *Wall Street Journal*, August 6, 2008.
2. Johnson (2003).

for public resources for public transport, and public opposition to the environmental and safety costs of the current freight distribution system.

In looking toward the future, we recognize that the production organization and place-based investments that have crystallized in the recent twenty years will continue to drive strategies of firms. Any changes are likely to be incremental rather than revolutionary. As we will discuss later in the chapter, this insight has important implications for regional economic development policies.

The Chicken-and-Egg Question of Policy and Technological Change

Changes in the geography of transportation networks and in the position of places in those networks typically assume that technological innovation is the major driver. In the case of the contemporary freight transport system in the United States, the explanations focus on containerization, bar code and radio frequency tracking devices, and logistics software. As some perceptive analysts of the relationship between society and technology have noted, however, technology is applied within a political and economic context.[3] The question of which technologies are adopted and how they are used requires an appreciation of pure invention but also an understanding of governance and policy.

Concretely, the adoption of one policy measure rather than another affects how managers attempt to cut costs or what they perceive as new opportunities for profit. For example, policy measures that restrict the option to save money by reducing wage costs may push managers to adopt productivity-enhancing technologies and practices. We argue that governance and policy decisions are as important as technological innovations in affecting the economic fortunes of cities and regions.[4] Indeed, the opportunities for new markets and profits created by policy decisions may stimulate technological change.

In addition, policies that change the relative power of actors in an industry (small firms, large firms, unions) or the relationships among firms in interrelated industries (manufacturing, retailing, transportation) have spatial consequences.[5] All investment (or disinvestment) decisions affect where economic activities occur and the relative importance of one location as against another. We can see this in key features of the contemporary U.S. freight transportation geography—concentration in port functions and the alienation of primary and secondary ports from their adjacent regions; the centrality of air transport facili-

---

3. Heilbroner (1996); Atkinson (2004).
4. Christopherson and Clark (2007).
5. Christopherson and Clark (2007); Sheppard (2002).

ties and highway access to metropolitan regional investments; and the move from urban to exurban locations for warehousing and distribution functions.

Our approach to understanding firm strategies and their implications for the spatial configuration of firm networks and nodes or hubs in the networks is both institutionally sensitive and industry oriented. From this perspective, policy decisions undertaken since the mid-1970s to liberalize trade and deregulate transport industries and industrial relations have been critical to firm strategies (including those that apply to particular technologies). They have affected the actions of shippers and carriers, creating aspects of what we now describe as "globalization."

To demonstrate how policies affecting industries are translated into location choices and investments, we examine how specific public policies, exemplified by trucking industry deregulation, have shaped the existing truck-oriented, time-sensitive freight transportation in the United States. Then, using a broad range of quantitative data and qualitative sources, including a small but important set of studies by economic geographers, we look at the implications of changing shipper strategies for metropolitan hubs in the air freight, trucking, and associated services and facilities industries.

What Policies Set the Stage for a Low-Cost, Flexible, Time-Sensitive, Import-Oriented Freight Transport System?

In the United States, the emergence and adoption of information and distribution technologies—bar codes; radio frequency identification; containerization—have reduced costs for major shippers.[6] The market for these technological innovations would not have developed, however, were it not for broader, policy-driven changes that restructured the freight transport industries and altered the power relations between domestic manufacturers and importers, between shippers and carriers, and between carriers and labor. By altering power relations in the freight transport industries, these policies changed firm incentives and behavior, including those related to the location of their activities. The two most important sets of policy decisions changing the strategies and investment decisions of firms in the United States since the 1970s have been those associated with trade liberalization and deregulation. Therefore, to understand how the freight transport system has evolved since the 1970s, we need to look at those policies and how they are reflected in the kind of freight transportation system that exists in the United States.

6. Cidell (2008).

Trade Liberalization

Trade liberalization achieved through global agreements, such as those organized through GATT and the WTO as well as regional trade agreements, enhanced the mobility of capital and reduced the risks of investment in production sites outside advanced economies. This regulatory liberalization process supported the development of global supply chains and the extensive use of outsourcing by U.S. retailers and a significant increase in outsourcing by United States–based manufacturers.

Multiple policies facilitated trade liberalization, but the reversal of national policies that supported manufacturers by allowing them to set the retail price of their product was among the most important. The removal of this protection set the stage for extensive international outsourcing and for the rise of discount retailers, such as Wal-Mart, which almost exclusively sell imported products.[7] In 2007, *The Journal of Commerce* reported that the three largest U.S. importers were Wal-Mart, Target, and Home Depot. Of the top 100 importers, 35 were retailers.

Another critical policy decision shaping the direction and content of trade liberalization was the passage of the Ocean Shipping Reform Act in 1998. This law eliminated public and transparent processes for setting shipping rates and allowed for secret service agreements between shippers and ocean carriers. The conferences that had previously set shipping rates became "advisory."[8] The Motor Carrier Act of 1980 followed the same model.[9] These kinds of policy decisions allowed the biggest shippers to make deals with carriers that were based on the volume of their shipments. Because these agreements were not public, smaller shippers (both importers and exporters) did not have access to similar rates or to regulatory recourse when their shipments were treated differently from those of the dominant shippers.

The largest shippers—in retail and in manufacturing—have benefited disproportionately from these new trade regulations. According to an interview with a reporter from *The Journal of Commerce*:

> "The giant retailers are dominating. You can count the most powerful on the fingers of one hand: Wal-Mart, Target, Home Depot, K-Mart, Payless Shoe Source. There are two categories of shippers: retailers and direct importers. They set the freight rates through contract negotiations. The rates are supposed to be secret, but the word gets around so that everyone knows what the rates are. . . .The smaller shippers do worse than the big ones. It all boils down to volume."[10]

7. Petrovic and Hamilton (2006).
8. Bonacich and Wilson (2008).
9. Belzer (2000).
10. Quoted in Bonacich and Wilson (2008, p. 88).

These decisions effectively increased the bargaining power of major retailing importers and their influence over the shippers who send products from manufacturers outside the United States to domestic consumers. Because of their shipping volume, these retailers dominate activity in U.S. seaports, particularly in the dominant ports of Los Angeles–Long Beach and New York–New Jersey.

To be effective for their constituent coalitions, however, trade liberalization agreements had to be accompanied by deregulation of national freight transport shipping industries. In the next section, we briefly examine the deregulation of the trucking industry to demonstrate how deregulation was related not only to decreasing freight transport costs, but to a redistribution of total costs from shippers to the trucking industry workforce and communities.

Deregulation of the Transport Industries and their Labor Markets

The legislative deregulation of transport modes—the Aviation Deregulation Act of 1979, the Staggers Act of 1980 (deregulating railroads), and the Motor Carrier Act of 1980—occurred primarily during the Carter administration. The second wave of deregulation included the Ocean Shipping Act of 1984 and the Federal Aviation Administration Authorization Act of 1994, which deregulated intrastate trucking. The deregulation process continued through the 1990s. Deregulation enabled mergers and acquisitions across freight transport industries and changed the contractual balance of power between carriers and shippers and between carriers and their workforce, particularly (but not exclusively) in the trucking industry.

New technological applications, including those deployed by third-party logistics providers (3PLs), developed in the wake of transport deregulation and enhanced competition by organizing logistics movements on behalf of shippers and consignees. These applications optimized freight transportation logistics on behalf of the shipper-customer by fostering collaboration among customers with the objective of intensifying competition among freight transport service providers. Third-party logistics providers also saved money for their clients by optimizing clients' load and routing characteristics. Although transport deregulation began with administrative deregulation, legislation created new permanent competitive forms of transport.

Deregulation of freight transportation industries also led to a loss of union membership and bargaining power across these industries; in trucking, de-unionization put wages in competition across the industry.[11] The changing bargaining power of workers in the transportation industries occurred within the context of what could be termed the deregulation of industrial relations, effected through administrative decisions of the National Labor Relations Board

11. Belzer (1994, 1995).

and changes in the common law made by the courts.[12] While demand for unionization has remained relatively high, union density in the public and private sectors combined has declined to 12.1 percent and union density among eligible private sector workers has dropped to 7.5 percent.[13] The trucking industry was particularly affected by court decisions that removed owner-drivers' rights to union representation.[14]

Deregulation has been credited with increasing productivity in freight transportation, but questions remain about the extent to which productivity increases have been achieved by allocating a portion of total cost to the public sector. Kenneth Boyer and Stephen Burks, for example, found that higher speed limits and a deregulated environment allowing for longer and heavier trucks, accounted for much of the apparent growth in truck transport productivity.[15] Certainly, productivity gains can be linked to lowered wages. Analysts in both Europe and in the United States have found that the reductions in intranational shipping costs were more attributable to low wages than to technological change.[16]

Changing conditions in truck transport have, in fact, had significant implications for the trucking services labor market. The widespread growth of subcontracting in trucking, especially in intermodal operations, allowed the price for truckload freight to drop significantly. A recent online survey of owner-operators found that, on average, those owner-operators (drivers) with one truck had annual earnings of $21,267 in wages and profits after expenses.[17] These drivers probably worked more than 3,000 hours per year.[18] While the owner-operator pays himself a below-market wage and classifies his earnings as profit, the combined wages-plus-profits of owner-operators is less than two-thirds of the wage earnings of nonunion truckload drivers in similar markets. By comparison with nonunion employee drivers, only a fraction of owner-operators have health insurance or pensions.[19] In intermodal *port drayage* (a trucking company freight charge for the pickup or delivery of an ocean container), few for-hire car-

12. Belman and Belzer (1997).

13. Concerning demand for unionization, see Freeman and Rogers (2006); for statistics on declining unionization, see Bureau of Labor Statistics, "Union Members in 2007," news release (www.bls.gov/news.release/History/union2_01252008.txt).

14. *National Labor Relations Board* v. *Deaton Truck Line, Inc.*, 502 F.2d 1221 (5th Cir. 1968); *United States Steel Corporation* v. *Fraternal Association of Steelhaulers*, 431 F.2d 1046, 1048 (3d Cir. 1970).

15. Boyer and Burks (2007).

16. Belzer (1994, 1995); Combes and Lafourcade (2005).

17. The survey, conducted in 2003–04, was based on 338 nonmissing observations. Combined annual wages and profits after expenses for owner-drivers with one truck ranged from $14,957 to $301,400, with a mean of $21,267 and a median of $17,989. See Belzer (2006).

18. Belman, Monaco, and Brooks (2004).

19. Belman, Monaco, and Brooks (2004); Belzer (2000).

riers can afford to send their nonunion employee drivers into the ports. Almost all port drayage is done by owner-operators.[20]

Owner-operators, more than three-quarters of whom are permanently contracted to a single carrier and who "operate" their "business" under that carrier's authority and depend on that carrier to secure loads, are prohibited from organizing a union because of a federal court ruling in the early 1970s.[21] This ruling changed almost 100 years of precedent—the International Brotherhood of Teamsters was created in substantial part by owner-operators—without any legal sanction under the Sherman Antitrust Act.[22] The inability of owner-drivers to secure protection for collective bargaining, including the right to strike, distinguishes them from similarly situated company drivers. Since the law now considers them independent businesses, owner-drivers do not have any protection under the Fair Labor Standards Act (FLSA). FLSA protections are weak for truck drivers who work in operations involved in interstate commerce; they must earn the minimum wage (calculated by dividing their gross compensation by the number of hours worked) and are not covered at all by the overtime provision.[23] Those protections do not apply to owner-operators, however. Other protections, such as workers' compensation and safety and health regulations, have little or no applicability to owner-operators, who technically are self-employed. Inclusion of independent contractors in workers' compensation varies from state to state. In combination, multiple asymmetries between employee and contractor drivers give carriers (and the shippers they serve) strong cost incentives to favor contracting to owner-operators whenever possible.

Transport industry experts estimate that deregulation, including its associated labor market policies, worked in tandem with trade liberalization to reduce overall U.S. freight transport costs by approximately 25 percent, to a 2004 rate of 11.5 percent.[24] Edward Glaeser and Janet Kohlhase argued that the transportation costs of goods fell dramatically during the twentieth century and that in more than 80 percent of global shipments, transport costs are less than 4 percent of total value.[25] Ultimately, deregulation of the freight transport service market enhanced the effects of trade liberalization.

20. Monaco (2005); Monaco and Grobar (2004).
21. *United States Steel Corporation* v. *Fraternal Association of Steelhaulers*, 431 F.2d 1046, 1048 (3d Cir. 1970).
22. Leiter (1957).
23. Fritsch (1981); DOL (2002).
24. Eno Foundation and Upper Great Plains Transportation Institute (2007).
25. Glaeser and Kohlhase (2004); Wilson (2001).

Implications for Shipping Costs

The question of shipping costs needs to be looked at in some detail to understand the implications for place-based distribution activities and facilities within the domestic market. Although policy-driven changes drove down overall transport costs, they did not wholly eradicate the importance of distance in the location of economic activities. Analyses of transport costs have focused primarily on the cost reductions associated with containerization and improved logistics affecting the *global* transport of goods. Less attention has been paid to changes in the cost of intranational movement of goods in North America and Europe. Research on intranational transport costs indicates that these costs have not decreased at the same rate as those in international shipping.[26]

Experts on the role of logistics costs indicate that there is compelling evidence that distance costs are persistent despite lower costs in freight transport.[27] One explanation for the persistence of distance costs is that the role of time in the transportation of goods has increased.[28] In commodity transport, time-space compression is the direct consequence of firm strategies to reach markets more quickly and minimize the costs of holding goods before manufacture or sale.

The higher cost of time comes from carrying stock (inventory costs) and also from the risk that longer transport times reduce the chance of reliable and predictable delivery.[29] Since the 1980s, the opportunity costs of time have become more important to households and industrial consumers.[30] This translates into more frequent goods shipments. Markus Hesse and Jean-Paul Rodrigue argued, for example, that the proportion of total cost in transportation (both logistics and goods movement) has actually increased because of the enhanced role of time in the delivery shipping process.[31]

The increased importance of time and the incorporation of just-in-time practices among shippers and in the customer industries (retail and manufacturing) served by freight transportation has led to the rise of air freight as a significant component of freight distribution services. Time—in delivery and of delivery—became an integral aspect of product value made possible, in part, by cheap freight transport and the capacity for a continuous stream of product delivery.[32]

As we have suggested, this time-sensitive, truck-based regime favored large-volume shippers. It also brought two freight shipment industries to the fore: air freight for high-value, low-weight products and trucking and containerized

26. Winston (1993).
27. Disdier and Head (2008).
28. Hummels (2001).
29. McCann (2005); Venables (2006).
30. McCann and Shefer (2004).
31. Hesse and Rodrigue (2004).
32. Bowen (2002); Zook and Brunn (2006).

intermodal transport for the majority of supply chain shipments. In the next section we examine some ways in which the time-sensitive, truck-based freight shipment system created a new spatial "logic" and opportunities for some metropolitan areas, especially those that could develop land-intensive facilities to serve the high-volume shippers.

A New Spatial Logic for Freight Shipping

The increasing importance of time in freight shipment (including more frequent shipments), the decrease in total shipping costs (derived from deregulation of transport industries and the use of new technologies), and the advantage both of these factors provide to major importers have had significant consequences for patterns of transport facility investment in U.S. regions, including in its major transport hubs.

The expert consensus is that the distribution function has been loosened from its previous moorings in regional economies. Freight distribution industries and facilities are not tied to regional industries but provide pass-through services. *Pass-through* refers to globally sourced freight shipments that are destined for national metropolitan retail markets and, to a lesser extent, manufacturing firms. The disengagement of freight transportation from regional economies and its transformation into a system serving high-volume importers is manifested in the concentration of transoceanic shipping in two key ports, the development of distribution hubs in the Midwest organized around economies of scale, and the peripheralization of freight transport facilities to the metropolitan fringe.

The role that seaports and inland ports had played in enabling value added processes in their adjacent regions did not disappear but decreased in importance in a pass-through transport system. And, overall, a rationalized national "import feed" system undermined the role of regional economies as distinctive end points for both imports and exports.

In a related process, the lower cost to shippers of using truck transport arguably contributed to a change in the spatial organization of a significant portion of manufacturing production in the United States.[33] In particular, the importer advantage changed the calculus involved in the spatial division of labor. This has been noted with respect to the increasing use of imported inputs, whose share in total U.S. shipping in capital goods producing sectors has doubled (to 18 percent) since the 1980s.[34] But there is also evidence that manufacturers were

33. Parr and others (2002).
34. Venables (2006). This suggests a connection between the policies that have fostered the reorganization of the freight transportation system in the United States and the inability

more able to divide up the production process to minimize costs, transporting inputs from one specialized establishment to another. This capacity was aided by another consequence of the policies associated with the wave of deregulation beginning in the 1970s: industry concentration through mergers and acquisitions.[35] Firms were able to move away from the costs they associated with agglomeration (higher wages, for example) using establishments in dispersed regions to carry out different parts of the production process. That produced economies of scale for the firm that were only possible with a low-cost freight transport system that moved half-finished goods among the establishments.

The reorganization of a significant portion of the supply chain for the North American auto industry in a band across Michigan, Indiana, and Ohio, reaching north into southern Ontario, illustrates this tendency. Original equipment manufacturers in the automobile industry (that is, final assemblers such as General Motors, Ford, and Toyota) benefit from the regionalized supplier network, global production networks, and logistics cost reductions. Within this production system, the potential for imports acts as a competitive device. Suppliers concentrate because they have to compete with cheaply transported imports.[36]

Through another series of policy actions, support mechanisms for the national transportation infrastructure also changed during the 1980s and 1990s, devolving more responsibility for upkeep of the critical transport infrastructure to states and localities. The responsibility for critical infrastructure maintenance became localized at the same time that economic returns to regions for investment in a nationally oriented transit infrastructure declined. Local responsibility for facilities serving national markets has exacerbated serious environmental and safety problems in the areas around the major import-oriented ports, It has inevitably led to deterioration in the transport infrastructure that serves intraregional trade and to massive private and public investments in nodal centers and infrastructure to serve the import segment of the economy.

Some locations are particularly prominent in the system of time-sensitive, truck transport services and facilities that has emerged since the 1970s. In the next sections we look at what is known about where economic development took place, among and within metropolitan areas.

---

of some regions and auto parts suppliers to compete globally. If increasing merchandise trade can be associated with increasing U.S. consumption of foreign-made goods (or incorporation of foreign-made components in U.S. goods), then deregulated freight transport has contributed to this disintermediation.

35. Hesse (2006); Parr and others (2002).

36. Rodrigue (2006).

Critical National Hubs in a High-Speed, Low-Cost Freight Transport Network

Documenting where different components of the transport network are located is surprisingly difficult. Although there are data and documentation of transport routes and on the quality and character of transport modes and systems, systematic analysis of investments and employment in places—within and across metropolitan areas—is rare.

Much of the literature on the consequences for places consists of journalistic accounts or case studies. The small analytical literature indicates three prominent features of the geography of freight transport under the time-sensitive, cheap trucking regime: seaport concentration, the emergence of major inland intermodal hubs built around air transport, and development of intermodal distribution parks at the fringes of major metropolitan areas.[37]

Seaport Concentration

The bargaining power of retail importers and the dominance of the import over the export trade has altered the function of the seaports, the gateways through which most imported commodities and production inputs enter the United States and which are the largest spatially fixed investments in the global freight transportation system. Although very expensive port development continues to take place along the East and West coasts, many ports no longer contribute to the economic development of the metropolitan areas in which they are located, in the way that they did in the mid-twentieth century.[38]

Before the era of containerization and the rationalization of the surface freight transportation system to favor expedited, low-cost freight transportation, seaports largely served their surrounding regions. They contributed to regional economic development by connecting sources of supply with intranational producers. Global sourcing has weakened intranational connections to domestic sources (that is, weakened input-output relationships). According to Scott Campbell:

> This situation is particularly significant on the Pacific Coast, where a shipper may send bridge cargo through Seattle, Portland, San Francisco-Oakland, LA/LB [Los Angeles–Long Beach] or Vancouver. Seattle benefits from having the shortest sailing distance to Asia, while Los Angeles is closer to many inland markets and does not need to send bridge cargo by rail over the Sierra Nevada. . . . This change in the geographic logic and

37. Bowen (2008); Cidell (2008); Hesse (2006); Rodrigue (2006).
38. Campbell (1993) describes such metropolitan areas as having been "disempowered by intermodalism." See also Cidell (2008); Hall (2004); Luberoff and Walder (2000).

scale economies of international shipping has led to the rise of Los Angeles and Seattle, and the resulting "squeeze" of Portland and San Francisco into smaller shares of Pacific trade, especially with imports.[39]

The transformation of seaports into points in a pass-through system alienated the port from its surroundings. The role of the port has been transformed from a center of regional economic activity to that of a single link in a complex transportation network.[40] This process has significantly favored concentration in the largest coastal ports, Los Angeles–Long Beach and New York–Newark.

"Footloose" Inland Ports

New inland ports have emerged whose form and functions derive from the time-sensitive character of many products and production inputs (speedy pass-through). Although truck transport enabled decentralization and flexibility, the increasing importance of the time dimension has encouraged the emergence and rising importance of hubs, such as those in the exurbs of Dallas–Fort Worth, Memphis, Columbus (Ohio), Chicago, and Indianapolis. These massive intermodal distribution facilities depend critically on accessibility to major interstate highways. Although the most important of them includes rail capacity, some of them rose in significance in the 1980s and 1990s because of air freight and the investments of major air freight carriers, such as Federal Express (Memphis) and United Parcel Service (Louisville), in their land ports.[41] Access to air freight service has also led to the concentrated location of warehousing and distribution centers for major retail importers.

An analysis of the major determinants of growth in warehousing and distribution employment between 1998 and 2005 indicates that access to air and highway transport was "significantly correlated with the distribution and growth of warehousing," although air transport was more important with respect to the total number of warehousing establishments than to the number of large establishments.[42] As Julie Cidell states:

> As freight traffic has both increased in volume and become more international in scope, it has concentrated in fewer ports and gateways. As those gateways have become congested, shippers have begun to move towards inland ports and distribution centers to free up dockside space for maritime activities. Mapping the location of freight establishments per capita for fifty of the largest U.S. cities confirms that there is a shift in the last

39. Campbell (1993, p. 222).
40. Campbell (1993, p. 222).
41. Bowen (2008); EEOC (2004).
42. Bowen (2008, p. 384).

twenty years towards concentrating freight activity in the Mississippi, Ohio, and Missouri River valleys. Highways, rail, and inland waterways, though themselves not significant predictors of freight establishments, are therefore of considerable importance both in these Midwestern cities and in the coastal gateways they are connected to.[43]

The Metropolitan Picture

To construct a set of data points that might shed light on how a time-sensitive, trucking-based regulatory framework has affected metropolitan areas in the U.S. transport hierarchy in the early 2000s, we used a proprietary database developed by Moody's Economy.com. We ranked 361 metropolitan areas with respect to total employment and specialization in freight transportation, which we define as air transportation (NAICS code 481), truck transportation (NAICS code 484), support activities for transportation (NAICS code 488), and warehousing and storage (NAICS code 493) combined.[44]

Although some might reasonably argue that the presence of employment in an industry does not necessarily signify future potential, especially as technologies change, high levels of employment across these four industries indirectly measure capacity, including the capacity to produce innovations in services and facilities. Levels of employment and specialization also signal investment by firms, which is likely to stimulate future investment if past success breeds future success. Information about levels of employment and specialization in freight transportation gives a sense of which metropolitan areas have benefited from the move to a time-sensitive, trucking-oriented system as it has evolved over the past twenty years.

Our analysis shows that the metropolitan areas that rank highest in total employment are, not unexpectedly, the largest sea and inland port regions: Los Angeles, New York, and Chicago (table 6-1). Table 6-2 ranks metropolitan areas according to their employment location quotients for freight transportation. The employment location quotient for freight transportation is a measure of the extent to which a metropolitan area specializes in freight transportation. It

43. Cidell (2008).
44. The data used are for 2005. County data were summed to obtain metropolitan area estimates. Summing all counties produced a comparable total for the entire United States. See North American Industry Classification System (NAICS) codes at the U.S. Census Bureau website (www.census.gov/epcd/www.naics.html). The Moody's Economy.com data were used because they include estimates of employment for workers not covered by unemployment insurance and thus not counted in publicly available Bureau of Labor Statistics (BLS) data and because they include estimates of employment that are suppressed in the BLS data to preserve employer confidentiality.

Table 6-1. *Top 40 Metropolitan Areas Ranked by Freight Transportation Employment, 2005*[a]

Rank	Metropolitan area	Freight transportation employment
1	New York–Northern New Jersey–Long Island, NY–NJ–PA	157,608
2	Chicago–Naperville–Joliet, IL–IN–WI	145,778
3	Los Angeles–Long Beach–Santa Ana, CA	125,204
4	Dallas–Fort Worth–Arlington, TX	101,477
5	Atlanta–Sandy Springs–Marietta, GA	92,290
6	Houston–Baytown–Sugar Land, TX	75,800
7	Philadelphia–Camden–Wilmington, PA–NJ–DE–MD	60,829
8	Miami–Fort Lauderdale–Miami Beach, FL	50,289
9	Riverside–San Bernardino–Ontario, CA	49,211
10	Detroit–Warren–Livonia, MI	46,826
11	Seattle–Tacoma–Bellevue, WA	44,117
12	Memphis, TN–MS–AR	43,929
13	San Francisco–Oakland–Fremont, CA	43,084
14	Phoenix–Mesa–Scottsdale, AZ	41,948
15	Indianapolis, IN	37,542
16	Columbus, OH	37,329
17	St. Louis, MO–IL	34,145
18	Washington–Arlington–Alexandria, DC–VA–MD–WV	33,856
19	Kansas City, MO–KS	31,761
20	Omaha–Council Bluffs, NE–IA	31,465
21	Boston–Cambridge–Quincy, MA–NH	30,495
22	Minneapolis–St. Paul–Bloomington, MN–WI	28,102
23	Baltimore–Towson, MD	27,975
24	Portland–Vancouver–Beaverton, OR–WA	27,373
25	Denver–Aurora, CO	25,208
26	Nashville–Davidson–Murfreesboro, TN	24,982
27	Charlotte–Gastonia–Concord, NC–SC	24,510
28	Jacksonville, FL	22,361
29	Cincinnati–Middletown, OH–KY–IN	22,249
30	Pittsburgh, PA	20,584
31	Virginia Beach–Norfolk–Newport News, VA–NC	19,486
32	Cleveland–Elyria–Mentor, OH	19,319
33	Chattanooga, TN–GA	18,864
34	Harrisburg–Carlisle, PA	18,628
35	Louisville, KY–IN	18,150
36	Fayetteville–Springdale–Rogers, AR–MO	18,098
37	Tampa–St. Petersburg–Clearwater, FL	17,909
38	Salt Lake City, UT	16,778
39	Orlando, FL	16,751
40	Sacramento–Arden–Arcade–Roseville, CA	16,022

Source: Authors' analysis of data supplied by Moody's Economy.com.

a. Freight transportation consists of air transportation, truck transportation, support activities for transportation, and warehousing and storage combined.

Table 6-2. *Top 40 Metropolitan Areas Ranked by Location Quotient for Freight Transportation, 2005*[a]

Rank	Metropolitan area	Freight transportation location quotient
1	Laredo, TX	5.955
2	Fayetteville–Springdale–Rogers, AR–MO	3.299
3	Joplin, MO	3.254
4	Chattanooga, TN–GA	3.055
5	Houma–Bayou Cane–Thibodaux, LA	3.032
6	Memphis, TN–MS–AR	2.618
7	Harrisburg–Carlisle, PA	2.261
8	Lakeland, FL	2.210
9	Decatur, IL	2.197
10	Savannah, GA	2.186
11	St. George, UT	2.136
12	Stockton, CA	2.095
13	Altoona, PA	2.041
14	Fort Smith, AR–OK	2.031
15	Cheyenne, WY	1.976
16	Springfield, MO	1.906
17	Iowa City, IA	1.882
18	Green Bay, WI	1.869
19	Anchorage, AK	1.868
20	Omaha–Council Bluffs, NE–IA	1.858
21	Kankakee–Bradley, IL	1.840
22	Cedar Rapids, IA	1.834
23	Atlanta–Sandy Springs–Marietta, GA	1.740
24	Dalton, GA	1.738
25	Springfield, OH	1.729
26	Harrisonburg, VA	1.715
27	Indianapolis, IN	1.678
28	Winston–Salem, NC	1.667
29	Morristown, TN	1.663
30	El Paso, TX	1.643
31	Lebanon, PA	1.641
32	Dallas–Fort Worth–Arlington, TX	1.612
33	Tulsa, OK	1.584
34	Fort Wayne, IN	1.582
35	Albany, GA	1.573
36	Little Rock–North Little Rock, AR	1.561
37	Roanoke, VA	1.555
38	Greensboro–High Point, NC	1.549
39	Salt Lake City, UT	1.538
40	Columbus, OH	1.500

Source: Authors' analysis of data supplied by Moody's Economy.com.

a. Freight transportation consists of air transportation, truck transportation, support activities for transportation, and warehousing and storage combined.

Table 6-3. *Metropolitan Areas in Top 40 for Both Freight Transportation Employment and Location Quotient for Freight Transportation, 2005*[a]

Metropolitan area	Location quotient rank	Employment rank
Fayetteville–Springdale–Rogers, AR–MO	2	36
Chattanooga, TN–GA	4	33
Memphis, TN–MS–AR	6	12
Harrisburg–Carlisle, PA	7	34
Dallas–Fort Worth–Arlington, TX	18	4
Omaha–Council Bluffs, NE–IA	20	20
Atlanta–Sandy Springs–Marietta, GA	23	5
Indianapolis, IN	27	15
Salt Lake City, UT	39	38
Columbus, OH	40	16

Source: Authors' analysis of data supplied by Moody's Economy.com.

a. Freight transportation consists of air transportation, truck transportation, support activities for transportation, and warehousing and storage combined.

equals the percentage of the metropolitan area's employment that is in freight transportation divided by the share of national employment that is in freight transportation. Table 6-2 identifies a group of mostly smaller metropolitan regions, such as Laredo, Texas, and Fayetteville, Arkansas, that have carved out specializations in air cargo–related business but also that have major trucking and warehousing industries. Table 6-3 shows the metropolitan areas that rank in the top forty in both freight transportation employment and freight transportation location quotient. These places, which are specialized and paramount in freight transportation, are the nation's leading freight hubs. They include Memphis, Fayetteville (Arkansas), Columbus (Ohio), and Indianapolis.

Behind each of the metropolitan areas in tables 6-2 and 6-3 is a story of real estate and economic development linked to trade liberalization and transport industry deregulation. For example, Laredo, the metropolitan area with the highest location quotient (see table 6-2), has become the fifth-largest customs district in the United States and a major U.S. point of entry and exit for the North American Free Trade Agreement trade with Mexico because of truck, rail, and air cargo. The Laredo airport has 390,000 square feet of warehousing space onsite, and there are over 60 million square feet of warehousing space within ten miles of the airport, which identifies itself primarily as a commercial service airport. Fayetteville is the largest commercial airport serving Bentonville, Arkansas, home to Wal-Mart's corporate headquarters. The growth of its air freight service is tied to the dominance of Wal-Mart in national and, to some extent, international retailing. Other metropolitan areas that are specialized in freight transportation are the headquarters of overnight cargo carriers including UPS (Louisville), and FedEx (Memphis).

Thus, although there are a number of different reasons for the emergence of these second-order metropolitan areas as specialized centers in a time-sensitive, truck-based transport system, their newfound prominence can be explained only partially by local and regional initiatives. To the contrary, these centers have grown as a consequence of their positions as nodes in an international trade system created by national policy decisions.[45]

The Intrametropolitan Perspective

A metropolitan perspective on national inland transportation hubs provides only part of the picture of transformation in the time-sensitive truck transport system, however. There have also been major shifts in where investments in the necessary facilities and services to serve the pass-through-oriented system are being located *within* regions. Their association with a city-centered metropolitan region is, in reality, quite tangential. The major investments have been primarily located on the periphery of the metropolitan area. They can be either in a county included in the metropolitan area but sparsely settled or in a nonmetropolitan county adjacent to a metropolitan region. This has implications for economic development policy and for job creation, subjects we address later in the chapter.

The proliferation of very large distribution center hubs at the fringe of major metropolitan areas is a consequence of the restructuring of the warehousing industry and its transformation into a *distribution* industry oriented toward major importers. According to John Bowen:

> In 1998, there were just 26 establishments (0.4% in the total industry) with 250 employees or more. By 2005, 4% of all establishments (522) had at least 250 employees. . . . Multi-establishment warehousing firms are increasingly common.[46]

An assessment of consultant reports for regional or metropolitan real estate ventures seeking assessment of the potential for distribution center siting suggests a trend toward larger distribution centers (more than a million square feet) on very large sites (more than 200 acres) and a search for locations proximate to major metropolitan markets. It is the availability of huge parcels of cheap land

45. Sheppard (2002).
46. Bowen (2008, p. 381).

that drove the emergence of exurban logistics hot spots at the beginning of this decade.

A systematic study of the location and hiring patterns of 589 distribution centers, analyzing 1982 and 2002 locations, supports this location pattern.[47] As the warehousing and distribution industry has become more concentrated and oriented toward serving large importers, it has also moved from higher-density urban locations to low-density exurban locations. According to the EEOC study, "If all of the low density categories are combined, 61.2 percent of the retail distribution centers are located in counties with population densities of less than 500 persons per square mile, and 21 percent of the retail distribution centers are located in counties with population densities of less than 200 persons per square mile."[48]

Major cities with important freight transportation industries, including San Francisco, Los Angeles, Houston, Denver, and Chicago, lost warehousing and distribution establishments and employment to outlying counties. The counties gaining establishments and employment typically have their own commercial airports and are located at or just beyond the edge of a major metropolitan area. As in the case of DuPage County, Illinois (in metropolitan Chicago), these types of counties may be adjacent to a major metropolitan airport (in this case O'Hare). They benefit from proximity to a major airport but avoid the direct costs associated with airport functions (for example, traffic control and public safety services). Other counties that have gained warehousing and distribution establishments in the era of the exurban port include San Joaquin (Stockton) in Northern California; Franklin in central Ohio (Columbus); and San Bernardino and Riverside Counties in Southern California.

In Indiana, exurban pass-through distribution ports have boomed because of a combination of highway accessibility, cheap land, low taxes, incentives, and low-cost labor.[49] Two counties have become critical exurban distribution nodes: Hendricks County, adjacent to the Indianapolis airport, and Boone County, twenty miles northeast of Indianapolis. Both exemplify how industry growth in transportation and logistics attributed to a metropolitan area is, in reality, at the semirural exurban fringe. Hendricks County has a population of about 130,000, but its distribution center, Plainfield, has 22 million square feet of warehouse and distribution space in more than forty warehouses and 5,000 truck bays.

Boone County has a population of only 52,000, but it also has millions of square feet of recently built warehousing space spread over thousands of acres of

47. EEOC (2004).
48. EEOC (2004).
49. O'Malley (2008).

cheap rural land. New projects include a 318,000-square-foot automated pharmacy complex and an Amazon order fulfillment center. These projects and others will add 15 million square feet of new industrial space. To continue the development spiral, the city of Lebanon (the county seat of Boone County) is annexing 3,655 acres bordering Interstate 65.

How should local policymakers think about the costs and benefits of investing in a nationally oriented transport hub built to handle the pass-through of imported goods? To date, the discussion of the impact of such an economic development project has been limited by a poor understanding of the costs and benefits. In the next section we look at one key arena that economic development policymakers should investigate when making decisions about whether and how to invest in transportation and distribution centers: the consequences for employment and earnings.

What Are the Employment Implications of Pass-Through Distribution and Transportation Centers?

When economic development initiatives are evaluated to determine whether they merit public investment, the primary criteria that many policymakers use are how many jobs they produce and whether those jobs are good jobs, that is, whether they pay above average wages and provide good working conditions. Supporters of investing public funds to expand infrastructure for seaports and inland ports, including emerging demands for rail spurs, point to the high-wage jobs associated with logistics, transportation, and warehousing.[50] The figures supporting the high-wage argument for public investment in pass-through centers are picked up by commentators, such as Joel Kotkin, and used to attack environmentalists and others who question their public costs.[51]

There are skeptics, however, including those witnessing very high growth in their own regions. In some cases, these skeptics go to the trouble to look more carefully at the employment data. For example, in an analysis of the potential economic development benefits of public investment in a multiregional distribution complex on the outskirts of Sacramento, Jock O'Connell examined the implications of the common practice of using average wage figures from the Bureau of Labor Statistics' Quarterly Census of Employment and Wages (QCEW) to project the income potential of jobs in the transport and logistics industries.[52] Because of wage bifurcation among workers, the QCEW reports

50. Husing (2006).
51. Joel Kotkin, "The Myth of Deindustrialization," *Wall Street Journal*, August 6, 2008.
52. O'Connell (2007).

provide an exaggerated measure of the wages actually received by the majority of people working in these industries.[53]

O'Connell used the Occupational Employment Statistics Survey (OES) to examine wage rates for particular occupations. These data, based on a semiannual survey of approximately 37,000 employers per year, provide average and median hourly wages and, most important, average wages earned by employees in the top and bottom quartiles in each occupational category. By contrast with studies using QCEW *averages*, which claimed that 81 percent of logistics jobs offered midlevel salaries—between $27,000 and $48,000 annually, O'Connell found a much different wage picture.[54]

> In 2006, the approximately one million Californians employed in the forty-five Transportation and Material Moving (T&MM) occupations received a mean hourly wage of $14.05. But the median hourly wage was significantly lower at $11.66. . . . Even worse is the wage plight of the lowest 25% of wage earners employed in the T&MM occupations. Their average hourly wage was $8.55, which annualizes to $17,784. . . . This is the quartile most likely populated by unskilled and poorly educated workers.[55]

O'Connell's findings are reinforced by a study of wages for logistics occupations for the Keystone Research Center in Pennsylvania. This study found that while regional distribution centers can be major employers, they do not pay high wages. Material handlers, the most common job title, earn under $13.00 per hour in Pennsylvania, and their annual earnings averaged $27,916.[56] In addition, these studies, as well as a study of alternative employment relations in Texas and one based on interviews in the "Inland Empire," found that distribution centers make intensive use of temporary help agencies to deal with seasonal differences in labor demand and to meet the labor needs associated with unpredictable just-in-time distribution systems.[57] This tells us that hourly wages may not translate into annualized salaries based on full-time employment. Many

---

53. O'Connell (2007). This is known as the "Bill Gates Gets on the Bus" statistical fallacy. If Bill Gates gets on a bus of poorly paid day laborers, the average or mean annual income of patrons on the bus would be over a billion dollars (O'Connell 2007). Because the mean is sensitive to the earnings of a few very high earners, it overstates the earnings of a typical worker, which would be more adequately represented by the median earnings (that is, the earnings of a worker in the exact middle of the earnings distribution). Median earnings are not available in the QCEW.

54. Regarding the use of QCEW averages, see Husing (2006).

55. O'Connell (2007, p. 7).

56. Belzer and others. (2005).

57. For the study in Texas, see Dalton (2002); for the "Inland Empire" study, see Bonacich and Wilson (2008).

workers may be able to work long hours at certain seasons of the year but may be unemployed during "trough" seasons.

Several studies noted that one of the most important factors separating low-paid logistics jobs from those that pay middle-class wages is union representation.[58] Union representation, however, is declining in these occupations. For example, from 1983 to 2002, the percentage of workers represented by unions fell from 31 percent to 14 percent in warehousing.[59] Union representation in trucking fell from approximately 60 percent overall during the early 1970s (and as high as 88 percent among class I common carriers of general freight in 1977) to 18 percent overall by the early 2000s.[60] Union representation in 2007 stood at 11.3 percent in the trucking industry as a whole and 15.6 percent overall among driver–sales workers and truck drivers.[61]

For economic development policymakers, then, the risks of investing in a multiregional distribution center complex are significant. Advising the Sacramento Area Council of Governments regarding the economic development potential of a multiregional distribution center, O'Connell summed up the dilemma:

> While the benefits of a robust logistics sector are felt regionally and sometimes nationally, the aesthetic and environmental downsides of facilities engaged in the movement and storage of goods are most directly experienced locally. This reality has prompted many public officials to call for greater equity in sharing the costs of ameliorating the consequences of air pollution, traffic congestion, and accelerated highway deterioration. The same imbalance as well to the dispersal of employment could be repeated. For example, a region seeking to attract enterprises engaged in wholesale trade may find that the high paying white-collar jobs which boost average wage figures are apt to be located in downtown office towers or suburban office campuses far removed from the warehouses, distribution centers and heavy rail or trucking venues where lower-paid blue collar work is performed.[62]

O'Connell's concerns are magnified by the EEOC study, which examined the changing location pattern of distribution and warehousing jobs and the implications of that shift for the employment of minorities and women.[63] The study found that as retail distribution centers grow in size (measured by number of employees), they tend to be located in less populated areas. In these less-

58. Belzer and others (2005); Bonacich and Wilson (2008); O'Connell (2007).
59. Bonacich and Wilson (2008).
60. Belzer (1995, 2002).
61. Hirsch and Macpherson (2009).
62. O'Connell (2007, p. 9).
63. EEOC (2004).

populated locations, the percentage of women and minorities in the relevant job groups (operatives and laborers) is lower than in urbanized locations. A comparison of the location of retail distribution centers and warehouses in 1982 with their location in 2002 suggests that had the locations remained in the same counties as in 1982, the relevant labor markets would have had 10 percent (based on EEO-1 data) to 14 percent higher (based on 2000 census data) minority representation as operatives and laborers.

Some policymakers in rural counties that are booming by virtue of attracting low-paid warehousing and distribution jobs because of their interstate highway and air cargo connections also raise concerns about the long-term implications of attracting a large workforce that earns low wages. One official from Boone County, Indiana, for example, worries that the incentives provided to the warehousing and pass-through distribution industries may pose long-term problems: "You need diversity in your job market. You need economic diversity. It's really important." An influx of low-paying jobs "puts additional burdens on the rest of the taxpayers" for supporting public services.[64]

These concerns with jobs as well as other public costs associated with pass-through hubs, in terms of road safety and environmental damage, raise critical issues for economic developers. They are faced with the difficult task of assessing whether investments in an infrastructure primarily oriented to delivering imports to national consumers provide enough local benefits to justify significant local costs.

As we indicated at the beginning of this chapter, however, the low-cost, truck transport–dominated era may be coming to an end. The combination of volatile fuel prices, along with environmental concerns about congestion, and competing needs for passenger transportation may change the calculus for freight transportation. In the next section we reflect on what is known about the existing system and speculate about the future and especially about the implications for regional economies.

The Problem of Integrating Different Infrastructures

Given the volatility in fuel prices, it is impossible to predict with certainty when the existing pass-through freight transportation mode will begin to experience severe cost pressure. Even with an extended period of cheap fuel, however, policy actions to reduce road congestion and limit the safety and environmental hazards associated with truck-based freight transport may contribute to cost increases and alter firm strategies. Changes in labor regulation may also make it possible for owner-operators to unionize, altering the bargaining power of the

64. O'Malley (2008).

workforce. And, while the spatial consequences of cost increases may differ depending on the source of increased costs, the presence of multiple sources is likely to change the behavior of shippers and, by extension, affect carriers and seaport and inland port operators.

Although shippers are not directly affected by congestion or the environmental impact of truck-based freight transport, the imposition of congestion fees or environmental impact regulation on carriers will raise their costs. These costs will be passed on to shippers, altering their practices, including what carriers they use, the spatial routing of shipments, and the location of distribution hubs. Volume shippers, such as Wal-Mart, may attempt to force the carriers to absorb all new costs, but because (as we have described above) the carriers are operating on very slim margins, some cost increases to the shipper may be inevitable.

The retail and manufacturing organizations built around economies of scale during the past thirty years of cheap truck transport are likely to resist significant change because of sunk costs in facilities. The same can be said of distribution hub operators. Thus, if truck–based transportation costs rise, we are likely to see moves to influence policy to maintain the existing system and to reduce costs strategically. Coalitions composed of high-volume retailers, megadistribution hub developers, and freight carriers may lobby for infrastructure investments that will maintain the efficiencies and low costs associated with the pass-through system.

Railroad transport is perceived as the major alternative to trucks and during this first decade of the twenty-first century, its share of freight transport has increased. Rail intermodal freight transport rose from 3.1 million trailers and containers in 1980 to nearly 10 million units in 2003. When examined carefully however, the railroad alternative is not a particularly good fit with the pass-through system because its infrastructure was intended to link up places and to serve passenger as well as freight needs.

Railroads tend to move through cities and so lack the advantages of the land-intensive distribution hubs in the metropolitan periphery that have grown up with the truck-based freight transport system. The Chicago hub, with its six railroads and massive congestion, is only the most egregious example of the problems that would emerge with a move to rail. The only way that rail could effectively serve the pass-through system is if new rail infrastructure (spurs, intermodal hubs, and so on) is constructed that is completely separate from traditional intercity rail service. Railroads are lobbying for such public investments in a new railroad infrastructure that would enable freight trains to move through cities rapidly via underpasses or overpasses. Infrastructure proposals also include plans to avoid cities altogether, linking existing exurban distribution hubs to rail networks.

Another set of changes may occur in those parts of the freight transport system that are consonant with maintaining economies of scale and the pass-through mode of operation. There may be a decentralization of seaport operations, for example, to take advantage of less expensive water transport to decrease the use of trucks to move freight to regions in the coastal megalopolis. This strategy would decrease the costs of congestion at the dominant ports, Los Angeles–Long Beach and New York–New Jersey, and potentially limit increases in environmental costs. This strategy is already evident in growing distribution and logistics industries in smaller ports, such as Albany, New York, which receives barge traffic from the New York port via the Hudson River.[65] Older industrial cities along water routes may receive some of this freight if they can provide the land facilities to handle pass-through traffic.

Overall, our analysis of import-driven, pass-through facilities and services indicates that positive local economic and employment impacts are likely to be minimal unless ways are devised to reconnect distribution facilities and services to local and regional economies. The potential to reconnect freight distribution with export-oriented manufacturing is, however, a difficult proposition because of the changes that have occurred in production organization and the dominance of freight transport by the high-volume retail shippers. Any shift toward a production organization that reestablishes regionally specialized industries is likely to have major forces arrayed against it. If it can happen at all, it is more likely to occur in those locations that retain a base of specialized expertise in industrial processes, such as Pittsburgh and Rochester (New York), or in globally connected advanced manufacturing, such as Detroit and Toledo. To realize this potential, however, will require working against the contemporary production organization of interconnected, dispersed plants organized to achieve economies of scale. Clever economic development strategies and public investments will be needed to rebuild regional supply chains and to find ways to make the freight distribution system work effectively for regional exporters. If effective, that could have significant benefits in bringing manufacturing and distribution multipliers back to the region.

Conclusion

Although federal policy has been critical in shaping the contemporary time-sensitive, truck-dependent freight transport system, state and local economic development policy has played a role, too. In the metropolitan regions that have risen in importance as freight transport centers, places such as San Bernardino, Laredo, Indianapolis, and Columbus, economic development policymakers

---

65. Christopherson and others (2008).

have fostered the construction of land-intensive, multimodal distribution hubs at the fringe of the metropolitan region. These hubs and the specialized seaports they are connected to primarily serve what is known as pass-through freight shipping.

The pass-through freight distribution system based on low-cost trucking and air freight is likely to face significant challenges in the near future. Fuel costs are predicted to increase over time and make imports and truck and air shipment more expensive. Freight shipping also may be affected by public demands to decrease the impact of truck-based shipping on the environment and to put more resources into public transportation. Finally, there may be policy interest in fostering U.S. exports, if the value of the dollar continues to decrease and if policymakers place more value on U.S. capacity in what is known as advanced manufacturing.

Our examination of the geography of transport nodes in the first years of this decade indicates both continuity and change. When looked at from 50,000 feet, we can see a pattern in which the established seaports and inland ports retain significant positions because of what Gunnar Myrdal described in the 1950s as initial advantage and circular and cumulative causation. The major transport centers for the East Coast megalopolis show up, as do the historic ports (New Orleans, Charleston, and Seattle), railroad towns (preeminently Chicago, but also Denver and Minneapolis–St. Paul) and river port cities (Memphis). All exhibit connections to earlier modes of transportation and logistics in the U.S. transport system. Their historic positions, based on site and situation, have spurred continuous investments in infrastructure, maintaining their specialization in freight transportation and logistics.

At the same time, there have been significant changes, wrought by policy decisions, to liberalize trade and deregulate transport industries. These changes are more in evidence in the secondary centers, some of which have risen in prominence beyond what might have been expected if conditions had remained constant. In many cases these metropolitan areas have risen to prominence because of their role in the dramatically expanded import trade and their willingness and ability to provide extensive land packages and inexpensive labor. Laredo, Indianapolis, and Columbus all fit this description.

The investments made during the era of cheap trucking and high-speed delivery are now "facts on the ground." Future policy goals to use less energy, reduce dependence on imports, and recapture production jobs within specialized regional economies will have to reckon with these massive import-oriented investments, the political coalitions that support them, and the limits they impose on our future choices.

References

Atkinson, Robert. 2004. *The Past and Future of America's Economy: Long Waves of Innovation That Power Cycles of Growth*. Northampton, Mass.: Edward Elgar.

Belman, Dale L., and Michael H. Belzer. 1997. "Regulation of Labor Markets: Balancing the Benefits and Costs of Competition." In *Government Regulation of the Employment Relationship*, edited by Bruce E. Kaufman, pp. 179–220. Madison, Wis.: Industrial Relations Research Association.

Belman, Dale L., K. A. Monaco, and T. J. Brooks. 2004. *Sailors of the Concrete Sea: A Portrait of Truck Drivers' Work and Lives*. Michigan State University Press.

Belzer, Michael H. 1994. "The Motor Carrier Industry: Truckers and Teamsters under Siege." In *Contemporary Collective Bargaining in the Private Sector*, edited by Paula B. Voos, pp. 259–302. Madison, Wis.: Industrial Relations Research Association.

———. 1995. "Collective Bargaining after Deregulation: Do the Teamsters Still Count?" *Industrial and Labor Relations Review* 48, no. 4: 636–55.

———. 2000. *Sweatshops on Wheels: Winners and Losers in Trucking Deregulation*. Oxford University Press.

———. 2002. "Trucking: Collective Bargaining Takes a Rocky Road." In *Collective Bargaining in the Private Sector*, edited by Paul F. Clark, John T. Delaney, and Ann C. Frost, pp. 311–42. Champaign, Ill.: Industrial Relations Research Association.

———. 2006. *OOIDA 2003–2004 Cost of Operations Survey: Report of Results*. Wayne State University.

Belzer, Michael H., and others. 2005. "Pennsylvania Logistics & Transportation." In *Workforce Choices*. Harrisburg, Pa.: Pennsylvania Department of Labor and Industry.

Bonacich, Edna, and Jake B. Wilson. 2008. *Getting the Goods: Ports, Labor, and the Logistics Revolution*. Cornell University Press.

Bowen, John T. 2002. "Network Change, Deregulation, and Access in the Global Airline Industry." *Economic Geography* 78, no. 4: 425–39.

———. 2008. "Moving Places: The Geography of Warehousing in the U.S." *Journal of Transport Geography* 16: 379–87.

Boyer, Kenneth D., and Stephen V. Burks. 2007. *Stuck in the Slow Lane: Traffic Composition and the Measurement of Labor Productivity in the U.S. Trucking Industry*. Bonn: Institute for the Study of Labor (IZA).

Campbell, Scott. 1993. "Increasing Trade, Declining Port Cities: Port Containerization and the Regional Diffusion of Economic Benefits." In *Trading Industries, Trading Regions: International Trade, American Industry, and Regional Economic Development*, edited by H. Noponen, J. Graham, and Ann R. Markusen, pp. 212–55. New York: Guilford.

Christopherson, Susan, and Jennifer Clark. 2007. *Re-making the Region: Labor, Power and Firms' Strategies in the Knowledge Economy*. London: Routledge.

Christopherson, Susan, and others. 2008. *Growing Your Own: Building Regional Economies through Targeted Workforce Development*. Report to New York State Association of Counties.

Cidell, Julie. 2008. "The Decentralization of Freight Transportation: Chicago in Context." Paper presented at 2008 Transport Chicago Conference (www.transportchicago.org/images/Freight-Cidell.pdf).

Combes, Pierre-Philippe, and Miren Lafourcade. 2005. "Transport Costs: Measures, Determinants, and Regional Policy Implications for France." *Journal of Economic Geography* 5, no. 3: 319–49.

Dalton, Elizabeth. 2002. "The Workforce in Alternative Employment Arrangements." IPED Technical Reports. University of Texas–El Paso, Institute for Policy and Economic Development.

Disdier, Anne-Célia, and Keith Head. 2008. "The Puzzling Persistence of the Distance Effect on Bilateral Trade." *Review of Economics and Statistics* 90, no. 1: 37–48.

Eno Transportation Foundation and Upper Great Plains Transportation Institute. 2007. *Transportation in America*. 20th ed. Fargo, N. Dak.

Freeman, Richard B., and Joel Rogers. 2006. *What Workers Want*. Ithaca, N.Y.: ILR Press and Cornell University Press.

Fritsch, Conrad F. 1981. "Exemptions to the Fair Labor Standards Act, Transportation Sector." *Report of the Minimum Wage Study Commission*. U.S. Government Printing Office.

Glaeser, Edward L., and Janet E. Kohlhase. 2004. "Cities, Regions and the Decline of Transport Costs." *Papers in Regional Science* 83: 197–228.

Hall, Peter V. 2004. "'We'd Have to Sink the Ships': Impact Studies and the 2002 West Coast Port Lockout." *Economic Development Quarterly* 18: 354–67.

Heilbroner, Robert. 1996. "Do Machines Make History?" In *Does Technology Drive History?* edited by Merritt Roe Smith and Leo Marx, pp. 53–66. MIT Press.

Hesse, Markus. 2006. "Global Chain, Local Pain: Regional Implications of Global Distribution Networks in the German North Range." *Growth and Change* 37, no. 4: 570–96.

Hesse, Markus, and Jean-Paul Rodrigue. 2004. "The Transport Geography of Logistics and Freight Distribution." *Journal of Transport Geography* 12, no. 3: 171–84.

Hirsch, Barry, and David Macpherson. "Union Membership and Coverage Database" (www.unionstats.com [February 4, 2009]).

Hummels, David. 2001. "Time as a Trade Barrier." GTAP Working Paper. Purdue University, Department of Agricultural Economics, Center for Global Trade Analysis.

Husing, John E. 2006. "Logistics: Southern California Has Competitive Advantages for a Major Blue Collar Sector for 1st Time since Defense Industry after WWII." Los Angeles: Southern California Leadership Council.

Johnson, Curtis. 2003. *Market Choices and Fair Prices: Research Suggests Surprising Answers to Regional Growth Dilemmas*. Report 17, Transportation and Regional Growth Study. University of Minnesota, Center for Transportation Studies.

Leiter, Robert D. 1957. *The Teamsters Union: A Study of Its Economic Impact*. New York: Bookman Associates.

Luberoff, David, and J. Walder. 2000. "U.S. Ports and the Funding of Intermodal Facilities: An Overview of Key Issues." *Transportation Quarterly* 54, no. 4: 23–46.

McCann, Philip. 2005. "Transport Costs and New Economic Geography." *Journal of Economic Geography* 5, no. 3: 305–18.

McCann, Philip, and Daniel Shefer. 2004. "Location, Agglomeration, and Infrastructure." *Papers in Regional Science* 83: 177–96.

Monaco, Kristen. 2005. "Wages and Working Conditions of Truck Drivers at the Port of Long Beach." Paper presented at the 2005 annual meeting of the Transportation Research Board. Washington, January 10–13.

Monaco, Kristen, and Lisa Grobar. 2004. *A Study of Drayage at the Ports of Los Angeles and Long Beach*. Los Angeles: METRANS.

O'Connell, Jock. 2007. "Growing the SACOG's Logistics Sector: How Much, How Fast." White Paper commissioned by the Sacramento Area Council of Governments (SACOG), California.

O'Malley, Chris. 2008. "Boone County Distribution/Warehousing Still Rule." IBJ.com: May 17 *Indianapolis Business Journal* (Downloaded December 1, 2008).

Parr, John B., and Suahasil Nazara. 2002. "Agglomeration and Trade: Some Additional Perspectives." *Regional Studies* 36: 675–84.

Petrovic, Misha, and others. 2006. "Making Global Markets: Wal-Mart and Its Suppliers." In *Wal-Mart: The Face of 21st Century Capitalism*, edited by Nelson Lichtenstein, pp. 107–42. New York: New Press.

Rodrigue, Jean-Paul. 2006. "Transportation and the Geographical and Functional Integration of Global Production Networks." *Growth and Change* 37, no. 4: 510–25.

Sheppard, Eric. 2002. "The Spaces and Times of Globalization: Place, Scale, Networks, and Positionality." *Economic Geography* 78, no. 3: 307–30.

U.S. Department of Labor (DOL). 2002. *Exemption from Maximum Hours Provisions for Certain Employees of Motor Carriers.* Washington: DOL, Wage and Hour Division.

U.S. Equal Employment Opportunity Commission (EEOC). 2004. "Retail Distribution Centers: How New Business Processes Impact Minority Labor Markets" (www.eeoc.gov. [November 4, 2008]).

Venables, Anthony J. 2006. "Shifts in Economic Geography and Their Causes." *Economic Review* 91, no. 4: 61–85.

Wilson, Rosalyn A. 2001. *Transportation in America 2000: Statistical Analysis of Transportation in the United States, with Historical Compendium 1939–1999.* 18th ed. Westport, Conn.: Eno Foundation for Transportation.

Winston, Clifford. 1993. "Economic Deregulation: Days of Reckoning for Microeconomists." *Journal of Economic Literature* 31, no. 3: 1263–289.

Zook, Matthew A., and Stanley D. Brunn. 2006. "From Podes to Antipodes: Positionalities and Global Airline Geographies." *Annals of the Association of American Geographers* 96, no. 3: 471–90.

7

How Might Inclusionary Zoning Affect Urban Form?

ROLF PENDALL

Housing affordability has been in crisis for at least a decade. Ever higher numbers of households find themselves unable to make mortgage payments or pay rent and cover utilities without forgoing other necessities. National policies have failed adequately to address these issues either directly—by increasing funds for tenant- or unit-based housing subsidies—or indirectly, through requirements for a living wage or an expanded Earned Income Tax Credit. In the face of federal neglect, local governments in many high-cost regions have become extraordinarily active and creative in affordable housing, shifting their regulations and even (especially in the case of New York City) investing portions of their discretionary local budget in housing.

One local program, inclusionary zoning (IZ), induces or requires private sector builders to provide affordable housing as a condition of project approval. Initially embraced by suburban areas with strong growth regulations, IZ "moved downtown" in the 1980s.[1] In the 1990s, local planning evolved from a "growth management" to a "smart growth" framework, adding high-quality neighborhood design to such long-standing regulatory goals as reducing sprawl, saving open space, protecting sensitive environments, and providing adequate infrastructure levels. This shift in emphasis raised concerns that smart growth is an elitist and exclusionary movement; in response, many smart growth advocates have added IZ to the smart growth toolkit, based largely on the example of Montgomery County, Maryland.[2] Jurisdictions in California and New Jersey have also used IZ extensively.[3]

1. Merriam, Brower, and Tegeler (1985).
2. Brown (2001).
3. Calavita (1998); Calavita, Grimes, and Mallach (1997).

223

Advocates for smart growth, however, have not yet examined deeply whether IZ and compact development are complements or substitutes for one another. Some critical observers characterize IZ flatly as a tax on market-rate development that will simply displace growth.[4] If they are right, then IZ would undermine, rather than support, goals for high-density development within and adjacent to established neighborhoods. But many characteristics of IZ suggest that it need not reduce development and may in fact support a higher-density development pattern, as supported by two recent studies.[5]

This chapter begins with a definition of inclusionary zoning in its narrowest sense—a program requiring builders to provide affordable housing—and in a broader sense, followed by discussion on the number of IZ programs in various parts of the United States. It then sets out a framework for understanding the conditions under which IZ would affect urban form at the scale of buildings, neighborhoods, jurisdictions, and housing market areas (regions). The impacts will depend on complex interactions between local IZ program design, other local regulations, housing market conditions, and the regulatory environment of surrounding jurisdictions within the housing market area. A review of studies on IZ and other regulations follows, with special attention to two studies by Gerrit-Jan Knaap, Antonio Bento, and Scott Lowe and Jenny Schuetz, Rachel Meltzer, and Vicki Been, and recent studies on development impact fees.[6] This recent work places IZ, like other development regulations, into the context of local government politics and the local built environment, showing that IZ adoption and design are at least as much a consequence as a cause of local development patterns.

How, then, should we understand IZ writ large? As I argue in the conclusion, IZ, similar to zoning, is a flexible tool that planners can design either to enhance compact development or to promote low-density, single-use development. In closing, with the hope that local governments will embrace IZ as part of a larger program promoting more compact, diverse, walkable, economically mixed neighborhoods, I offer suggestions about how to design an IZ program that will accelerate the attainment of such a pattern.

Toward a Sustainable Urban Form

Before beginning the review of the definition and impacts of inclusionary zoning—the "cause" that motivates this chapter—it will be helpful to review a few aspects of urban form—the "effects" that have not, to date, been explored

4. Ellickson (1981); Powell and Stringham (2004).
5. Knaap, Bento, and Lowe (2008); Schuetz, Meltzer, and Been (2007).
6. Knaap, Bento, and Lowe (2008); Schuetz, Meltzer, and Been (2007).

with regard to IZ. For at least 100 years, planners and architects have had concerns with the nature and arrangement of urban development. Starting in the late 1990s, urban sprawl became not only an abstract issue for academics and planners but a concrete political concern. In response to the emergence of sprawl on the national political agenda, many advocates began exploring in greater depth which characteristics of urban form related most closely to such negative outcomes as disappearing open space, excessive driving, and ugly streetscapes. Interest in a different land use pattern has grown yet more in the past five years, as observers have come to associate sprawl with public health issues (for example, obesity or automobile-related casualties) and with global climate change.

Advocates seek changes in several characteristics of urban form as a means to promote sustainable cities; many of these characteristics of urban form might also be influenced in some way by IZ, as I will discuss shortly. The density of urban development (the number of residents or jobs per acre of developed land) affects vehicle miles traveled, the consumption of agricultural land and habitat, and the characteristics and amount of storm water runoff. The mix of land use at the neighborhood or block level may affect people's willingness and need to drive as opposed to walking or cycling. The mix of housing types in the neighborhood might provide visual relief and interest that will sustain reinvestment in the community. The design of streets and block fronts, including anything from the way that doors and windows meet the street, the number of doorways fronting the street, the nature of the street wall (the portion of the buildings fronting the sidewalk), and the uses of ground or upper-story floors, may also influence people's desire to walk and use transit.

Inclusionary Zoning: Definitions and Policy Goals

Confusion about IZ begins with its very definition. Is it any inclusive housing policy? Any program resulting in a developer's contribution of affordable housing? Or a mandate for developer contributions? Here, I define the program, focusing first on the narrowest definition and then broadening the scope more generally to inclusive land use planning and regulations.

In the Narrowest Sense

In its narrowest definition, *inclusionary zoning* is a mandate in which local governments require residential builders to provide a share of housing that will be affordable over a long term to people earning low to moderate incomes. Presumably, the prices or rents for these units will fall below market rates at least at the time of construction. Narrowly defined local IZ programs have a long history in the United States, dating back to the 1960s or early 1970s. Montgomery County adopted the most famous one in 1973.[7] Newton, Massachusetts, had an informal IZ program as early as the 1960s but did not adopt a formal ordinance until 1977.[8]

Even though they may seem straightforward, mandatory IZ programs feature significant complexity. IZ responds to at least two policy goals: first, encouraging the production of as much affordable housing as possible and second, integrating low-income families into neighborhoods otherwise affordable to only the middle and upper classes. In some states, especially New Jersey, IZ also began from the desire of advocates to provide housing choices for black families in mostly white suburbs, but the civil rights connection has been absent from recent policy agendas. Even within goals, there is complexity; for example, all else being equal, there will be a trade-off among the depth of affordability, the number of units being made available, and the length of time during which units must remain affordable.

The nature and evolution of these goals traces back to the contexts within which IZ developed. First, a series of IZ programs (especially those that offered density bonuses to builders) emerged in response to exclusionary zoning in affluent suburbs. The outstanding examples of these programs are what might be considered state-mandated IZ in New Jersey as a result of the *Mount Laurel* rulings and the Massachusetts so-called anti-snob zoning provisions enacted as chapter 40B.[9] These programs differ dramatically from local programs, because they tend to enjoy strong support from builders and opposition from local governments (the opposite of most locally initiated programs). Second, some politically liberal suburbs adopted IZ themselves in an effort to become more economically integrated and to balance the potential negative impacts of their growth management programs on housing affordability: Montgomery County is probably the best known of these latter examples.[10] Third, a number of large cities—led by Boston and San Francisco—have adopted IZ, energized by organizations and residents who want to avoid gentrification.[11] Within each of these three contexts, some concern exists over rising inequality at the local and neigh-

---

7. Brown (2001); for the formal ordinance, see Engler (2002).

8. For a discussion of the informal IZ program, see Engler (2002). For the formal ordinance, see Horsley Witten Group, "Inclusionary Zoning Urban Case Study," prepared for the Massachusetts Office of Environmental Affairs as part of the Smart Growth Toolkit (n.d.) (http://www.mass.gov/envir/smart_growth_toolkit/pages/CS-iz-newton.html).

9. For a discussion of the Mount Laurel rulings, see Haar (1996). For the anti-snob zoning provisions, see Krefetz (2001).

10. Brown (2001).

11. Merriam, Brower, and Tegeler (1985).

borhood levels, although motivation to adopt IZ is also based on worries over the availability of low-cost labor to fill jobs in high-cost places.

The theory of change behind IZ is that the appropriate application of government incentives and mandates can induce landowners and builders to shift housing production from exclusively middle- and upper-income units to a wider range of housing types and price levels. IZ cannot usually meet many of its possible goals equally well and in the same location, however, because it is a local program (that is, it does not apply to entire housing markets) and because it uses the private sector to achieve social goals. An IZ program that seeks deep, long-lasting affordability of many units integrated into market-rate development is, in most places, a program that will drive landowners to use their land for nonresidential purposes and builders to ply their trade elsewhere.

Because of these complexities and the sensitivity of private sector actors to real or perceived disincentives, decisionmakers must answer a series of questions as they decide how to design IZ in their locations. As has been recognized for at least twenty-five years, the answers to all these program design questions will have varying effects on developer decisionmaking.[12]

What share of units must be affordable, and for how long must they remain affordable? Inclusionary zoning programs range in their requirements from an almost token share of units—as little as 5 percent—to a very high share of units. Bridgewater, New Jersey, for example, required for several years that 40 percent of its new housing units be affordable.[13] Like other affordable housing programs, IZ programs can have units with affordability terms that sunset after a short time or that last practically forever. For example, Pleasanton, California, shifted to a ninety-nine-year affordability requirement, also the case for Santa Monica, California. In Montgomery County, at the other end of the scale, many of the affordable dwellings have already exited the affordable housing inventory.

Will base densities be raised to accompany and offset the inclusionary mandate, and will developers be able to take advantage of those higher permitted densities? In and of itself, the answer to the "percent mandate" question makes little difference to developers without a sense of whether the mandate will be offset by higher permitted density. A 5 percent mandate with no density bonus, for example, might be less appealing than a 20 percent mandate with a 40 percent density bonus. But builders' ability to capitalize on a density bonus depends on other development requirements. A large increase in permitted density will often shift development from one structure type to another. For example, presented with an apparently astronomical 50 percent density bonus, a developer can build single-family houses at eight dwellings per acre or at twelve per acre, which is not as

12. Mallach (1984).
13. Mallach (1984, p. 107).

comfortable as the former—and certainly not for the same market. A shift from thirty to forty-five units per acre will probably also entail a shift from a wood-frame, walk-up building to a steel-frame structure with an elevator, which might reduce or even eliminate a project's feasibility. Local development standards can also limit the utility of a density bonus; most important for multifamily projects, onerous parking requirements might result in a need for structured parking, which like steel frame housing construction could make a project unfeasible.

What will be the target level of affordability for the units? Closely related to the question of the breadth of affordability is that of the depth; any program design will grapple with this issue, and IZ is no exception. The least demanding local programs typically require developers to provide housing aimed at those earning less than 80 percent of the area median income (AMI). On the one hand, since the median incomes of renters, Latinos, and African Americans generally fall between 50 and 70 percent of the area median, an 80 percent standard tends to serve better-off households among those who might benefit from IZ. On the other hand, some IZ advocates explicitly push for programs advertised as "work-force housing" programs. David Rusk, for example, suggests the slogan "anyone good enough to work here is good enough to live here."[14] As Rusk notes, after the construction of inclusionary rentals, some assisted tenants can use portable subsidies (for example, housing choice vouchers) to live there affordably, especially if local governments make deliberate efforts to open the new units to voucher users.

Will the units be aimed at renters or homeowners? Practically unexamined in the literature is the question of how and whether local IZ programs target tenure. Affordability problems are much more severe for low-income renters than for low-income homeowners. Even so, some local governments perceive a range of important benefits in aiming their IZ programs either exclusively or partly at homeowners. Pasadena, California, matches the tenure of the affordable units to that of the market-rate ones.[15] Pleasanton and Newton recently moved in opposite directions, toward favoring rental housing and homeownership, respectively.[16]

Is there a minimum development size to which IZ will apply? Montgomery County, widely cited in the literature, at first exempted all developments of fewer than fifty units from its IZ program.[17] Other jurisdictions apply the requirement

14. David Rusk, "Nine Lessons for Inclusionary Zoning: Keynote Remarks of David Rusk to the National Inclusionary Housing Conference, Washington, DC, October 5, 2005" (www.gamaliel.org/DavidRusk/keynote%2010-5-05.pdf [October 2005]).

15. City of Pasadena, *Pasadena Municipal Code*, ch. 17.42, "Inclusionary Housing Requirements" (2008) (http://cityofpasadena.net/zoning/P-4.html#17.42 [2008]).

16. Pendall (2008b).

17. Brown (2001).

to practically everything; for example, Santa Monica applies its inclusionary requirement even to two-unit projects, which must pay a fee in lieu of building the units.[18] Any IZ program with a threshold will create some incentive at the margin for strategic scaling of projects to slip in under the IZ threshold.

What options do builders have if they do not want to provide units on site? Many local governments provide a range of options apart from on-site construction to allow developers to meet their inclusionary obligation. Some of the more common options include the construction of affordable dwellings in a different location, the payment of a fee in lieu of construction, participation in the purchase or rehabilitation of an existing development to provide long-term affordability, and the donation of a site suitable for affordable development. All else being equal, IZ will produce a larger number of affordable dwellings when builders have more options with which to respond. Some jurisdictions, however, aspire to economic integration at the level of subdivisions and buildings and not just to a total production goal; no alternative works as well as on-site construction in integrating by class. Moreover, some jurisdictions with IZ have exhausted the development capacity of their zoning ordinances, limiting the effectiveness of several options. New York City responded to such conditions by emphasizing construction and rehabilitation of rental apartment buildings as an option to new construction in Williamsburg and Greenpoint neighborhoods.[19] Pleasanton attempts to shift the balance in favor of on-site development without necessarily foreclosing alternatives.

To what extent must the affordable units be equivalent to the market-rate units? (*That is, must they be identical in every respect? Can they be of lower quality? Can they be smaller? Can they be located in different parts of the same development?*) While this may seem a second-order question, it can have a big effect. In Montgomery County, for example, builders were able to meet the inclusionary requirement (at least in the early years of the program) by providing houses meant for sale that were smaller and featured modest-quality appliances, fixtures, and cabinets. This predictably made the units less expensive for builders to provide but created identifiable differences from the market-rate units that some observers might find distasteful. Even after the affordability period ended, however, these units retained a lower cost because of their smaller size.[20] Units built with the proceeds of in-lieu fees or on alternate sites, similarly, would practically never be identical to the market-rate units that generated the offsets.

18. Andy Agle, director of housing and economic development, city of Santa Monica, "FY06/07 Annual Report to the City Council Concerning the City's Affordable Housing Production Program" (S.M.M.C., sec 9.56) (2007) (www.smgov.net/housing/reports/Prop_R_Report_FY06-07.pdf [December 2007]).
19. Mintier (2007).
20. Brown (2001).

Getting a clear understanding of the answer to any of these questions is very complex at any one time. In a case study of jurisdictions in California and Massachusetts, Rolf Pendall showed that program features evolve, following no clear pathway.[21] Pleasanton shifted from a shallow subsidy program aiming to provide affordable homeownership opportunities toward a more deeply affordable rental housing program; both versions have featured substantial flexibility in the construction of new units. Newton has arguably shifted in the other direction, toward a program favoring homeownership. In their study based on interviews with program administrators, Schuetz, Meltzer, and Been suggested that programs in the San Francisco Bay Area (hereafter, the Bay Area) have generally become more stringent, by requiring deeper and longer affordability terms, through time, while those in Maryland and Virginia have a more mixed record.[22]

Broadly, local governments will design their IZ programs, if they are rational at all (and some may not be), according to a calculus that weighs a series of factors. First, does the locality really want affordable housing, or does it want to create the appearance of sympathy to affordable housing with no real impact? The three states where IZ has become most common—New Jersey, California, and Massachusetts—all require local governments to demonstrate their commitment to affordable housing through planning requirements and anti-NIMBY legislation.[23] Some exclusive, and exclusionary, jurisdictions might design an IZ program as a convenient smokescreen that will divert attention from its underlying hostility to low-income housing. In fact, Alan Mallach noted that the aggressive IZ ordinance in Bridgewater had not produced a single unit of affordable housing as of 1984.[24] Localities have ample opportunity to design an IZ program that not only will fail but also will discourage all new residential development: large and deep affordability requirements, no offsets, application to all new development types, no waivers of other standards, and so on.

Second, a jurisdiction's attitudes toward growth rates will also affect its IZ design and evolution. Jurisdictions that accommodate or even want to accelerate growth might take the path opposite that of a hypothetical anti-affordable housing jurisdiction. What about those jurisdictions in which decisionmakers prefer not to add too many new residents but want deeper affordability for households

---

21. Pendall (2008b).

22. Schuetz, Meltzer, and Been (2007).

23. Concerning planning requirements, see, for example, California State Housing Element Law, *California Government Code*, sec. 65580 *ff.* (2008). For anti-NIMBY (Not in My Backyard) legislation, see, for example, the New Jersey Fair Housing Act, *New Jersey Statutes, Annotated*, 52:27 D-301 (2008), and Massachusetts's Regional Planning: Low and Moderate Income Housing law, *General Laws of Massachusetts*, ch. 40B, sec. 20–23 (2008).

24. Mallach (1984, p. 107).

who live there?[25] Such jurisdictions might logically adopt IZ as a redevelopment mechanism for the gradual reconstruction of established high-density neighborhoods into moderate-density, mixed-income areas; the conversion of apartments into mixed-income condominium projects; or the conversion of existing below-market-rate apartment developments to mixed-income projects at the end of their affordability terms. If it wants to achieve any of these three objectives, a slow-growth pro-affordability jurisdiction has plenty of points in the planning and regulatory process at which it can impose inclusionary requirements.

A third and related factor concerns the jurisdiction's degree of support for higher-density housing construction through supportive regulations, infrastructure, and attitudes. Generally speaking, the support structure for high-density housing in the San Francisco Bay Area—home to the highest concentration of IZ programs in the United States—and in suburban Washington, D.C.—home to some of the earliest programs—far exceeds that in either New Jersey or Massachusetts. Zoning ordinances in the Bay Area and metropolitan Washington widely accommodate residential development at densities exceeding thirty dwellings per acre and rarely exclude moderate-density garden apartment developments entirely. The majority of jurisdictions in New Jersey and Massachusetts, by contrast, restrict density to fewer than fifteen dwellings per acre and would seldom allow a moderate-density apartment development.[26] The regulatory environment for high-density housing development is reinforced by, and in turn reinforces, infrastructure systems: the regions that allow high-density housing tend to have better-developed public sewer and water systems than those that avoid it. These infrastructure investments raise land values, increasing developer expectations for density; they influence those local officials who wish to make best use of infrastructure investments; and they probably reduce pressure from local residents who would oppose high-density development mainly on the basis of infrastructure adequacy issues.

A fourth factor in program design, one that also acts upon the other factors influencing IZ design, is the size and complexity of the jurisdiction. A medium-sized or large jurisdiction with a complex mix of land uses—for example, Montgomery County—cannot perpetually assume "someone else" will house its low-wage workers, teachers, and firefighters. A small, primarily residential jurisdiction can easily make that assumption and thus might be less concerned with designing an IZ program that works. A larger and more complex jurisdiction also usually has professional dedicated staff, organized constituents for affordable housing, and a series of housing programs within which IZ is only one (and often a

---

25. Here, I have in mind such jurisdictions as Cambridge, Massachusetts; Berkeley, California; and Santa Fe, New Mexico.

26. Pendall, Puentes, and Martin (2006).

small) strategy. It can therefore more easily design a context-sensitive and results-oriented IZ program that it monitors and adapts through time.

A local government's IZ design will also respond largely to its state context. In New Jersey, local governments can "immunize" themselves against builder's remedy challenges by enacting a state-certified housing element. Usually, certified elements incorporate inclusionary zoning with density bonuses, and often they follow very similar models because of the state requirement and because of the initial language in the *Mount Laurel II* ruling.[27] In the three southern New England states (Massachusetts, Rhode Island, and Connecticut), municipalities face builder's remedy challenges until at least 10 percent of the housing is subsidized. Since 2000, however, Massachusetts and Rhode Island have modified these provisions to encourage the integration of land use planning and housing planning, thereby erecting hurdles to some builder's remedy challenges and potentially creating new incentives for local governments to adopt IZ as a defense mechanism. In August 2003, Illinois adopted a threshold-based statute that integrated housing planning and IZ as mechanisms for local governments to protect themselves from builder challenges.[28]

California's laws exert an especially strong effect on its local governments' IZ program design. Redevelopment agencies in the state are required to incorporate low- and moderate-income housing in new developments within project areas, and the California Coastal Act requires inclusionary units in new housing in the coastal zone.[29] Both requirements establish thresholds and inclusionary percentages. California's discretionary local IZ programs also respond to state signals and pressures. The state requires local governments to offer a prescribed density bonus if builders volunteer to provide specified levels of affordable housing, as discussed later in this chapter. This requirement may induce some local governments to impose IZ with deeper affordability levels than builders would voluntarily provide. In addition, the state requires local governments to adopt housing elements as part of their mandatory general plans and that these elements incorporate an array of programs to address affordable housing needs. While this second requirement probably does not have a direct effect on program design, it probably results in the adoption of more IZ programs than would occur in the absence of a strong housing element requirement. One aspect of housing element law may affect program design: the review of draft housing elements by the state's Department of Housing and Community Development

27. *South Burlington County N.A.A.C.P. v. Township of Mount Laurel*, 92 N.J. 158 (1983) (*Mount Laurel II*).

28. Meck (2003). For an early appraisal of the act in the Chicago area, see Hoch (2005).

29. California Coastal Act, *California Public Resources Code*, sec. 30600.1 (1982) (www.coastal.ca.gov/ccatc.html [January 2008]).

(HCD), which requires local governments to analyze whether their IZ programs may constrain development or raise the cost of housing rather than facilitating housing construction.[30]

Regional context also can affect program design. Schuetz, Meltzer, and Been noted that in the Bay Area and Boston, jurisdictions appear to adopt inclusionary ordinances resembling those of their neighbors, something not as true in metropolitan Washington (where jurisdictions are generally larger in area).[31]

Local programs are, in sum, products of local political processes, embedded within the larger, complexly constrained context of policymaking. Local program design might contribute visibly to urban form but more likely is only one small constituent of the many forces shaping the local built environment.

Broader Definitions: Inclusive Housing Policy and Programs

Local governments can encourage affordable housing without necessarily requiring it. Such encouragement can range from modest to aggressive and from targeted to broad ranging. Most common in the United States is the incentive density bonus, which resembles the offset density bonus used in mandatory IZ programs. Incentives obviously would need to be more aggressive than offsets to persuade otherwise unwilling developers to provide affordable housing units. California law, for example, now requires local governments to offer a density bonus of up to 35 percent plus additional concessions, in exchange for providing as few as 5 percent affordable housing units.[32] Many of the program design questions for mandatory IZ apply as well to incentive IZ programs, especially those allowing a range of options for providing affordability (for example, off-site construction and in-lieu fees), affordability targets, and associated waivers and amendments to local fees and development standards.

The encouragement of affordable housing can also be embedded within the structure of a jurisdiction's or a region's land use regulations. In some jurisdictions and entire metropolitan areas, local governments decline to adopt or are prevented from enacting regulations that obstruct the development of affordable housing types (for example, apartments and small single-family houses). Houston, Texas, is perhaps the outstanding example of a metropolitan area whose regulatory environment has historically allowed the unfettered development of hundreds of thousands of apartments spread very widely across the metropolitan

---

30. See, for example, letter from Lynn L. Jacobs, director, California Department of Housing and Community Development, to Ms. Kristine E. Thalman, chief executive officer, Building Industry Association of Orange County (California), December 13, 2007 (www.hcd.ca.gov/hpd/thalman_inc121307.pdf [December 2007]).

31. Schuetz, Meltzer, and Been (2007).

32. Kautz (2006).

area; Houston and the second-largest city in its region, Pasadena, have no zoning, and counties are prohibited from zoning unincorporated land outside city
limits. Consequently, landowners have wide latitude to anticipate market
demand and to respond to national and state regulatory and tax incentives for
apartment construction. Two huge waves of apartment development in the early
1970s and early 1980s resulted in a vast supply of rental housing that continues
to accommodate working households with a wide choice of modest-quality
dwellings. Even in the face of massive in-migration of evacuees from New
Orleans after the devastation of Hurricane Katrina in 2005, Houston's rental
housing vacancy rate did not dip below the mid-teens, where it has been with
few exceptions since the early 1980s.[33]

Among areas with greater local control and a stronger tradition of planning
than those in Texas, none has been more aggressive about requiring local governments to accommodate multifamily housing than metropolitan Portland.
Oregon's long-standing growth management program has nineteen statewide
planning goals that all local governments (cities and counties) must meet when
they develop their mandatory comprehensive plans and development regulations.[34] To carry out goals 10 and 14, for housing and urbanization, respectively,
Portland's elected metropolitan government adopted the Metropolitan Housing
Rule (MHR) that requires local governments to zone so that attached single-
family and multifamily dwellings account for at least half their zoned capacity
for potential housing units. In addition, the MHR requires almost all the cities
in the region to aim for average housing densities of eight to ten dwellings per
acre. (The MHR sets the target at six units per acre in five small cities.)[35] Oregon's homebuilders convinced the state legislature to block IZ in 1999, however,
and the high base densities mandated by state law have limited the potential for
incentive bonus density to produce deep affordability.[36] Pennsylvania—whose
politics and planning laws have not been reformed to the extent that Oregon's
have—also has restricted local governments' ability to use zoning to exclude
multifamily housing.[37]

33. Pendall (2008a).

34. *Oregon Administrative Rules*, 660-015-0000(10), adopted December 27, 1974, last
amendment effective March 31, 1988; *Oregon Administrative Rules*, 660-015-0000(14),
adopted December 27, 1974, last amendment effective April 28, 2006 (http://www.lcd.
state.or.us/LCD/adminrules.shtml).

35. *Oregon Administrative Rules*, 660-007-0035, LCD October 1981, f. & ef. December
11, 1981; LCDC January 1987, f. & ef. February 18, 1987 (http://arcweb.sos.state.or.us/
rules/OARS_600/OAR_660/660_007.html [October 2008]).

36. Kennedy Smith, "Lobby Group Looks to Repeal Oregon's Ban on Inclusionary Zoning," *Daily Journal of Commerce* (Portland, Ore.), February 7, 2007.

37. See, for example, *Surrick* v. *Zoning Hearing Board of Upper Providence Township*, 476
Pa. 182, 382 A.2d 105 (1977) (www.preservationist.net/laws_you_should_know/padocs/
Surrick_%20v_Upper_%20Providence.pdf [1977]).

Performance: Research on IZ and Density Bonus Adoption and Production

My 2003 mail survey of local governments in the fifty largest metropolitan areas in the United States offers a view on how many local governments used IZ, offered density bonuses for affordable housing, and adopted other regulatory affordable housing programs at the beginning of the decade. The survey was mailed to planners or elected officials in all jurisdictions with at least 10,000 residents. In seventeen metropolitan areas, where jurisdictions with more than 10,000 residents accounted for a small share of the metropolitan population or land area, I also sampled smaller jurisdictions.[38]

Only about 5 percent of the jurisdictions in the fifty biggest metropolitan areas are estimated to have mandatory IZ; these jurisdictions include 14 percent of the metropolitan population and 5 percent of the land area. California again leads the nation in the adoption of IZ, with over 35 percent of jurisdictions (124 jurisdictions) estimated to be using IZ. Jurisdictions with IZ are mainly bigger cities, with 45 percent of the metropolitan population in the "big four" metropolitan areas (Los Angeles, San Francisco, San Diego, and Sacramento) and only 10 percent of the land area. In San Francisco and Sacramento, over half the jurisdictions had IZ in 2003, a much higher share than that in San Diego (40 percent) or Los Angeles (22 percent). Interpretation of the survey for California is complicated, however, by California's IZ requirement in redevelopment areas: some jurisdictions reporting IZ may have been referring to the redevelopment requirement, while others not reporting IZ but with substantial redevelopment programs may have failed to report it.[39] These findings are, however, generally consistent with those of other studies.[40] A 2007 report from the California Coalition for Rural Housing found that the share of jurisdictions with IZ statewide had jumped to 32 percent (170 in all).[41]

An estimated 10 percent of jurisdictions offer a density bonus for affordable housing, making this the single most important regulatory affordable housing program. The impact of density bonuses, however, far outstrips its incidence at the jurisdictional scale, since they are available in jurisdictions accounting for 35 percent of the population in these fifty metropolitan areas and 21 percent of the land area. Because of its state mandates, California is the density bonus leader,

38. For more details on the survey, see Pendall, Puentes, and Martin (2006).

39. This is also a shortcoming of other studies of IZ in California. Schuetz, Meltzer, and Been (2007), for example, reported that seven of ten counties and 48 of 104 incorporated cities have adopted "some form of IZ"; but it is not clear whether this count specifically refers to citywide IZ beyond redevelopment requirements.

40. Calavita (1998); California Coalition for Rural Housing and Non-Profit Housing Association of Northern California (2003).

41. California Coalition for Rural Housing (2007).

with 81 percent of jurisdictions estimated to be using them.[42] Between a quarter and a third of jurisdictions offer density bonuses in Massachusetts, Connecticut, Washington State, and Delaware.

In New Jersey, about a quarter of jurisdictions (143 in all) have IZ; these jurisdictions account for 27 percent of the population and 36 percent of the land area. These statistics show the impact of the *Mount Laurel* rulings, which essentially mandated IZ in "developing" suburban townships that had not yet accommodated much affordable housing. The surprise in New Jersey, however, is that only an estimated 11 percent of its jurisdictions offer density bonuses. In Maryland, well-known for IZ because of Montgomery County's pioneering program, only an estimated four jurisdictions (18 percent of those for which estimates were made), which compose about a quarter of the state's metropolitan population and land area, now have IZ. Jurisdictions in Massachusetts also had a high incidence of IZ, with 14 percent of jurisdictions containing 35 percent of the metro area's population. In twenty-one of the thirty-seven states, none of the respondents had IZ, and most of these states were in the South and Midwest but also included Pennsylvania, Arizona, Oregon, and the District of Columbia.

How do jurisdictions with IZ differ from those without it? Considering that state policies tend to target different kinds of jurisdictions for policy interventions, it is appropriate to consider this question separately within the three states where the largest number of jurisdictions that responded to the survey has IZ: California, Massachusetts, and New Jersey. In California, 71 of 172 city respondents had IZ in 2003, 17 of the 97 respondents from Massachusetts cities and towns had it, and 30 of 101 New Jersey municipalities reported that they had IZ. In these three states, median contract rent is higher in jurisdictions with IZ; jurisdictions with IZ appear also to have higher shares of white non-Hispanic (in California and New Jersey) and Asian (Massachusetts and New Jersey) residents and lower shares of Hispanic residents (California and New Jersey). New Jersey jurisdictions with IZ also have significantly lower shares of black residents than those without IZ. IZ localities also have higher incomes and newer housing stock in California and New Jersey and higher shares of housing in single-family, detached stock and owner-occupied tenure in New Jersey. Massachusetts departs somewhat from these patterns, with lower shares of single-family housing, higher shares of renters, and slightly older housing stock.

Reliable data on the total production of IZ programs are difficult to get, but some sources have tried. The most recent reports on IZ in California suggest

42. Since California law requires that local governments provide a density bonus to affordable housing developers, we must also treat responses to this question with caution. Schuetz, Meltzer, and Been (2007) reported that only four Bay Area jurisdictions have a voluntary density bonus program, which suggests a lack of precision in the wording of questions and survey instruments (including my own).

that it has been responsible for producing at least 29,000 units.[43] Programs in the Washington, D.C., metropolitan area had produced at least 15,000 units by 2003, mainly in Montgomery County, but many of the Montgomery County units have since shifted to market rate because of their short affordability terms.[44] IZ therefore ranks as a minor, but not unimportant, player in the creation of affordable housing in these high-cost regions.

How Might IZ Affect Urban Form?

Considering the wide variety of meanings associated with inclusionary zoning, as shown in the introductory sections of this chapter, it should come as no surprise that the answer to the question "How might IZ affect urban form?" would be "It depends." Even for a single jurisdiction, IZ might increase, have no effect on, or decrease a jurisdiction's total new residential supply, density, and unit mix. The result will depend on the characteristics of the jurisdiction's housing market, the IZ program design, the nature of other land use regulations, and the availability of acceptable alternative locations that lack IZ. Since the built environment takes a long time to evolve, and since all four of these factors change often rapidly, identifying the precise contribution of IZ will be very challenging.

Housing Market Conditions

As discussed often and at length in the literature on development impact fees, the effect of a local exaction (including affordable housing) or development standard (for example, parking) on development depends on the strength of demand for residential development in that jurisdiction. Assuming that the IZ requirement lowers the potential profit from development (an assumption that depends on program design, as discussed below), builders will avoid IZ jurisdictions where demand is modest, especially when prospective buyers of market-rate units have large numbers of alternative locations. In such situations, builders cannot pass along the cost to market-rate buyers; landowners in the IZ jurisdiction, perhaps expecting a change in demand or regulations, will (according to economic theory) withdraw their property from the market rather than accept lower prices for their land.[45]

Of course, the assumption that local governments will adopt IZ or any other regulation in the face of weak market conditions is itself subject to question.

43. California Coalition for Rural Housing (2007).

44. For affordable housing units, see Fox and Rose (2003, p. 15). For units changing to market rate, see Brown (2001).

45. The true decisionmaking calculus of landowners is probably not nearly this rational, however; in many situations, landowners will probably accept a "satisfactory" price for their property that falls below their desired price.

Typically, local governments adopt regulations in response to problems and market conditions. Local governments in weak-market regions such as Buffalo and Pittsburgh do not adopt IZ; rather, IZ is popular in strong-market regions such as metropolitan Washington, D.C.; the San Francisco Bay Area; and (until recently) hot markets in Florida. Furthermore, one cannot realistically assume that prospective buyers face multiple alternative locations without any IZ program; as noted earlier, local governments appear to mimic their neighbors' decisions to adopt IZ.[46]

IZ Program Design

IZ program design can affect urban form by influencing builders' decisions about whether to build housing at all, and if so, how much, what housing types, and where in the jurisdiction. These decision sets can potentially affect urban form at the scale of buildings, block fronts, neighborhoods, jurisdictions, and housing submarkets.

Except in very hot local markets, an IZ program that offers no offsets and requires long and deep affordability commitments would probably send most builders to other markets and might encourage landowners to withdraw their properties from the residential market (since such land would fetch lower prices than would many other potential uses). But the housing impacts of stringent IZ (or any IZ, for that matter) will depend on the complex interplay among landowners and their decision calculus (that is, whether to sell now or to wait, questions based on very imperfect information about the implications of waiting), the jurisdiction's commitment to relax other requirements or otherwise facilitate construction, the builder's sense of his or her own market and profit requirements, and the willingness of consumers of market-rate housing to pay more.

If a strong IZ results in a withdrawal of builders and land from the residential market, the implications for the jurisdiction's urban form depend on what happens on parcels where housing would have been built absent the IZ program. Many property owners would try to persuade the jurisdiction to rezone their land to accommodate nonresidential development, perhaps resulting in commercial, office, or industrial development. Some property owners might work with developers of subsidized housing. Most new subsidized projects require at least the consent, and more often the active participation, of local government. Thus, their success would depend on whether the local government in question really does want affordable housing. The dwelling style and street fronts in neighborhoods with assisted housing might differ substantially from the residential development that would have occurred there in the absence of IZ. In either of these cases (shift to nonresidential development or construction of

46. Schuetz, Meltzer, and Been (2007).

affordable housing types), building footprints, streetscapes, and transportation impacts would likely differ somewhat, and perhaps dramatically, from the pre-IZ regime.

An IZ program at the other end of the spectrum (with high-density bonuses or other offsets or with shallow and short-term affordability requirements) might appear so attractive to builders that they would flock to the jurisdiction. This would increase supply, perhaps delaying price increases in market-rate segments consequently and increasing the quantity of housing demanded in the jurisdiction. Land markets generally might adjust in ways that increase density in other (nonresidential) land uses.

Generally, any IZ program that allows builders to meet affordability requirements through a range of alternative approaches would also tend to reduce their inclination to avoid the jurisdiction. Beyond providing a possible boost to supply, a generous palette of alternative mechanisms for meeting the affordable housing requirement could reinforce the separation of housing types into discrete neighborhoods. Most IZ program designers see on-site construction of identical dwellings as a means for social integration, but such a requirement can also influence neighborhood design. Take as an example the construction of a golf course surrounded by large, single-family houses. A jurisdiction might require the builder to provide one of these houses as a four-unit affordable structure mostly indistinguishable from the single-family houses. It might also allow the builder to donate land so that another developer could build affordable housing someplace else in the jurisdiction, build the housing himself in a different location, or pay an in-lieu fee; any of these alternatives would almost certainly yield a different structure type than the four-unit building or buildings integrated into the golf course development.

Some IZ programs apply specifically to either single-family or multifamily development. A stringent or punitive policy applying only to single-family houses would tend to shift interest toward multifamily housing, whereas a program with strong incentives would pull builders toward the single-family market. Again, the precise impacts of this aspect of program design depend on the program's other aspects (as well as on the other three factors discussed here).

Other Characteristics of the Existing Local Regulatory and Built Environment

Similar to the effect of any affordable housing program, the effect of IZ will depend fundamentally on the regulatory regime and the built environment in the IZ jurisdiction and in its neighboring jurisdictions. On the regulatory side, nothing is more important than the base zoning, but it is hard to predict how zoning will affect the performance of IZ. As mentioned above, regulatory incentives (such as a density bonus) will attract builders, in part, depending on whether building and parking construction methods need to change to attain the bonus. For example, unless parking requirements were relaxed, a builder might need to shift from surface parking to much costlier structured parking before the builder could take advantage of the bonus. Attaining the full bonus density might also require the installation of elevators or even a shift from wood frame to steel construction. Under these circumstances, builders might decline a voluntary density bonus or might avoid a project entirely (if IZ is mandatory). In jurisdictions where the zoning ordinance requires large-lot development in most new growth areas, however, most builders would prefer to provide an alternative site or pay in-lieu fees, especially if on-site construction meant they would have to build an affordable "monster home." In jurisdictions that already feature a very complex regulatory environment, IZ might be the last straw for some builders. It might work well, at the same time, for other experienced players in the jurisdiction. From the perspective of urban form, the addition of yet another criterion or layer of complexity might delete players or actors from the local development market, perhaps resulting in more uniform design and development.

The existing built environment will also indirectly influence the urban-form impacts of IZ. Probably most important is the availability of centralized sewer and water. Developers need larger lots to accommodate on-site wells and septic systems as opposed to the size of lots they need to build on sites with public sewers and water. The impact of IZ on urban form in Boston (where centralized infrastructure is comparatively sparse), then, might diverge substantially from that in the San Francisco Bay Area (where public sewers and water are nearly omnipresent). The type of housing in both areas might even be identical (for example, garden apartments), but each development in Boston would require larger lots than each one in San Francisco and therefore would contribute to a more scattered development pattern. It is hard to judge whether Boston's pattern with IZ including density bonuses would be more scattered than that without it, but such would be the risk unless deliberate efforts were made to integrate IZ into a broader program for local compact development.

Availability of Substitute Jurisdictions

The impact of IZ on urban form will also depend on the regulatory environment in jurisdictions that builders view as potential substitutes for the IZ jurisdiction. Builders who see their locations as unique would assume that their potential market households will pay a high enough premium (in either more crowding of public facilities or higher housing costs) to offset any potential losses to themselves or to the landowner. If builders can go elsewhere and provide a similar product to a similar market segment but not have to provide inclusionary units, they would do so. A jurisdiction wanting its IZ program to succeed (that is, to provide affordable housing) would need to provide a sweeter set of incentives under these conditions than if the location were unique. Assuming that displacement occurred to substitute jurisdictions, however, the impacts on urban form would depend on the location and predominant built form(s) of the alternative(s). If the next best alternative is a little denser and closer to established development, for example, then the jurisdiction's IZ program will contribute (probably modestly) to compact development; otherwise, it could either be neutral or reduce compactness.

How Might Urban Form Affect IZ? Complexity and Endogeneity

Inclusionary zoning is clearly not just a cause of changes in the urban environment but also a consequence of certain kinds of change in the urban environment. In Pleasanton, for example, local residents urged the city to adopt IZ because of their concern that the community was becoming so affluent that it no longer resembled the city they had moved to over a decade previously.[47] Part of this shift entailed the creation of a large business park, proposals for high-density development on a large vacant parcel close to the downtown, and a struggle over the adoption of a redevelopment agency and area. In New York City, IZ is emerging as a measure to mitigate intensified land use and rapid gentrification of formerly working class and ethnic neighborhoods.[48] Schuetz, Meltzer, and Been also contend more broadly that IZ, like other regulations, must be treated as endogenous in econometric specifications: if IZ is a product of the housing changes one thinks IZ is creating, then we researchers mistakenly may be classifying as an effect something that is, in fact, a cause.[49] In this way, IZ resembles zoning more generally; political scientists and planners have known for decades that land use regulation is a political outcome.[50] Economists have caught up to this reality in the last twenty years, but the full import has not yet completely penetrated work on the impact of land use regulations, including IZ.[51]

From the standpoint of local politics, IZ resembles rent control even more than it does zoning in general. Teitz and Barton both point out that local governments tend to adopt rent control in response to a combination of rapidly rising rents and constrained housing supply.[52] Looking back at the proliferation of "second-generation" rent control ordinances in the 1960s, Teitz writes (in par-

47. Pendall (2008b).
48. Mintier (2007).
49. Schuetz, Meltzer, and Been (2007).
50. See, for example, Babcock (1966); Dubbink (1984).
51. Pogodzinski and Sass (1994); Wallace (1988); Quigley and Rosenthal (2005).
52. Teitz (1998); Barton (1998).

ticular about New York City): "After a period of oversupply in the early 1960s, a hiatus in construction and consequent rent increases led to a short-term upward movement in rents in the non-regulated stock and demands for regulation of the previously non-regulated, newer sector of the rental housing stock."[53] Many localities that have imposed strong rent controls have strong neighborhood preservation movements that limit new construction of apartments and small, single-family houses, restricting the supply of new entry-level housing even before rent controls are imposed; this was especially true in New Jersey but also in Berkeley and Santa Monica in California.[54]

Under the "permissive" conditions of strong home rule, and absent other signals from the state (for example, builder's remedy, affordable housing planning requirements), local governments usually adopt IZ in response to demands from progressive citizens and planners for more affordable housing, especially when rezoning allows landowners to capture increased land value. Such has been the case in Boston, San Francisco, Washington, D.C., and New York City, all of which have citywide or neighborhood-specific IZ programs. In these jurisdictions, concessions to affordable housing advocates are part of the cost of doing business and therefore a prerequisite to increased density in high-density parts of the metropolitan area. To measure or estimate how IZ would affect density and urban form in such progressive cities, analysts would need to follow the logic outlined in figure 7-1. In the absence of IZ, would the project be built at all? If housing advocates are strong enough, their opposition to a project without affordable units could either kill a project or delay it so long that it misses its expected market. If household demand exists for the market-rate component of the project, then presumably builders would meet that demand elsewhere in the city or region, potentially producing a less compact urban form. Under these circumstances, IZ politics echoes the politics of impact fees described more than a decade ago by Alan Altshuler and José Gómez-Ibáñez.[55] Rather than slowing growth, impact fees enable growth because they help quiet established residents' concerns that new growth will degrade their quality of life and force them to accept higher property tax rates.

Other jurisdictions might adopt IZ because they wish to use it as an anti-growth smokescreen. As discussed above, IZ can be so punitive that it makes residential development entirely impossible. In such cases, however, it would be hard to argue that IZ is uniquely responsible for slow or no growth; a jurisdiction in a state whose land use laws allowed the adoption of such an aggressive IZ

53. Teitz (1998, p. 70).
54. For a discussion of the situation in New Jersey, see Baar (1998, p. 142); for Berkeley and Santa Monica, see Clavel (1986).
55. Altshuler and Gómez-Ibáñez (1993).

Figure 7-1. *IZ in Progressive City Politics*

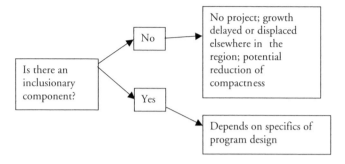

requirement (California being an example) would have a vast array of other tools as well for hindering or stopping housing. Rather than being the cause of slow growth, a smokescreen IZ ordinance represents a symptom of a slow-growth environment that would not disappear even if the ordinance were rescinded.

In summary, then, it is quite difficult to tell even in a case study setting exactly what would have happened in the absence of IZ. And even in the best-designed quantitative study, the many complexities involved in local IZ design and its evolution, and the regulatory environment of neighboring communities and their evolution, leave the results open to dispute.

What We Know about the Impacts of IZ from Recent Studies

The literature on the impacts of IZ is still quite new, partly because the program is new. Much of it has been produced in service of political agendas and sometimes paid for by interested parties.[56] Regardless of the quality of such studies, their funding sources ought to concern us and raise the level of scrutiny just as in the case of research funded by interests in debates over tobacco or fast food.

Most studies to date have concerned two main impacts of IZ: its impact on housing production in the jurisdictions that use it and its putative impact on the price or cost of single-family housing in these jurisdictions. The two most recent, and most rigorous, studies of these impacts of IZ are by Knaap, Bento, and Lowe and Schuetz, Meltzer, and Been.[57] They find little, if any, average

56. One example of such research is Powell and Stringham (2004), produced for the Reason Foundation. Schuetz, Meltzer, and Been (2007) and Basolo and Calavita (2004) discussed some key theoretical and methodological shortcomings of this study; in particular, the article fails to compare IZ to non-IZ jurisdictions, concentrating instead only on a "before-after" comparison of IZ jurisdictions.

57. Knaap, Bento, and Lowe (2008); Schuetz, Meltzer, and Been (2007).

impact on overall production and modest, if any, effects on housing prices. Both studies, however, are worth a closer look because they are models for future research, and the data on which they are based might provide more answers to the questions raised in this chapter. They are also both bound to enter into the highly charged public policy arena in municipalities, counties, and states that are considering the desirability of IZ.

The Knaap study, a nearly twenty-year retrospective, was based on IZ programs in California.[58] Knaap, Bento, and Lowe collected data on the existence and year of adoption of IZ programs, housing production by unit type, and a series of control variables in 369 cities. They also collected information on a series of IZ characteristics: whether developers were allowed to meet the affordability requirement through off-site building, in-lieu fees, or land dedication; the income range targeted by the IZ program; the affordability period; the minimum project size; and the percentage of units required to be affordable. Finally, they had access to a sales database containing price, dwelling-unit, and other data for nearly 300,000 new housing units in the San Francisco and Sacramento metropolitan areas built from 1988 to 2005.

Knaap, Bento, and Lowe's most important finding for those interested in urban form was that builders decisively shifted their production toward multifamily housing in California cities with IZ when compared with their production in non-IZ jurisdictions. After holding constant other characteristics of the city, IZ was associated with an average shift of more than 6 percentage points away from single-family and toward multifamily housing. That is, in a jurisdiction where builders started 1,000 dwellings in a given year, IZ would be associated with the production of about 69 more multifamily and 69 fewer single-family units. Bolstering this finding, Knaap, Bento, and Lowe found that the relationship held only in jurisdictions with strong (strict) IZ. An inclusionary mandate of more than 10 percent is associated with a shift of 12 percentage points toward multifamily housing, and an IZ threshold below ten dwellings is associated with a shift of nearly 10 percentage points.

The density shift occurred, moreover, without any significant relationship between IZ and total housing production. In fact, the authors found a small *positive* relationship between IZ and housing starts. Cities with IZ had 0.15 percent more total housing starts than other jurisdictions and 0.36 percent more multifamily housing starts; single-family starts were modestly lower in IZ cities (0.19 percent lower on average).

---

58. Knapp, Bento, and Lowe (2008), funded by the National Association of Home Builders, nonetheless appears to be rigorous and is neutral and measured in its writing style, not a "hit piece" like some other industry-funded studies have been.

Builders may have chosen to continue producing similar levels of housing even in the presence of IZ because they could pass along part of the costs to buyers in the hot housing markets where the programs concentrate. Knaap, Bento, and Lowe found that the average price of a subset of houses that sold for more than $187,000 (in 1988 dollars) was 5 percent higher in IZ jurisdictions than in non-IZ jurisdictions. The average price of the less expensive subset of houses dropped, in fact, but so did their average size. Thus, housing consumers at the low end helped pay for IZ by getting a little less space.

Knaap, Bento, and Lowe used strong cause-effect language when they contended that IZ shifts housing composition and raises prices, but their data could also support alternative hypotheses about the relationship between IZ and local housing markets. Housing starts in California occur only after lengthy planning and permitting processes, which often give jurisdictions a clear sense of the nature of future residential growth. It is plausible to hypothesize that some jurisdictions would impose IZ as they anticipate the construction of a large number of high-cost houses. (This was, in fact, the case in Brooklyn, where affordable housing advocates knew that the rezoning of Williamsburg–Greenpoint was about to deliver hundreds of new million-dollar apartments to the waterfront.) A jurisdiction where builders plan lower-cost housing, by contrast, might not even consider IZ. On the compositional effect of IZ, one would expect builders to oppose IZ ferociously in jurisdictions where they plan to build large, single-family houses; they might embrace it where they plan to build apartments, especially if they received density offsets and cooperation from planners. In both cases, IZ could be considered at least as much a consequence as a cause of shifting residential markets. Knaap, Bento, and Lowe also did not account for the possibility that local IZ programs might have changed through time.[59] If a jurisdiction adopts a mild (weak) form of IZ and sees that builders are still producing a large number of high-priced housing units, planners and decisionmakers might conclude that the IZ program could become stronger without killing market-rate production. Finally, the Knaap, Bento, and Lowe study did not account for changes in the rest of the regulatory environment in the city that may well accompany the imposition of IZ; as in Williamsburg–Greenpoint, IZ may be imposed only because of a dramatic broader change in the zoning ordinance that is itself primarily responsible for observed changes in housing supply.

Schuetz, Meltzer, and Been attempted to deal with some of the problems of endogeneity and overall regulatory complexity that leave open questions in the Knaap, Bento, and Lowe study. They used a combination of data on IZ from independent studies of the San Francisco; Washington, D.C.; and Boston met-

59. They measured IZ program features when they collected their data but asked only when IZ was first adopted; they did not ask about amendments to the program over time.

ropolitan areas, all collected initially by other groups but rounded out by their own follow-up interviews and analyses. Controlling more carefully for endogeneity in these three housing markets than Knaap, Bento, and Lowe did, Schuetz, Meltzer, and Been found evidence of a relationship between IZ and permits only in metropolitan Boston—production was lower in IZ jurisdictions—but once they controlled for market and other regulatory variables, IZ became statistically insignificant. Schuetz, Meltzer, and Been also noted that Boston's programs were generally too new to have had an effect on affordable housing (two years old at the median, as of 2006). This supports the hypothesis that IZ in Boston is a sign of an affluent jurisdiction that wants to control growth rather than a constraint on production in an otherwise open regulatory environment. They found no systematic (average) relationship between IZ programs and either housing permits or prices in San Francisco or Washington, D.C. Unlike Knaap, Bento, and Lowe, Schuetz, Meltzer, and Been did not examine the multifamily market (rents or housing permits and starts) at all, dismissing multifamily permits as unimportant in the overall new housing supply in all three regions between 1980 and 2005.

In summary, then, the two studies move a little closer to the answer to the question—"How does inclusionary zoning affect urban form?"—compared with where I was at the beginning: It depends, but if anything, IZ is associated with a shift toward higher-density housing types and not (on average) displacement of development. At the very least, it appears that the notion that IZ inevitably raises housing prices and depresses supply can be categorically dismissed, but neither does it seem to lower prices or increase supply, and under some circumstances, it might raise housing prices. (Recall, however, that the better-controlled Schuetz, Meltzer, and Been study found no average independent impact of IZ on housing prices.) By itself, therefore, on average, as applied in California and Massachusetts, IZ neither promotes nor discourages development in the jurisdictions that adopt it. It might raise housing prices in some segments of the market, but in others, it reduces house sizes, thereby potentially increasing the density of dwellings per acre. As applied in California, IZ is associated with shifts within jurisdictions toward multifamily housing. At the very least, one can assert with confidence that program design matters to outcomes and that research design that fails to account for varying program design appears to draw inaccurate inferences.

Do studies of other regulations give us any more insight into the IZ–urban form question? As Schuetz, Meltzer, and Been noted, impact fees—which resemble IZ somewhat in their requirement that new development bear some of the cost of community infrastructure—have been studied in greater detail than IZ has. Two recent fee studies give some insight into the relationship between

IZ and urban form because they evaluate the effects of impact fees on single-family and multifamily housing construction.[60] Their long-term analysis of development trends in Florida suggested that impact fees lead to higher housing production in both single-family and multifamily structure types. Most impact fees increase construction, they argued, because fees increase project approval rates and therefore decrease developer costs. Impact fees shift the financial burden of new development away from existing residents, Gregory Burge and Keith Ihlanfeldt contended; therefore, they reduce resistance to multifamily housing construction in inner suburban areas. Such is not the case in outer suburbs, however, because these more racially and economically homogeneous areas continue to exclude multifamily housing even if impact fees mitigate fiscal motivations for exclusion.[61]

Some observers might question the parallel between IZ and impact fees. After all, IZ pays for something many homeowners do not want and would not pay for in the absence of IZ (in fact, they may pay to avoid it), whereas impact fees help pay for infrastructure that homeowners do want and would often have to pay for in their absence. But in some jurisdictions, citizens do consider affordable housing a fundamentally important part of the community infrastructure. Perhaps they see the prospective residents of the new subsidized units as being important members of their community; IZ is one ingredient in what many advocates now call "workforce housing"—places for our teachers, nurses, and firefighters to live. Perhaps, too, they see that unless key workers can live near their jobs, the businesses that operate in their cities as well as their local governments will have to pay higher wages—wages that will translate into higher prices and taxes. Although this argument may be farfetched as applied to citizens and homeowners, planners and elected officials in many jurisdictions embrace IZ because they believe it makes their jurisdictions more economically competitive and provides a mechanism that allows future rounds of growth to continue. In this way, IZ does resemble impact fees as a precondition, rather than an obstacle, to growth over the medium to long term.

While IZ might create labor market conditions that support long-term growth, it also can have spillover effects that cause neighborhood backlash, especially when a local IZ program induces construction through density bonuses, exceptions to height limits, and parking requirements. Such has been the case in Berkeley, where twenty-eight large residential projects were built between 1995 and 2006, mainly in its downtown and along two important mass transit routes, resulting in almost 1,500 new dwellings (200 affordable units within the twenty market-rate projects) after two decades of very little

60. Burge and Ihlanfeldt (2006a, 2006b).
61. Burge and Ihlanfeldt (2006a).

Figure 7-2. *Berkeley Density Bonus Project: The View from the Transit Corridor*

Photo: Kristin Perkins.

new housing construction.[62] Applications and new construction continue on perhaps ten more projects (figure 7-2). All these projects received density bonuses following hearings at the Zoning Adjustment Board (ZAB), where neighbors often objected to the concessions in height (figure 7-3), massing, parking, and open space that project sponsors called essential to the viability of their projects.[63] The ZAB felt obliged by the state law to approve these projects. Dissatisfied, the adjacent residents have pressured elected officials to reduce the permitted base density and increase setbacks in districts where developers had used the density bonus most aggressively. A city task force is still considering whether to do so: affordable housing advocates and some environmental groups oppose reductions in density, but neighborhood activists also have a very strong voice.[64]

IZ does not only galvanize neighbors against density and affordable housing, however. It can also serve as a potent rallying cry and as a key plank in a local

62. Dan Marks, "Development Standards Related to Density Bonus." Prepared for the Berkeley City Council, September 19, 2006; attached as an appendix to "Staff Report" for the Planning Commission hearing, April 8, 2008 (www.cityofberkeley.info/uploadedFiles/ Planning_(new_site_map_walk-through)/Level_3_-_General/20080408%20Item%209%20 density%20bonus%20report_complete.pdf [2006]).

63. Richard Brenneman, "Neighbors, ZAB Blast University Ave. Project," *Berkeley Daily Planet,* May 3, 2005; Richard Brenneman, "University Avenue Project Clears ZAB," *Berkeley Daily Planet,* November 2, 2005.

64. Jordan Harrison, associate planner, "Staff Report" for the Berkeley Planning Commission hearing, April 8, 2008.

Figure 7-3. *Berkeley Density Bonus Project: A Neighborhood View*[a]

Photo: Kristin Perkins.
  a. This view shows the same University Avenue project (background) from within the adjacent lower-density neighborhood. Note the abrupt change in height from one-story bungalow to four-story apartment construction.

political platform. In Brooklyn, the District of Columbia, San Francisco, Los Angeles, and Louisiana, advocates—often supported by research from PolicyLink, a national organization dedicated to the introduction of social justice into the smart growth agenda—have rallied residents to respond to gentrification by supporting IZ. Such an approach differs dramatically from a NIMBY reaction; it may create the basis for new constituencies and opinions about urban redevelopment that would not have arisen otherwise.

Building a Stronger Linkage: IZ and the Compact City

This final section shifts from fact-finding to design. The previous sections have shown that well-designed studies have discerned little if any average effect of IZ on housing supply and price. IZ is a product of local development politics, woven into a broader regulatory and market environment; it is a product of design, probably more than it is a driver of design. This programmatic openness offers policymakers a great opportunity to weave affordability and inclusion into their broader planning for compact and sustainable development, if they wish to do so.

Local Strategies: Making IZ Work for Compact Development

Local governments can make IZ and compactness work together by answering five critical questions in a strategic way.

When should IZ be adopted? First, use proposals to increase density as critical opportunities for IZ. Every day, at least one local government in practically every metropolitan area in the United States is considering at least one proposal—either generated by property owners or initiated inside local government—to raise residential density, whether for a small project or a large planning area. In some regions, Portland outstanding among them, density increases occur systematically throughout a region as a matter of state or regional policy. Such has also been the case in Maryland, with its smart growth planning system, and may soon characterize some new developments in Massachusetts. Local governments have extraordinary power during rezoning to impose development conditions; after approval, however, that power often evaporates. When a municipality or county is considering raising density as a general policy issue, it can prevent backlash because it can require mitigation of the negative effects and reinforcement of the benefits of higher density. When approving individual projects, local governments usually have less latitude to mitigate all the negative effects of higher density.

Should the program be voluntary or mandatory? The obvious answer to this question, for local governments that wish to promote both compactness and affordability, is mandatory. A voluntary program will never produce as much affordable housing—or as high an ultimate density—as a mandatory one will, because some developers will decline to take any bonus. In the face of uncertainty about developers' decisions to take the bonus, jurisdictions will struggle to plan the public facilities necessary to accommodate growth under a voluntary program. For some infrastructure systems, this will mean either congestion or excess capacity, both of which impose unwelcome costs on local residents.

How much density bonus should be offered? A comprehensive local rezoning, with substantial increases in permitted density, provides a political environment in which a mandatory IZ program can be made to work even without a density bonus, because the higher permitted density and the affordability mandate would be capitalized into land values both at once. Without a comprehensive rezoning, density bonuses should be ample, especially in the program's early years, when builders might otherwise mount the fiercest resistance to IZ. But the Berkeley case should reinforce caution about backlash.

How does IZ fit into other local development policies? The pairing of compact and inclusionary development will prove much more effective if it forms part of the central vision of a local comprehensive plan. Comprehensive plans aim to attain a vision supported by internally consistent goals, policies, and programs; within the plans, chapters (elements) on land use, transportation, public facilities, housing, and open space all can help integrate IZ into compact and equitable development policy. The plan can help jurisdictions with at least two levels of integration. First, the jurisdiction can use the housing element to place IZ within the context of a broader local housing strategy. Such a strategy documents current and future housing needs; identifies local constraints and opportunities for matching housing supply and demand; and describes the programs and policies that the jurisdiction will use, including but not limited to IZ, to meet a variety of housing needs. Second, the jurisdiction can use the plan to identify competing agendas (growth versus conservation, preservation versus renewal, and so on) and address them directly with deliberate programs and policies in public facilities, open space, and transportation. Otherwise, backlash may quickly target affordable and high-density housing, resulting in a complete policy shift in a less equitable direction.

What happens after IZ is adopted? Most jurisdictions that adopt IZ modify it over time, either because their goals for the program change or because they find it has not met their expectations. Local governments should anticipate that their IZ programs will never work perfectly, that their own goals for the program will change, and that they will need to devote resources periodically to analyzing and fine-tuning IZ along with other housing and development programs. Monitoring and evaluation can be written into an IZ ordinance or a general plan, and funds to allow staff reviews of programs can be written into budgets just as preventive maintenance appears in a capital improvement plan.

State Strategies: Fostering Integration between IZ and Compact Growth

The literature on IZ also makes it clear that states can foster integration between IZ and compact development. States can do so by integrating IZ with planning reform, passing IZ-enabling legislation, and monitoring and evaluating local IZ programs.

Integrate IZ with planning reform. In Oregon, the growth management system, which was designed in the early 1970s, did not build IZ into the package, believing that compactness and federal subsidies would solve any affordability problems that might arise in a low-cost state. By the late 1990s, Oregon had become much less affordable, but the coalition that would have been necessary to add IZ to the growth-management mix was fighting tooth and nail just to save the system from property rights advocates. Affordable housing advocates could not prevent the Oregon legislature from passing a bill prohibiting IZ; real estate agents and the construction lobby outgunned them. Thus, Oregon jurisdictions can use density bonuses, but jurisdictions in the area covered by Portland's metropolitan government (Metro) are required to set fairly high minimum densities; Metro also periodically requires cities to boost zoned density even further. These requirements render density bonuses practically superfluous.

Set the terms for local IZ. States can also set the terms of local IZ by passing legislation governing the program. Concerns that IZ will be used as a smokescreen for local exclusion can be addressed with guidelines established in state legislation about the circumstances under which IZ may be imposed, the minimum density bonuses that project sponsors must receive, and additional concessions that local governments must offer. In the wake of Hurricanes Katrina and Rita, a coalition in Louisiana convinced the state legislature to pass IZ-enabling legislation. This bill, HB 974, established rules for project thresholds, required affordability levels and control periods, and minimum density bonuses, among other program-design elements.[65] Legislation that enables IZ will always be necessary in "Dillon's Rule" states, where local governments cannot pass ordinances unless authorized to do so by their state legislatures. Even in home rule states, legislatures can establish rules for local IZ to reduce the impression that local governments can use, or are using, IZ as camouflage for preventing growth.

Monitor local use of IZ. When California's Department of Housing and Community Development reviews the housing elements of local general plans, it requires local governments to demonstrate that their IZ programs do not hinder housing development. For example, a 2006 review letter on the housing element for Goleta in Santa Barbara County noted that the city's 55 percent inclusionary requirement on five key multifamily sites might "impact the cost and supply of housing in Goleta" and asked the city to "describe the types of incentives or regulatory concessions the City will be proposing . . . to ensure these requirements will not unduly impede overall housing production and supply."[66]

Conclusions: Prospects for IZ in the Compact City

Research on IZ is still in its infancy. Only in the last few years have a large number of places in any state adopted it. California, the nation's leader, has about a one-third rate of adoption among its cities and counties, but this is up from

65. PolicyLink, "Support HB 974: Inclusionary Zoning to Address Louisiana Housing Needs" (www.policylink.org/documents/HB974_onepager_permissive.pdf).

66. Cathy Creswell, deputy director of housing policy development, California Department of Housing and Community Development, letter to Ken Curtis, director, Planning and Environmental Services, city of Goleta, March 27, 2006 (www.hcd.ca.gov/hpd/hrc/plan/he/he_review_letters/sbbgoleta032706.pdf [March 2006]).

between 10 and 20 percent as little as ten years ago. The widely varying array of policy goals that motivate IZ, and the corresponding diversity of program design options that local governments face when building their programs, make it—like zoning writ large—a tremendously flexible tool, able to produce significant numbers of units, deep subsidies, and mixed-income housing projects, although additional subsidies are usually necessary to accomplish all these goals at once.

The diverse motivations for adopting IZ and the varying program designs also make IZ frustratingly difficult to evaluate even where its direct impacts (those on affordable housing) are concerned. The best studies thus far find that its effects on affordable housing supply are appreciable, helping build tens of thousands of low-cost houses and apartments at a time of dire housing cost burdens.[67] The programs' incentive structures, however, often appear to blunt or eliminate the need for cross-subsidy from market-rate units.

As far as the most careful analysts have been able to measure thus far, IZ has little or no average effect on market-rate housing production; its indirect average effect on urban form, therefore, must be even more difficult to detect. At the same time, however, the absence of an average effect does not mean the absence of any effect anywhere. In some places and for some periods of time, IZ can either induce housing construction where it would not have otherwise occurred or obstruct housing construction altogether.

For local governments that want to adopt mandatory IZ as a mechanism to induce the construction of housing that both is more affordable and attains higher densities, the recipe may appear obvious: just offer a very healthy density bonus. The experience of Berkeley, however, underscores the risk of such a program design and suggests that program designers need to think about whether and how to mitigate higher density. In some locations, especially built-up cities like Berkeley, local governments (or, more accurately, taxpayers at some scale beyond the high-density projects themselves) will have to shoulder at least part of the burden of mitigation. How, if at all, will a city pacify single-family homeowners who abut high-density projects along a major transit spine? Can the city afford to ignore them? Should it, if it could? This subject clearly needs more research, and not only because of the higher densities that often pay for IZ. Increasing numbers of metropolitan areas are investing in mass transit and linking transit with land use along key corridors, often boosting transit service in or near single-family neighborhoods built between 1950 and 1970. Maximizing the potential ridership on these lines and inducing a shift in transportation mode will require higher densities that neighbors will certainly resist in many

67. Schuetz, Meltzer, and Been (2007); Knaap, Bento, and Lowe (2008).

areas. As much as transit-oriented development heightens the urgency of working on density mitigation, though, it also heightens the opportunity to include new measures that will compensate neighbors for new IZ-related density.

For states whose leaders want to ensure that local governments embrace IZ but also use it responsibly rather than as a smokescreen for exclusionary intentions, past research on policy offers important lessons. Enabling legislation with specific guidelines on the use of IZ (the recent Louisiana model) might be one way to promote the program and to reduce abuse, but resolutely exclusionary local governments could still find ways around such a statutory approach, for example, by reducing base density, imposing additional restrictions, or rezoning residential land to industrial and commercial designations. States could instead offer technical assistance to local governments and an appeals process to allow would-be builders to initiate complaints against localities they consider exclusionary (even with IZ). Similar to what is done in California, states could also enhance the housing-planning context within which local governments adopt IZ programs. And they could tie state infrastructure funding, especially for transportation, to inclusionary programs. When states fund infrastructure for regional and local transportation, sewer, and water—even by lending money— they enhance land value and, ultimately, shift the balance of political power within the regions they fund. An inclusionary mandate from the state level broadens the beneficiaries of these investments and helps to right some of the imbalance between haves and have-nots in U.S. metropolitan areas.

All this implies that we need to continue to pay attention to the *Z* part of IZ: it starts and ends as a zoning tool. Like zoning in general, it is tremendously flexible. It can foster compact development; it can kill development entirely. Compared with other programs, policies, investments, and regulations that can either induce compactness or kill development, however, IZ is an indirect and weak instrument. But since it has such wide potential, properly designed IZ should absolutely continue to be one of the elements in local and regional programs to promote compact, mixed-use, pedestrian-friendly development.

References

Altshuler, Alan A., and José A. Gómez-Ibáñez. 1993. *Regulation for Revenue: The Political Economy of Land Development Exactions.* Brookings and Lincoln Institute of Land Policy.

Baar, Kenneth K. 1998. "New Jersey's Rent Control Movement." In *Rent Control: Regulation and the Rental Housing Market,* edited by W. Dennis Keating, Michael B. Teitz, and Andrejs Skaburskis, pp. 142–50. New Brunswick, N.J.: Rutgers Center for Urban Policy Research.

Babcock, Richard F. 1966. *The Zoning Game: Municipal Practices and Policies.* University of Wisconsin Press.

Barton, Stephen E. 1998. "The Success and Failure of Strong Rent Control in the City of Berkeley, 1978 to 1995," In *Rent Control: Regulation and the Rental Housing Market,* edited by W. Dennis Keating, Michael B. Teitz, and Andrejs Skaburskis, pp. 88–109. New Brunswick, N.J.: Rutgers Center for Urban Policy Research.

Basolo, Victoria, and Nico Calavita. 2004. "Policy Claims with Weak Evidence: A Critique of the Reason Foundation Study on Inclusionary Zoning in the San Francisco Bay Area." Discussion paper written at the request of national and California housing advocacy organizations. University of California–Irvine, Department of Planning, Policy, and Design.

Brown, Karen Destorel. 2001. "Expanding Affordable Housing through Inclusionary Zoning: Lessons from the Washington Metropolitan Area." Brookings.

Burge, Gregory S., and Keith R. Ihlanfeldt. 2006a. "The Effects of Impact Fees on Multifamily Housing Construction." *Journal of Regional Science* 46, no. 1: 5–23.

———. 2006b. "Impact Fees and Single Family Home Construction." *Journal of Urban Economics* 60, no. 2: 284–306.

Calavita, Nico. 1998. "Inclusionary Housing in California: The Experience of Two Decades." *Journal of the American Planning Association* 64, no. 2: 150–69.

Calavita, Nico, Kenneth Grimes, and Alan Mallach. 1997. "Inclusionary Housing in California and New Jersey: A Comparative Analysis." *Housing Policy Debate* 8, no. 1: 109–42.

California Coalition for Rural Housing. 2007. "Affordable by Choice: Trends in California Inclusionary Housing Programs." Sacramento (www.calruralhousing.org/system/files/SampleIHReport.pdf).

California Coalition for Rural Housing and Non-Profit Housing Association of Northern California. 2003. "Inclusionary Housing in California: 30 Years of Innovation." Sacramento and San Francisco (www.nonprofithousing.org/knowledgebank/publications/Inclusionary_Housing_CA_30years.pdf).

Clavel, Pierre. 1986. *The Progressive City: Planning and Participation, 1969–1984.* Rutgers University Press.

Dubbink, David. 1984. "I'll Have My Town Medium-Rural, Please." *Journal of the American Planning Association* 50, no. 4: 406–18.

Ellickson, Robert C. 1981. "The Irony of 'Inclusionary' Zoning." *Southern California Law Review* 54, no. 6: 1167–216.

Engler, Robert. 2002. "An Inclusionary Housing Case Study: Newton, Massachusetts." In *Inclusionary Zoning: Lessons Learned in Massachusetts. NHC Affordable Housing Policy Review* 2, no. 1. Washington: National Housing Conference.

Fox, Radhika, and Kalima Rose. 2003. "Expanding Housing Opportunity in Washington, D.C.: The Case for Inclusionary Zoning." Oakland, Calif.: Policy Link, p. 15.

Haar, Charles M. 1996. *Suburbs under Siege: Race, Space and Audacious Judges.* Princeton University Press.

Hoch, Charles. 2005. "Suburban Response to the Illinois Affordable Housing and Planning Act." Chicago: Board of Trustees of the University of Illinois.

Kautz, Barbara. 2006. "A Public Agency Guide to California Density Bonus Law." Adapted from presentation for County Counsels' Association of California, Land Use Study Section Conference. Oakland, California, Fall 2005.

Knaap, Gerrit-Jan, Antonio Bento, and Scott Lowe. 2008. "Housing Market Impacts of Inclusionary Zoning." College Park, Md.: National Center for Smart Growth Research and Education.

Krefetz, Sharon. 2001. "The Impact and Evolution of the Massachusetts Comprehensive Permit and Zoning Appeals Act: Thirty Years of Experience with a State Legislative Effort to Overcome Exclusionary Zoning." *Western New England Law Review* 22, no. 2: 381–430.

Mallach, Alan. 1984. *Inclusionary Housing Programs: Policies and Practices.* New Brunswick, N.J.: Rutgers University, Center for Urban Policy Research.

Meck, Stuart. 2003. "Illinois Enacts Housing Appeals, Planning Statute." *Zoning News* 20, no. 6: 6.

Merriam, Dwight H., David J. Brower, and Philip D. Tegeler. 1985. *Inclusionary Zoning Moves Downtown.* Washington: Planners Press, American Planning Association.

Mintier, Sophia. 2007. "New York City's New Approach to Affordable Housing: An Evaluation of the Greenpoint-Williamsburg Inclusionary Housing Program." MRP thesis, Cornell University.

Pendall, Rolf. 2008a. "Does Land-Use Deregulation Promote Social Mobility through Home Ownership? Lessons from Laissez-Faire Houston." Working Paper. Cornell University, Department of City and Regional Planning.

———. 2008b. "From Hurdles to Bridges: Local Land-Use Regulations and the Pursuit of Affordable Rental Housing." In *Rethinking Rental Housing,* edited by Nicolas Retsinas and Eric Belsky, pp. 224–73. Brookings.

Pendall, Rolf, Robert Puentes, and Jonathan Martin. 2006. "From Traditional to Reformed: A Review of the Land Use Regulations in the Nation's 50 Largest Metropolitan Areas." Research Brief. Brookings, Metropolitan Policy Program.

Pogodzinski, J. M., and Tim R. Sass. 1994. "The Theory and Estimation of Endogenous Zoning." *Regional Science and Urban Economics* 24, no. 5: 601–30.

Powell, Benjamin, and Edward Stringham. 2004. "Housing Supply and Affordability: Do Affordable Housing Mandates Work?" Policy Study 318. Los Angeles: Reason Public Policy Institute.

Quigley, John M., and Larry A. Rosenthal. 2005. "The Effects of Land Use Regulation on the Price of Housing: What Do We Know? What Can We Learn?" *Cityscape* 8, no. 1: 69–137.

Schuetz, Jenny, Rachel Meltzer, and Vicki Been. 2007. *The Effects of Inclusionary Zoning on Local Housing Markets: Lessons from the San Francisco, Washington DC and Suburban Boston Areas.* New York: New York University, Furman Center for Real Estate and Urban Policy.

Teitz, Michael B. 1998. "The Politics of Rent Control." In *Rent Control: Regulation and the Rental Housing Market,* edited by W. Dennis Keating, Michael B. Teitz, and Andrejs Skaburskis, pp. 61–78. New Brunswick, N.J.: Rutgers Center for Urban Policy Research.

Wallace, Nancy E. 1988. "The Market Effects of Zoning Undeveloped Land: Does Zoning Follow the Market?" *Journal of Urban Economics* 23, no. 3: 307–26.

Index